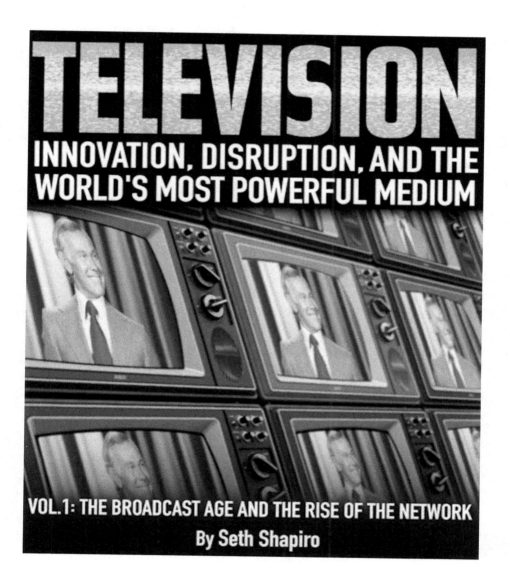

TELEVISION

INNOVATION, DISRUPTION, AND THE WORLD'S MOST POWERFUL MEDIUM

VOL.1: THE BROADCAST AGE AND THE RISE OF THE NETWORK

By Seth Shapiro

TELEVISION

INNOVATION, DISRUPTION, AND THE
WORLD'S MOST POWERFUL MEDIUM

VOLUME 1: THE BROADCAST AGE AND THE RISE
OF THE NETWORK

Seth Shapiro

ISBN-13: 9780997304206
ISBN-10: 0997304200
Library of Congress Control Number: 2016940167
New Amsterdam Media LLC, Los Angeles, CA

Advance Praise for *TELEVISION: Innovation, Disruption and the World's Most Powerful Medium, Volume 1* by Seth Shapiro

"If you ever wanted to know how the television
industry began, this is your primer."

—GARTH ANCIER

FORMER ENTERTAINMENT PRESIDENT, FOX BROADCASTING COMPANY

PRESIDENT, NBC ENTERTAINMENT

CHAIRMAN, THE WB TELEVISION NETWORK

PRESIDENT, BBC WORLDWIDE AMERICA

"From this point forward when I'm asked what inspired me to
pursue a career in broadcasting I will recommend this book.
Seth Shapiro masterfully chronicles the evolution of television
and prepares us for the explosion of options that some call
'Peak TV.' It was like seeing my life pass before my eyes."

—PRESTON BECKMAN

SENIOR STRATEGIST, FOX NETWORKS GROUP

EVP, PROGRAM PLANNING AND SCHEDULING, NBC ENTERTAINMENT

"The word 'TV' today is a loaded term. With the exponential growth
of access and quantity of content, *TELEVISION: Volume 1* brings
much-needed context and perspective to how we got here. A must
read for anybody even thinking about the media business today."

—JOHN CANNING

VP, INTERACTIVE EXPERIENCES, NBC ENTERTAINMENT DIGITAL

"Seth Shapiro teaches THE class on the media business.
Now, he's writing THE book. He's THE expert."

—RYAN HOLIDAY

EDITOR-AT-LARGE, *THE NEW YORK OBSERVER*

BEST-SELLING AUTHOR OF *TRUST ME I'M LYING* AND *THE OBSTACLE IS THE WAY*

"Seth is a spectacular storyteller with extraordinary perspective and real world experience. If you want to truly understand the TV business, *TELEVISION: Volume 1* is a must read."
—SHELLY PALMER
BUSINESS ADVISOR, AUTHOR AND COMMENTATOR

"Seth Shapiro nails it. With an eye for keen detail, insider's access, and a gift for analytic storytelling, Shapiro weaves a powerful tapestry of the formative days of the TV network business. With a dynamic energy that makes it a great read, *TELEVISION: Volume 1* delivers a spectrum of insight all along the way, and Seth creates one of the most engaging accounts of the origin history of arguably the most powerful medium ever invented. *TELEVISION: Volume 1* stands to become a must-read for all industry participants, students of electronic media, and viewers who have ever wondered how this global phenomenon called TV came to be."
—JOHN PENNEY, CHIEF STRATEGY OFFICER, STARZ

"Seth Shapiro has crafted a delightful, story-filled history of television that is as entertaining as the medium itself. Shapiro brings to life with rich detail the characters behind the scenes that transformed our culture and our world. As the media landscape continues to evolve in the 21st Century, *TELEVISION: Volume 1* is a must read for all those looking to comprehend the future of video."
—JAY SAMIT
COLUMNIST, THE WALL STREET JOURNAL
AUTHOR OF *DISRUPT YOU: MASTER PERSONAL TRANSFORMATION, SEIZE OPPORTUNITY AND THRIVE IN THE ERA OF ENDLESS INNOVATION*

With a keen understanding of both its history and its future, Seth is the perfect author to tell the story of television. And the story is a fascinating combination of art and business, of technology and culture.

—JEFF SHULTZ

SENIOR VICE PRESIDENT BUSINESS DEVELOPMENT, CBS

"This is THE fascinating and comprehensive history of Television. And it contains so many fantastic stories that you won't find anywhere else. Seth really brings forward the lessons we can learn from how technology and media innovation come together."

—HARDIE TANKERSLEY

SVP OF INNOVATION, FOX BROADCASTING COMPANY

"The most powerful medium of the twentieth century now has a book that does justice to its rich history. Bravo to Seth Shapiro for this fascinating, informative, comprehensive and most importantly entertaining chronicle."

—TERENCE WINTER

Executive Producer of THE SOPRANOS, BOARDWALK EMPIRE and VINYL

The history of the television industry is a fascinating one and Shapiro does an excellent job of bringing it to life, providing insider information that should appeal to laymen and insiders alike.

—ALAN WOLK

AUTHOR OF OVER THE TOP. HOW THE INTERNET IS (SLOWLY BUT SURELY) CHANGING THE TELEVISION INDUSTRY

CONTENTS

For Ann Marie,
Kate, Ollie,
Nancy and Ed

FOREWORD

The story of television, like radio before it and digital video today, has indelibly affected four generations of Americans. We are all the product of its constant evolution during our time on Earth. If you ask anyone to name their favorite show of all time, as I often do, the answers often depend on when you grew up—and range from *Howdy Doody* to *Pokémon,* and from *Mission: Impossible* to *Game of Thrones.*

Television has always delighted and fascinated us, as well as held a mirror to our society through times good and bad. And accident or fortune has often been part of that story. Just a few examples, out of literally thousands:

I Love Lucy, which finished its run in 1957, is known by just about everyone today for only one reason: in an era when most sitcoms were done live, Desi Arnaz chose—against the advice of most others and at additional cost—to shoot his show on film.

Star Trek, which aired only from 1966 to 1969, was canceled—then brought back after a massive letter-writing campaign to NBC—and then canceled, again. Today, after four subsequent revivals on TV and three successful reboots in feature films, a new version is set to launch on CBS digital next year. Go figure.

Family Guy, which aired from 1999 to 2001, was also canceled, twice. But this time, the savior was Cartoon Network, where the show gained a mass of new followers and was once again launched on FOX in 2005, where it remains a hit today. (I have a stake in this one, as I bought the canceled episodes at Turner for a song in 2002, and all of the reruns still live today).

And it just gets weirder. When I left my job at NBC in 1986 to start a "fourth network" at FOX, my NBC colleagues told me there would NEVER be a fourth network. That didn't turn out to be true, but none of us could envision the 300+ networks we have today. These were brought to us in the cable era, which will be covered in *TELEVISION: Volume 2*.

And now, of course, linear TV is colliding with the "watch anything you want, when you want it" of digital video platforms. That story will be told in *TELEVISION: Volume 3*.

The story of television continues to evolve. But don't expect an ending. That ending has yet to be written. That's why Seth's series on television is so important.

If you want to understand how television evolved, *TELEVISION: Volume 1* is your primer.

—Garth Ancier
Founding President, FOX Broadcasting Company
Former President, NBC Entertainment
Former Chairman, the WB Television Network
Founding President, BBC Worldwide America

PREFACE

istory is always disappearing. Like the horizon line, it recedes in the distance, as generations and their times pass away. At some point we learn that the past can be instructive—because what's happened before will happen again.

Meanwhile, we're all born in the middle of a story, then spend years trying to figure out where we came in.

That's why we need *common* stories. Stories put life in context. They ground us and give us a sense of what's possible.

Each generation gets a chance to tell its stories. Each is thrown the same basic pitches: childhood, parents, siblings, school, the unrequited love of the most beautiful girl in town. Every generation comes to the plate and tries to fashion a response.

Some generations leave more than others: Vienna circa 1800; Impressionists in the 1870s; London in the 1960s. But most generations disappear without a trace.

We are lucky. Our stories are told on television.

This book is an attempt to capture *that* overarching story: how an absurd technological fantasy became the most powerful medium on Earth.

It began with three events.

———

When I was little, my mother took me on the NBC tour, at 30 Rockefeller Plaza in New York City. The NBC page explained that most TV shows were recorded on tape, then broadcast afterward.

"What do they do with the old Johnny Carson shows?" I asked.

"Well, if Mr. Carson really likes them, they save them for *The Best of Carson.* Otherwise, they erase them, and use the tape again."

This was the stupidest thing I'd ever heard, even at age eight. They erased *Johnny.* Did these NBC people not know that Johnny should be *preserved?*

"They probably do," said my mom, "but maybe it's expensive. They're probably trying to save money."

The TV business seemed insane.

———

In 2011, I began teaching at the University of Southern California's School of Cinematic Arts. When I looked for course materials, I was surprised to discover that no one book seemed to capture the evolution of television. The *stories* are the main thing students should read, I thought: not just *what* had happened during the evolution of TV, but *how* it had happened, and *why.*

———

In 2013, I attended the Television Academy's 22nd Hall of Fame Awards, as a member of its Board of Governors. One Hall of Fame Award that year went to the family of Philo T. Farnsworth.

Based on my limited understanding at the time, this made as much sense as NBC's erasing Johnny. Farnsworth had *invented* television—or at least part of it. Why had it taken us, the home of the Emmys, nearly seventy years to recognize him?

That question began a three-year journey, the result of which is this book.

———

TELEVISION: Volume 1 is not an encyclopedia of television. It's meant to the capture the amazing, undervalued story of TV through the great innovators who created it, believed in it, and often bet their lives on it. Hopefully, it's a story of our times as well.

Seth Shapiro
Los Angeles
April 2016

PART 1

NBC AND THE BATTLE FOR TELEVISION

All of this has happened before, and it will all happen again.
—J. M. Barrie, *Peter Pan*, 1904

CHAPTER 1

PROMETHEUS

P hilo Farnsworth was in trouble.

He had been first. It didn't matter. He had been right. It didn't matter.

Sarnoff had power. Sarnoff destroyed people.

But that didn't matter. Philo could not give in. He would hold onto his life's work, no matter what the price.

He could not have known how high that price would be.

———

As a young boy in Utah, Philo had dreamed of being an inventor. The dream was electrified when the family moved from Idaho to a Utah farmhouse, where he discovered a pile of scientific journals in the attic. These journals predicted a fantastic world revolutionized by technology, in which the dreariness of farm life would be replaced by a magical new world.

One of these predictions intrigued Philo above all: the quixotic dream of "television."

And one night in 1920, at fourteen, Philo T. Farnsworth figured out how to make television work.

Unknown to Farnsworth, inventors in at least six countries were working feverishly to make television a reality.

His epiphany that night put him a decade ahead of them all.

Unfortunately for Philo, one other man soon reached the same conclusion. And that man would be hired by David Sarnoff.

CHAPTER 2

DAVID SARNOFF

All life is a risk. I learned it earlier than most.
—DAVID SARNOFF

I n 1900, the International Congress of Electricians coined the strange
new term "television."

If you were born in 1900, you grew up hearing about the idea of
television the way recent generations grew up hearing about jet packs.
"Remote seeing" was a futuristic, fantastic daydream, evangelized by
technologists, visionaries, and thieves. It would burrow into imagina-
tions for decades, as the advent of telegraph, telephone, and radio each
brought the ultimate medium closer to reality.

If you were born in 1900, you would not see TV until you were fifty.
But you'd know the name Marconi. Everybody did.

Marconi

One hundred and fifty years ago, everything took forever. Information
traveled on horseback and was stale before it arrived. That began to
change in the 1840s when Samuel Morse's telegraph made instant
communication possible for the first time. Morse became America's
"Lightning Man," one of the first technology heroes since Ben Franklin
(see Appendix).

But the telegraph required *wires.* That's where Marconi came in.

Born in Italy in 1874, Guglielmo Marconi caught the inventor bug early, and had a family wealthy enough to buy him the equipment he needed.

In the 1880s, scientific journals were a pop culture force, teaching inventors, students, and fans about new technology. From these journals, as from "how-to" YouTube channels, Marconi studied and replicated Benjamin Franklin's experiments with electricity. He went on to study Heinrich Hertz's wave theories, and became convinced that telegraph messages could be sent without wires.

Marconi got lucky: when Hertz died, his research was widely reprinted in the journals. This gave young Marconi the material he needed to begin his experiments in wireless communication. His experiments worked, but his home nation of Italy didn't see a future in them.

So Marconi and his mother went to England, where they got interest from the British Post Office. By 1895, Marconi was the first to transmit a radio signal over a mile. In his ongoing experiments, he expanded the distances farther and farther.

At age twenty-three, he founded the British Marconi Company, and his fame began to spread. "The calm of my life ended then,"[1] he would later say, as wireless telegraphy became radio, the technology that would connect the world.

In 1899, Marconi set up an office in New Jersey, and the Marconi Wireless Company of America was born. Marconi, already famous, became an icon—the world's second technology superstar, behind New Jersey's Thomas Edison.

America

On July 2, 1900, a destitute nine-year-old boy arrived at Ellis Island from Uzlian, a tiny Jewish village near Minsk. He spoke no English, and had spent his first years preparing to become a rabbi.

Instead, he followed his father to the new world, traveling as baggage in the bowels of the ship. In America, his sickly father struggled to make a living, so young David began working as soon as they arrived.

Within weeks of arriving in New York City, David was selling Yiddish newspapers on the Lower East Side, attending school, and reading discarded newspapers to learn English. On the Sabbath, his only day off, he picked up extra money by singing in a synagogue choir.

David's father became incapacitated with tuberculosis in 1906. So at age fifteen, David Sarnoff needed a full-time job to support the family. He dreamed of a job in journalism, and headed for an interview at the *New York Herald*, but fate intervened. According to historians, he ended up at a telegraph company, the office of the Commercial Cable Company.

Sarnoff's son Thomas corroborates the legend: "The story is true. He went to get a job at a newspaper, and he turned left instead of turning right. He wound up in the telegraph place and he got a job there instead."[2]

The lost fifteen-year-old was offered a job as a messenger. It wasn't the newspaper business, but it *was* the communications business.

So David started out on the lowest rung on the ladder, and immediately set his sights on becoming a telegraph operator. Telegraph operators were the gamers of their day, banging out messages in Morse code as quickly as they could, competing to beat their coworkers with more messages per day, in the equivalent of a modern leaderboard.

Sarnoff bought a telegraph key of his own, learned Morse code, and practiced clicking out messages until late in the night. Then he'd get up at 4 AM, make newspaper deliveries, and report to work at Continental.

On one fateful occasion, Sarnoff asked for three days off for the Jewish High Holy Days, since he made more money singing in the synagogue choir. His boss, Mr. Shea, understood the boy's dilemma, but told him to turn in his bicycle—he was fired.

It was a short-term blow, but a long-term gain.

Thirteen years later, Shea applied for a job at the newly created Radio Corporation of America. He was called in to meet one of the company's leading executives, David Sarnoff, who said:

> Mr. Shea . . . I am very much indebted to you. Back in 1906, on the eve of the High Holy Days, you fired me as a messenger boy. This led to my entering the wireless field. To show you I'm really grateful, you're hired. You can start at once.[3]

6

If he hadn't been fired, Sarnoff might never have moved from telegraphy to radio.

Wireless and Radio

Marconi finally managed to send wireless telegraph messages across the Atlantic in 1901. In 1903, he facilitated telegraphs between Teddy Roosevelt and King Edward VII. By 1904, wireless telegraph stations were cropping up all over the world, competing with the telegraph cables laid at the bottom of the ocean. Wireless was coming into its own, and Marconi was its star. The world saw him the way it saw Edison: as a transformer of reality itself.

No one wanted to change reality more than David Sarnoff.

After losing his job in 1906, Sarnoff went for an interview at the American Marconi Company. He asked for a job as a telegraph operator, and was offered one as an office boy. Sarnoff used it to learn every aspect of the business: studying technical journals, interviewing operators, taking night courses to catch up on the business.

In an anti-Semitic era, Sarnoff had no friends at Marconi. Extra jobs were heaped on him, and he did them without complaint. He recalled later:

> I knew that I would have to work twice as hard as most other boys. . . . I didn't think it unfair and I wasn't bitter. I accepted the handicaps calmly, as facts of life, to be faced and overcome.[4]

Soon he knew more about the company than anyone in the office. And he was ready for the audition of his life.

———

When Guglielmo Marconi next visited his office at the American Marconi Company, David Sarnoff was waiting. He proudly showed the founder the telegraph key that he'd bought with his own money, and volunteered to help Marconi during his stay.

Sarnoff won Marconi over, and became his assistant in New York: smoothing the capo's path, sending flowers to his girlfriends and arranging his meetings.

The relationship was mutually beneficial. Everyone wanted something from Marconi, but here was a kid who helped with *everything*. Sarnoff wanted to *be* Marconi, and got to learn from the man he would always revere.

Marconi liked him. "David," Marconi told him, "we know how things work, but we don't know why they work."[5] So Sarnoff began studying engineering and math.

Soon Sarnoff had the trust of the most powerful man in the company.

As it would for generations of young executives to come, the affection of the big boss paved the way for a steady climb. Soon, Sarnoff was a telegraph operator, in time for the next big break of his career.

The Titanic

By 1912, the term "wireless" was replaced by "radio." American Marconi had been scraping by for a decade, but that changed in 1912, as the world saw the power of its new technology.

David Sarnoff was now manager of a Marconi station at Wanamaker's department store. On Sunday, April 14, 1912, his station received a message: "*Titanic* sinking fast."

From here, accounts differ. According to legend, Sarnoff stayed on duty for three days straight, manning the telegraph key—the main point of contact between America and the world-famous ship. It was the biggest story in the world, and Sarnoff was right in the center of it.

Company PR would also claim that Sarnoff was the only operator present that Sunday:

> The eyes of the whole world . . . were fixed on young Sarnoff and his earphones. For three days and three nights, without sleep and virtually without food, Sarnoff remained glued to his earphones, while a horrified world hung on his every word. . . . Not until he had given the press the names of the last survivors, seventy-two hours after he had picked up the first distress signal, did the exhausted operator relinquish his earphones.[6]

Some researchers doubt that Wanamaker's would have been open on a Sunday. Others doubt Sarnoff (its manager) would have been on duty on a Sunday—and if he had, other operators would have been there too. Some say Sarnoff would have come to the office on Monday, and joined the effort then.

On balance, it's hard to believe that Sarnoff would have been alone on duty for seventy-two hours straight.

What we know is that the story was told until everyone believed it.

Sarnoff himself was more candid years later: "The *Titanic* disaster brought radio to the front—and also me."[7]

In any event, Sarnoff could not have had better timing. Radio saved the lives of 30 percent of the *Titanic*'s passengers, helping prove that radio was indispensable at sea. In 1914, World War I began, catapulting radio into the stratosphere.

Sarnoff saw a way to take radio in a completely new direction: into America's homes.

"Radio Music Box"

In 1915, Sarnoff was named chief inspector of American Marconi. Radio was spreading fast, but largely as a business and military medium. As the personal computer industry would do one day, Sarnoff saw that the bigger opportunity was in selling to *consumers*. He wrote a visionary memo to his bosses:

> I have in mind a plan of development, which would make radio a "household utility" in the same sense of the piano or phonograph. The idea is to bring music into the home by wireless. The "radio music box" can be supplied with amplifying tubes and a loudspeaking telephone, all of which can be neatly mounted in one box. The box can be placed on a table in the parlor or living room, the switch set accordingly, and the music received. There should be no difficulty in receiving music perfectly when transmitted within a distance of 25–50 miles.[8]

The memo proposed that radio could become a home appliance, bringing electronic entertainment and news to the country for the first time.

RCA management reviewed the proposal, but thought it was far-fetched. Five years later, Sarnoff's vision came into being almost exactly as described.

It led to the creation of a giant.

CHAPTER 3

RADIO CORPORATION OF AMERICA

The Radio Corporation does not pay royalties. We collect them.
—DAVID SARNOFF

Once the *Titanic* and other events made the military value of radio clear, many nations made radio a government-owned asset. The U.S. government and the Navy tried as well, with a bill to nationalize ownership of the medium. This would have meant the end of the American Marconi Company, and a huge blow for General Electric, AT&T, and others.

In Washington, allies of the industry fought the move to nationalize radio: "Having just won a fight against autocracy," declared one congressman, "we would start another autocratic movement with this bill."[1]

But the federal government was clear on one thing: radio would *not* be owned by a foreign power. America was *not* going to cede key technology to Europe. The days of foreign-owned Marconi were numbered.

In a compromise, the Navy, General Electric, AT&T, Westinghouse, and Marconi pooled their patents, agreed to share use, and created a new entity. It was called the Radio Corporation of America.

RCA was incorporated on October 17, 1919. It was, effectively, a private monopoly. And its commercial manager was twenty-eight-year-old David Sarnoff.

The Radio Craze

In the early 1920s, radio became a national craze, much as the World Wide Web would be in the 1990s. Hobbyists bought wireless gear and set up home stations, creating a miraculous din that enveloped cities and hamlets. America had never experienced anything like it.

The radio band of each town was full of competing auteurs, citizens unleashed to say anything to unseen audiences in the dark. Radio fans huddled over the gear, spinning the dial in hopes of a skip to parts unknown. In 1922 alone, more than 500 stations rushed to the air. The media age had begun.

Throughout the United States, hundreds of amateurs began assembling and selling radio kits and transmitters. Soon, these homemade transmitters began moving from garages and attics to newspapers and department stores. Amateur operators began broadcasting in droves. The big four—RCA, GE, AT&T, and Westinghouse—watched from the sidelines. Not surprisingly, they disliked being on the sidelines when money was involved. They complained to the government—loudly—and a new agency was born.

The Radio Act of 1927

Like land and other physical resources, the "spectrum" on which radio waves are broadcast is finite. As there is today for cellphone carriers, there were only so many frequencies available for radio companies. As the number of radio broadcasters increased, so did competition for frequencies, as stations crowded on top of each other, often drowning each other out.

In 1927, Congress responded to this by creating the Federal Radio Commission (FRC). The FRC was given control over radio spectrum and all radio stations. Its five commissioners had the power to grant and revoke radio licenses, and to assign the frequency and power level associated with each license. The FRC would eventually be renamed the Federal Communications Commission (FCC) and would regulate TV and the Internet as well.

The FRC ruled against the crowd in 1927, issuing mandatory licenses, and pushing amateurs to the grim regions at the bottom and the top of the dial. The Free Radio era was over, and the programming business was gathering steam.

Sarnoff wanted in.

Having been ignored by his bosses more than a decade before, Sarnoff resubmitted his Radio Music Box concept. His RCA bosses were intrigued, but pointed out that they did not have any programming for radio.

Sarnoff saw that radio *content* was critical for RCA, and for his own ascension. He feared that RCA would lose out to its competitors, and looked for a way to make his case.

In 1921, he saw an opportunity.

The Dempsey-Carpentier fight was an international event, the "Battle of the Century." Georges Carpentier was a fighter pilot and a war hero. Jack Dempsey was a draft dodger. The prizefight was characterized as a contest between good and evil. The crowd at the ring was going to be 90,000 strong.

Sarnoff rolled the dice. Operating on his own initiative without help from his bosses at RCA, he decided to broadcast the fight.

As the fight time approached, Sarnoff knew that if any link in the chain of equipment failed him, he would have a public relations disaster. Where possible, he arranged for backup systems, and drafted an employee to man the microphone for a blow-by-blow commentary.

At ringside on July 2, 1921, Sarnoff paced, checked the microphone and telephone link. He was attempting something his superiors had dismissed as crazy: a live sports broadcast to an estimated 300,000 Americans. If successful, the broadcast would vault RCA into a new commercial business. If it failed, Sarnoff would be disgraced.

During the fourth round of the fight, as Dempsey pummeled Carpentier, the RCA transmitter started to overheat. It soon blew out, but not until after Carpentier hit the canvas. Had the fight gone another round, the broadcast would have been a disaster. Instead, it was a triumph. Sarnoff had pulled off the first broadcast sports spectacular.

In 1922, rewarding his initiative, RCA chose Sarnoff to run domestic operations.

Something else had happened at the Dempsey fight: Sarnoff's beloved secretary, Marion McInnes, had attended at ringside. So had a radio inventor named Edwin Armstrong. Armstrong swept McInnes off her feet, and drove her away in his French sports car. They were married the next year. Armstrong gave his wife the world's first portable radio as a wedding gift.

When Sarnoff and Armstrong had met years ago, they'd been united by their belief in radio. Watching his secretary fall in love with Armstrong couldn't have helped Sarnoff's feelings toward his onetime friend. Whether that contributed to their eventual end is impossible to know.

CHAPTER 4

SARNOFF VS. ARMSTRONG

After Marconi, Edwin Howard Armstrong was radio's most important inventor. As an undergrad, he created a series of circuits that greatly simplified radio's complicated controls. He invented much of the technology that put radio in airplanes for the Allies in World War I, making radio an essential factor in winning the war. In many cases, Armstrong went into the planes and wired the radios himself. During both world wars, Armstrong gave the U.S. military free use of his patents.

When the radio craze swept America, future president Herbert Hoover gave the credit to Armstrong, "the genius of the American boy."[1]

Edwin Armstrong met David Sarnoff in 1913, when Sarnoff was dispatched by the Marconi Company to evaluate one of Armstrong's breakthroughs. They quickly became friends, and bonded one freezing night, huddled in a small shack with Armstrong's radio gear. For thirteen hours, they were lost in the dream of the technology they were leading, pulling in signals from Ireland, Germany, and Hawaii.

They were together on the crest of the wave, and they knew it.

Years later, Sarnoff wrote to his friend:

Well do I remember that memorable night at the Belmar station when, by means of your "magic box," I was able to copy the signals from Honolulu. . . . Whatever chills the air produced were more than extinguished by the warmth of the thrill.[2]

When the industry entered a dogfight for control of radio, the value of Armstrong's radio patents went through the roof. He battled AT&T in one of the longest patent lawsuits ever litigated, then eventually sold AT&T the patents, becoming a millionaire overnight.

AT&T eventually sold Armstrong's patents to Westinghouse, who sold them, inevitably, to RCA.

RCA and AT&T eventually reached an agreement that would shape the next century of media. AT&T would command the phone lines, but stay out of radio hardware and programming.

For Sarnoff, the message was clear: whoever controlled the patents controlled the industry.

That maxim would drive him for the next twenty-five years.

The Birth of FM

As Sarnoff had predicted, RCA's radio patents became a gold mine. In 1921, thirty-two broadcast licenses were granted. By 1922, there were over 600. That year, the RCA group went into high gear, as Americans spent $60 million on radios. Broadcasting became the chief source of RCA's income.

Sarnoff and Armstrong remained close friends, with Armstrong dropping over for coffee so often that the Sarnoff kids called him "the coffee man." Armstrong was the war hero/inventor, and Sarnoff the up-and-coming industrialist who needed him. Like Apple's Jobs and Wozniak decades later, Sarnoff and Armstrong became a powerful team of opposites, the ambitious executive and introverted inventor. They balanced each other, supported each other, and helped each other—for the time being.

One of the persistent limitations of radio was that it was accompanied by a constant stream of static. As they sat over coffee, Sarnoff had one request of Armstrong: find a way to get rid of all the noise.

For the next decade, Armstrong worked steadily on the noise problem at his Columbia University laboratory. Still wealthy from his patent royalties, he taught at Columbia for $1 a year, and steadily worked on a solution.

In 1933, Armstrong called Sarnoff. He had solved the noise problem.

When Sarnoff and his entourage made their way to Armstrong's lab, they were shocked by what they heard. The difference in quality was incredible: Armstrong had replaced a waterfall of noise with a whisper.

What Armstrong had invented was a new kind of radio. Called "Frequency Modulation," or FM, it was patented on December 26, 1933. It replaced the "Amplitude Modulation" (AM) technology that powered radio to that point with a completely new end-to-end system.

Sarnoff told Armstrong that FM was "revolutionary." But it was not a compliment. Like iOS and Android platforms in the future, Armstrong's FM and AM were warring formats. If FM rolled out, it would make every piece of RCA hardware in the field obsolete.

FM may have been a technological masterpiece, but for Sarnoff it was a business nightmare.

"A new kind of radio," responded Sarnoff, "is like a new kind of mousetrap. The world doesn't need another mousetrap."[3]

There was another force at play. In the ten years that Armstrong had been working on FM, Sarnoff had seen the future, again.

In 1923, Sarnoff wrote his second visionary memo, once again predicting the future of media. MIT scholars later referred to it as the "First Television Prophecy":

> I believe that television, which is the technical name for seeing instead of hearing by radio, will come to pass in due course. . . . We shall be able actually to see as well as hear in New York, within an hour or so, the event taking place in London, Buenos Aires, or Tokyo.[4]

Sarnoff used his position as a leader in radio to become the great evangelist for a future medium called television. In 1926, in *The Saturday Evening Post*, he took his vision to the public:

> The greatest day of all will be reached when not only the human voice but the image of the speaker can be flashed through space in every direction. . . . Mothers will attend child-welfare clinics in their own homes. . . . A scientist can demonstrate his latest discoveries to those of his profession even though they be scattered all over the world.[5]

Sarnoff saw, before any of his competitors, that the future was no longer in radio. Radio was now a cash machine to be milked until the next great medium was ready.

As radio had dwarfed the telegraph, television would dwarf radio.

Sarnoff would exploit every resource, bend every rule, do whatever it took to control television. He would fight every competitor, manipulate an industry, and bring his considerable power to Washington.

Edwin Armstrong had outlived his usefulness.

CHAPTER 5

NATIONAL BROADCASTING COMPANY

I don't get ulcers. I give them.
—DAVID SARNOFF

David Sarnoff had been right about the market for radio programming. The radio boom had created a huge market for programming—feeding the government's concern about monopoly. Sarnoff had first considered the idea of a "network" early on, as a library of assets that radio stations could share.

This "shared library" concept became a big issue, as the federal government considered antitrust actions. Under Sarnoff's leadership, the Big Four considered their options. As the federal government moved against them, Sarnoff dropped the idea that content should be a "sacred public trust." That ship had sailed.

In 1926, AT&T, GE, RCA, and Westinghouse agreed to set up a new entity. It would be co-owned by RCA (50 percent), GE (30 percent), and Westinghouse (20 percent).

It was called the National Broadcasting Company.

AT&T would get out of radio, but would monopolize the lines, the backbone that allowed the new networks to function. It surrendered the AT&T radio network to RCA, as well as its transmitting facilities.

This gave RCA two networks of radio stations: the one that they'd had all along, and the one that they got from AT&T. The first NBC network would be known as NBC Blue; the former AT&T network would be NBC Red.

The government would soon force NBC to sell NBC Red. Its new owners would rename it the American Broadcasting Company. NBC, ABC, and another new network called CBS would begin a competition that would dominate America for the rest of the century.

The Depression

In 1929, the stock market crashed, and public opinion turned against large corporations. In 1930, the Department of Justice notified the Big Four that it would investigate them for collusion and antitrust, for exploiting their interlocking patent access to monopolize radio.

In the month of that announcement, 305 banks went bankrupt. The following month, 522 more banks folded. Across America, farm foreclosures, land seizures, suicides, and crime increased. As RCA moved into Rockefeller Center, the future looked grim.

Not wanting to deal with potential disaster, AT&T withdrew from the broadcast business. It would stay out for nearly 100 years. For the three remaining companies, this situation was perilous—for the Radio Corporation, most perilous of all.

The Radio Act of 1927 contained antimonopoly provisions, which gave the federal government the right to revoke radio licenses. Losing their broadcast license would be a disaster for RCA, and the end of Sarnoff's rise.

The Big Four dreaded something even more ominous: the potential election of a "socialist" president in 1932. The former undersecretary of the Navy and governor of New York was running for office on a tide of massive indignation. If elected, it wasn't clear what Franklin Roosevelt might do. The clock was ticking for RCA.

With his former boss exhausted by the struggle, David Sarnoff jumped into the breach. He took over communications between the Big Four, and with the federal government. He urged GE and Westinghouse to "unify" their radio manufacturing, under RCA's control.

They agreed, and what could have been a disaster turned out to be a triumph. RCA consolidated its power, and evaded the government once again.

It was largely due to the immigrant from Uzlian, who had fished newspapers from the garbage to learn how to read.

In 1930, after twenty-four long years, David Sarnoff was made president of the Radio Corporation of America.

CHAPTER 6

FROM RADIO TO TELEVISION

I thought Armstrong would invent some kind of a filter
to remove static. . . . I didn't think he'd . . . start up a
whole damn new industry to compete with RCA.
—DAVID SARNOFF

In March 1934, Sarnoff allowed Edwin Armstrong to install his FM transmitter on the top of the Empire State Building, RCA's premium test location. The receiver was seventy miles away.

The results exceeded Armstrong's boldest claims. Defying thunder and lightning, FM transmitted a range of sound never heard before, and virtually noise-free. The log from the first transmission on June 16, 1934, by an RCA engineer, stated that a great new era was now underway.

Armstrong waited anxiously for word from Sarnoff. It took ten long months.

Sarnoff's terse note of April 1935 instructed Armstrong to move out of the Empire State Building immediately. The Radio Corporation of America was no longer interested in FM.

Armstrong was shocked by the rejection, but rationalized it, assuming that his old friend was busy with other things. When Armstrong spoke at RCA's 1935 stockholder meeting that questioned some of Sarnoff's behavior, Armstrong publicly defended the man who had shut him down. Sarnoff wrote to thank Armstrong the next day:

> Doubtless I have made many mistakes in my life, but I am glad to say they have not been in the quality of the friends I selected for reposing my faith.[1]

It may have been the last civil word between them.

Armstrong resolved to soldier on, and started presenting FM radio to various organizations. He took his case to the FCC. Meanwhile, RCA announced an allocation of $1 million—to television.

The FCC began evaluating the demands for spectrum from FM and television. There was, after all, only so much bandwidth to go around.

That's when the scope of the nightmare may have sunk in for Armstrong.

Sarnoff had asked Armstrong to create a quieter form of radio. Armstrong had spent a decade doing so. And now Sarnoff was trying to kill it.

Armstrong asked the FCC for an experimental FM license. When he got one, he sold his RCA stock to build the first FM station. Though news of FM's incredible sound quality made headlines, the FCC gave FM no spectrum for trials. It was focusing on a new medium called television, and trying to keep up with change.

Radio had transformed America, and Sarnoff had been its greatest steward. He had dodged an antitrust bullet after the crash, but eventually Roosevelt and Congress weighed in.

The Communications Act of 1934

In 1934, Congress passed landmark legislation that would define much of the media business. The Federal Communications Act of 1934 broadened the government's authority to regulate radio, telephone and television, and eventually, the Internet. The act declared that the American public owned the airwaves, and that spectrum was a public resource. Going forward, telecommunications and broadcasting would be regulated in a manner similar to that of railroads and interstate commerce.

While other government controlled the airwaves themselves, the FCC would grant licenses to *private* firms, which would serve the public interest.

A new round of dogfights began—between the FCC, RCA, AT&T, and a host of other would-be leaders.

RCA hammered the FCC for television spectrum—represented by Sarnoff and a new RCA employee who had been the FCC's chief engineer just a few weeks earlier. FM, RCA said, was a diversion from the real game of television.

Senator Charles W. Tobey of New Hampshire tried to help Armstrong:

> "RCA has been doing everything it can to keep Armstrong down. They did their damnedest to ruin FM. At the same time, they were supplying free TV sets to commissioners of the FCC."[2]

But a congressional inquiry went nowhere. In 1945, RCA lobbied the FCC to take away the FM spectrum it had eventually granted to Armstrong. They won, and all of Armstrong's FM radios instantly became worthless.

In 1946 the FCC ruled that television could use Armstrong's FM system as an audio standard. But RCA refused to pay royalties to Armstrong, and encouraged other TV makers not to pay either. Armstrong turned to the courts, charging theft and patent infringement. RCA responded with an army of lawyers and tied the case up for six years.

Then RCA unleashed its nastiest piece of business. It claimed to have invented FM itself. Sarnoff testified that he himself had "done more to develop FM than anybody in this country, including Armstrong."[3] RCA's patent on FM was granted, leaving Armstrong unable to claim royalties on the technology he had invented.

Armstrong sold off his assets, including what was left of his RCA stock. By 1954, bled dry, he was finally willing to settle. He asked RCA for $2.4 million. RCA countered with $200,000, less than Armstrong's outstanding legal fees.

Armstrong appealed to his wife for some of the money he'd given her in the past. She refused; that money was for their retirement.

Armstrong lost control and struck her in the arm with a poker. She fled to stay with her sister. Overcome with remorse, Armstrong wrote her a note:

> I am heartbroken because I cannot see you once again.
> I deeply regret what has happened between us. I cannot

understand how I could hurt the dearest thing in the whole
world to me. I would give my life to turn back to the time
when we were so happy and free. God keep you and may
the Lord have mercy on my soul.[4]

In January of 1954, Edwin Armstrong put on his hat, scarf, and gloves; removed the air conditioner from the window of his thirteenth-floor apartment; and jumped to his death.

Decades later, courts ruled for Armstrong and awarded his widow, Sarnoff's former secretary, millions in retroactive fees.

On hearing of the death of his old friend, Sarnoff responded, "I did not kill Armstrong." He is reported to have wept at the funeral.

CHAPTER 7

THE ALPHA AND BETA OF TELEVISION

Throughout the early twentieth century, inventors from all over the world struggled to create a working system of television. One hundred years later, the process for technology development is more fully defined. It often goes through a series of phases: pre-alpha, alpha, and beta.

Pre-alpha is the phase in which basic goals are defined. *Alpha* is the phase in which actual prototypes are created and tested. In *Beta*, an early version of the product is refined and revised, until a *beta version* is ready for a small audience of users called *beta testers*. The early days of television followed this model with a series of inventors that lasted over forty-five years. Notable among them are Paul Nipkow, John Logie Baird, and Charles Jenkins.

Pre-Alpha: Paul Nipkow

The major inventor of pre-alpha television was Paul Nipkow. In Germany in 1885, he patented a method for displaying images via a perforated spinning disk. The first method for producing a TV picture, it became the template for decades of prototypes. When a "Nipkow disk" revolved, light shone through the holes, which created a series of moving images. The first television broadcasts would use the mechanical picture-scanning method Nipkow helped create with his disk.

Nipkow created the *concept* for the disk, but he didn't create the actual prototype. That took another four decades. Nipkow first saw his handiwork in Berlin in 1928:

> Hundreds stood and waited patiently for the moment at which they would see television for the first time. Finally I reached the front row; a dark cloth was pushed to the side, and I saw before me a flickering image. . . . I waited among them, growing ever more nervous. Now for the first time I would see what I had devised 45 years ago.[1]

In a global race to take credit for television, the Nazis claimed that it had been invented by Nipkow. Britain gave that credit to the man who built the system that Nipkow saw that day. His name was John Logie Baird.

British Alpha: John Logie Baird

John Baird was a sickly Scotsman who spent his life searching for the next big invention—in his own words, "a wretched nonentity working with soap boxes in a garret."[2]

An inveterate inventor and marketer, Baird created a motley pageant of projects. He marketed hemorrhoid ointment. He tried manufacturing diamonds from cement and inadvertently blew up the electric lines at his workplace. His first successful invention was a fabric layer called the "Undersock," which succeeded in keeping his very cold feet warm. He also invented "pneumatic soles," boots with tires in them.

Hating the dampness of Scotland, Baird moved to Trinidad, where he tried to support himself by making jam. That failed too, so he moved back home and tried to invent a new kind of soap. He took up with his former girlfriend, and when her new husband found out, talked his way into a shared arrangement that lasted for years.

Like many of his generation, Baird had been inspired by the idea of "remote seeing." One afternoon, spurred by the buzz around wireless, he went for a walk on the moor and returned with a decision: he would invent television.

When Baird told a friend that he would invent a means of sending pictures through the air, his friend dismissed him and said he hoped

Baird wouldn't become another one of those wireless idiots. He would, and it would earn him a piece of immortality: in a global horse race of inventors, Baird would be the first to publicly demonstrate television.

With the help of a few volunteers, Baird built a crude television set—from darning needles, scissors, a hatbox, wax, and glue.

In 1923, he succeeded at transmitting a picture of a volunteer's hand via his version of Nipkow's spinning disk. In 1925, he was able to view one of his ventriloquist dummies. He then paid an office boy to take the place of the dummy, and could clearly see the boy's face in the transmission.

It was a landmark moment, and Baird was terrified: "I was extremely nervous in case while I waited, someone else achieved television and gave a show before I did."[3] His investors also worried that he would be copied.

On January 26, 1926, Baird finally demonstrated his technology. It went so well that the *New York Times* reported that the international race for television had been won, by Great Britain.

Baird found an investor, and swore that the Baird Company held a virtual monopoly on television. One year later, he was proven very wrong. In 1927, Baird's achievements were overshadowed by three competitors: AT&T, and two other inventors named Charles Jenkins and Philo Farnsworth. The American media, with nationalistic pride, seized on these domestic winners, and promptly forgot about Baird.

In his own country, Baird fought for a deal with the newly formed BBC—which suspected (rightly) that the mechanical TV of Nipkow's disk was not a long-term answer.

Instead of winning a client, Baird wound up paying the BBC to broadcast his programming at midnight, once a week, for fifteen minutes. It was not a shrewd arrangement.

Next, Baird tried his hand in the United States. He broke up with his girlfriend and got married in America. But RCA asked the FCC to block foreign broadcasters, and Baird Television was banned.

"The only way to get anything done in America is to sell out for what you can get to an American company, and let Americans fight Americans," Baird would later say.[4]

Baird returned to England to reengage with the BBC, where he faced an even bigger nightmare: the entry of British firm EMI into the TV fray. EMI was using *electronic*, rather than *mechanical*, television.

Baird, recognizing he needed to adapt, sent out a call for electronic TV assistance. American inventor Philo Farnsworth came to the rescue. Facing his own economic troubles in the States, Farnsworth allowed Baird to use his electronic TV technology, for a price.

Unfortunately, Baird attempted to combine the two systems, and created a hopeless mess. Farnsworth visited Baird to help a second time, then left for a long-needed vacation. The laboratory promptly burned to the ground, destroying Farnsworth's chances in Europe, and Baird's overall.

When the BBC set up a contest between Baird and EMI, Baird lost.

Like leagues of latter-day Silicon Valley entrepreneurs, Baird spent the rest of his life wishing he'd sold when he'd had the chance.

During World War II, Baird was arrested when police thought he was a German spy. He told them he was John Logie Baird, the inventor of television. It meant nothing to them. His wife convinced them that he was an odd and harmless inventor, which was true enough. Baird died in 1945.

American Alpha: Charles Jenkins

> *It's the old story over again. The inventor gets the experience*
> *and the capitalist gets the invention.*
> —CHARLES JENKINS

Inventor Charles Jenkins was prolific. At one point, he owned over 400 U.S. patents, for products including a wagon wheel greaser, a bean-shelling machine, a disposable paper milk bottle, and a horseless carriage.

Jenkins had learned the harsh realities of being an inventor early, at the foot of the master. In the 1890s, Jenkins had created a version of Edison's kinescope, an early motion picture viewing device. A thief—likely one of Jenkins's investors—stole the prototype.

Frank Gammon's cinema company purchased the stolen device, and it became the "Edison Vitascope." Though the Franklin Institute credits Jenkins as the inventor of the film projector, Jenkins lost popular credit to Edison, forevermore.

Jenkins fought the theft of his invention in court, and won $2,500. In 1921, he used the money to open Jenkins Laboratories in Washington, D.C., and joined the race to invent television.

By 1922, he had an early version of mechanical television. He applied for a patent the following year. He promoted mechanical television heavily, contributing to the buzz that swept America in the late 1920s.

Jenkins claimed to have made the first demonstration of "seeing by radio" in 1925—an extended image of a windmill. This was disingenuous; Jenkins certainly knew that Baird had come first. Nonetheless, the *New York Times* dubbed Jenkins "the father of television." That appellation would shift from person to person for at least ninety years.

Jenkins was granted the first license for a TV station in 1927. He began broadcasting in May of 1928. Like Sarnoff, he saw the vision for television early:

> Folks in California and Maine, and all the way between, will be able to see the inauguration ceremonies of their President in Washington, the Army and Navy football game in Philadelphia.[5]

As with Baird, it did not end well. The Jenkins Television Corporation was demolished by the stock market crash of 1929. It limped along until 1932, when it was purchased by the DeForest Radio Company.

Jenkins died in 1934. The Television Academy eventually named a Technical Emmy Award in his honor.

DeForest Radio was eventually bought by the company that bought everyone worth buying: David Sarnoff's RCA.

By the time RCA bought Jenkins's patents, Sarnoff had gone beyond them. He had discovered his new Armstrong in an evangelist of electronic television.

Sarnoff's new lieutenant had a revolutionary idea. The idea, though not his alone, would be television's beta phase.

Sarnoff's new lieutenant was Vladimir Zworykin.

Beta Phase: Vladimir Zworykin

As radio matured, Sarnoff turned his focus to television, looking for an inventor to help him build the Next Big Thing. For a time, he worked with an engineer named Ernst Alexanderson. But Alexanderson's concept, like Baird's and Jenkins's, was based on mechanical television. It became clear to Sarnoff that the spinning Nipkow disk was simply not RCA quality. The picture integrity was limited by the disk itself, which flickered and wobbled and eventually wore out. Even if the audience forgave the inconstancy, the service requirements might infuriate consumers. Sarnoff decided that he would not sell a television that was built on the technical equivalent of a PEZ dispenser.

So Sarnoff kept an eye on all potential breakthroughs. In 1929, the innovation came to him.

Vladimir Zworykin had arrived from Russia in 1919. He had studied under Boris Rosing, an early TV pioneer. From Rosing, Zworykin had seen the earliest experiments in electronic television, and a technology called the cathode ray tube. He knew where the future lay.

In America, Zworykin got a job at Westinghouse, and continued Rosing's experiments.

In 1923, Sarnoff had issued his new visionary memo, declaring that television was RCA's future. That same year, Vladimir Zworykin filed a patent on an electronic television technology called the Iconoscope.

How much of the Iconoscope he actually built would be a subject of debate for decades.

In 1925, Zworykin pitched Westinghouse on investing in electronic television. His bosses were unimpressed, and selected someone else to lead TV development. The rejected Zworykin began looking for greener pastures. He set up one meeting with David Sarnoff—and another with a man in San Francisco, who seemed to have found the Grail.

CHAPTER 8

PHILO FARNSWORTH

There are certain inventions which, although not yet existant
[sic], we take for granted will be invented some day. . . .
Television, or "remote seeing" is one such invention.
—HUGO GERNSBACK, *ELECTRICAL EXPERIMENTER MAGAZINE*, 1918

P hilo Farnsworth was born on August 19, 1906, in Indian Creek, Utah. His family was poor and moved frequently, searching for a better life. In 1918, as Hugo Gernsback predicted television, the three wagons of the Farnsworth family arrived at their new farmhouse home in Rigby, Idaho. Philo was ecstatic to discover that, unlike their previous homes, this one had electricity.[1]

It was a pivotal moment in twelve-year-old Philo's life. In a period Edison called "the renaissance of invention," inventors were the idols that rock stars would be fifty years later, that tech founders are today.

At age six, Philo had announced to his family that he was going to be the next Edison. The contents of the new farmhouse attic put him on his way. Here, Philo discovered a pile of scientific magazines. They detailed the secrets of electronic devices, with schematics and explanations of how to construct them. They also postulated theoretical inventions, many of which would come to pass in the coming years.

In addition to the scientific journals, he found magazines by Hugo Gernsback, the man widely considered to the father of science fiction, whose visions of technology inspired both writers and inventors for decades. The Science Fiction Awards—the Hugos—are named after him to this day.

One of Gernsback's themes intrigued Philo above all, the quixotic dream of television:

> That such an invention is urgently required is needless to say. Everybody would wish to have such an instrument, and it is safe to say that such a device would revolutionize our present mode of living.[2]

"I was only thirteen when I began studying the problem," Farnsworth would say later. "It wasn't long before I realized that whoever solved it would make a fortune."[3]

The Field

One night in 1920, fourteen-year-old Philo was plowing the field, thinking about various inventions, while he absentmindedly brought the horses back and forth in rows. His eyes wandered along the field, lost in a dream.

Then it hit him.

The rows he plowed were alternating, reversing direction as the plow came around. One row was created left to right, the next right to left. And each row was part of a larger canvas, sequentially building a larger square.

What if he could create a device that would "mow" rows of electrons on a screen, as the plow mowed rows in the field? And what if the electrons refreshed the image faster than the eye could perceive?

With the right kind of tube, you could do it. And Philo knew he could design that tube, modeled on things he had read about in the journals.

That would be electronic television, right there.

In one intuitive leap, the fourteen-year-old vaulted over decades of thinking, past Nipkow, Baird, Jenkins, Alexanderson, and Rosing.

But it was just an initial concept. To bring it to life, Philo needed a prototype. And to create a prototype, Philo desperately needed to supplement his science education in ways that the magazines could not do.

So every day after his morning chores, Philo went to Brigham Young High School early—and begged science teacher Justin Tolman to let him into his class.

At first, Tolman refused. Farnsworth had just moved to town and was pitifully behind. But eventually, Tolman gave in, and discovered that Farnsworth was the best student he'd ever had. When Philo asked questions hinting at his experiments, Tolman gave Philo a book on the cathode ray tube, which the boy devoured.

At the end of the semester, Farnsworth asked Tolman for his opinion on something he was working on. He then filled the boards with a series of equations.

Thunderstruck, Tolman asked what all this meant. Farnsworth said it was his plan for creating electronic television. What should he do next?

Tolman, beginning to see the implications, considered the boy's situation. He was David in the face of Goliaths RCA, AT&T, Westinghouse, and GE. He told Philo to keep studying—and to tell *no one* of his plans.

The Farnsworths soon moved to Provo, where Philo attended Brigham Young University. In early 1924, his college time was cut short when his father died young. Farnsworth decided to join the Navy and went to Annapolis. He soon faced a conflict: if he stayed in the Navy, the government would own his patents. That was off the table; Philo would never give away his inventions. Still, Farnsworth feared that he was running out of time.

Philo left Annapolis and moved back to Utah, where he made a living as a radio repairman. By 1925, his fears were realized, when Baird, Jenkins, and Ernst Alexanderson each made headlines with their versions of television.

In the spring of 1926, Philo got a job working for two professional fundraisers, George Everson and Leslie Gorrell. When Everson's car broke down, Philo picked it up from the mechanic and brought it back to town. He then proceeded to explain to Everson what the mechanic had done wrong.

Impressed, Everson asked Philo about his future plans. Farnsworth told the men that he was raising funds to bring television to America.

"Telly-who?" asked Everson.

When Farnsworth explained, both men were skeptical, assuming that one or more of America's electronics giants must already be on the case.

But Farnsworth won them over. Everson and Gorrell gave Farnsworth $6,000 for equity in the venture.

During this period, Philo got engaged, then abandoned his new bride at their hotel on the wedding night to work on deal terms with Everson and Gorrell. When he returned early in the morning, he made a confession: "Pemmie, I have to tell you there is another woman in my life—and her name is Television."[4]

The Lab

Soon, Farnsworth, Everson, and Gorrell moved to Los Angeles to establish a lab in the entertainment capital of the country. Like many aspiring young people before and since, Farnsworth thought his arrival in Hollywood would be life changing. It was not. Though he had some meetings, the studios paid little notice.

Meetings at Caltech were more fruitful. One banker at Crocker National Bank opined, "This is a damn fool idea, but somebody ought to put money into it. Someone who can afford to lose it."[5] Eventually, the Crocker group itself backed Farnsworth.

In 1926, the Farnsworth group established the Crocker Research Laboratory in San Francisco. Crocker First National put up $25,000—over $300,000 in 2016 dollars.

And in 1927, Farnsworth submitted a patent application for "electronic television." Although it was filed four years after Zworykin's, it had the benefit of being backed by actual prototypes.

Philo became the first inventor to transmit moving images by electronic television. Like Morse and Bell before him, he immediately sent a message. His telegram read, "The Damned Thing Works!"

As the Roaring Twenties progressed, buzz increased around the idea of television. The *New York Daily News* speculated on the fortune awaiting whoever won the race. In 1928, Farnsworth cast aside Tolman's words of caution. The company needed money, and publicity would bring it. So Philo unveiled his invention to the world.

The *San Francisco Chronicle* soon heralded its new local hero, with the headline "S. F. Man's Invention to Revolutionize Television":

> Farnsworth's [electronic] system employs no moving parts whatever. Instead of moving the machine, he varies the electric current that plays over the image and thus gets the necessary scanning. The system is thus simple in the extreme, and one of the major mechanical obstacles to the perfection of television is thereby removed.[6]

Media coverage spread. Farnsworth was extolled as a new Marconi. Though his patents had not yet been granted, his lawyers were optimistic.

But in 1928, as the experiments went on, Crocker decided not to extend further funding to the startup. So in the manner of many startups, the lab crew began working more or less for free.

Philo Farnsworth got his patent approval in August of 1930.

Farnsworth vs. Zworykin

> *This is a beautiful instrument. I wish that I might have invented it.*
> —VLADIMIR ZWORYKIN, TO PHILO FARNSWORTH

A few months prior to getting the patent, Farnsworth received exciting news: Vladimir Zworykin himself wanted to meet! Farnsworth was jubilant. He had been following news on Zworykin's cathode ray tube experiments, and thought Zworykin might bring funding from his company, Westinghouse. Farnsworth knew he'd need deep pockets for a potential patent battle with RCA.

In a now-legendary show of openness, Philo hosted Zworykin for three days.

He had Zworykin over for dinner, introduced him to his wife, and showed his competitor the full contents of his lab.

Zworykin took copious notes, especially concerning Farnsworth's crown jewel: the Image Dissector tube. This was Philo's version of the picture tube, and it was light years ahead of Zworykin's version. When he saw it, Zworykin commented tellingly: "I wish that I might have invented it."

Arguments have raged for decades about that three-day tour. Skeptics say that Farnsworth was hopelessly naive, opening his shop for an enemy to plunder. Farnsworth responded that had been a calculated risk; he needed capital, and Zworykin's Westinghouse was the best bet he had.

What Farnsworth could not know was that Zworykin wasn't representing Westinghouse anymore.

———

Zworykin said goodbye to Farnsworth, took a train back to Westinghouse, and dictated a 700-word memo, describing a device he wanted his lab staff to build. When he arrived, the device was ready. It was Zworykin's version of the Image Dissector tube.

In 1933, Zworykin created his first working TV system. It was very different from what he'd previously described. The new system was much more like the systems built by Farnsworth.

Then Zworykin packed up his office, left Westinghouse forever, and prepared to start his new job—for Sarnoff at RCA.

Sarnoff and Zworykin

At their first meeting in 1929, Zworykin had pitched Sarnoff on the idea of electronic television. When Sarnoff asked Zworykin how much it would cost, Zworykin said he would need $100,000. His estimate was about $50 million short, but by then it didn't matter. In Zworykin, Sarnoff saw an Armstrong he could manage.

What's most intriguing is that Sarnoff, the most powerful man in radio, had already gone to see the Farnsworth lab himself.

He had done it in one of the worst periods of his life, as the Depression was bringing RCA to its knees. At the time of the visit, according to Alex Magoun, director of the David Sarnoff Library:

RCA was in chaos. Radio and phonograph sales were plunging. The Depression led to a price war and the $10 radio. The government forced RCA to slash its licensing fees. And RCA's stock lost more than 90 percent of its value. Sarnoff had this desperation. He was probably thinking, "I'm going to buy this Farnsworth guy."[7]

For reasons never fully explained, when the most powerful man in media came to see him, Philo Farnsworth was not there. Investor George Everson gave Sarnoff the tour, after which Sarnoff went home.

Sarnoff eventually offered Everson and Farnsworth $100,000 in exchange for all of Philo's patents, for the Crocker Research Lab, and for Farnsworth's services as an employee—the same amount he initially gave Zworykin.

It was less than Everson and Farnsworth had built up in debt, and they rejected the offer. There's no evidence they made any attempts to negotiate a better deal.

It's not clear how Farnsworth thought Sarnoff would take the rejection. But anyone who paid attention to Sarnoff would have known that the rejection was an act of war.

Deep in debt, with no source of funding, Farnsworth knew he was in trouble.

But he would not give in.

CHAPTER 9

FARNSWORTH VS. SARNOFF

No great invention is ever wholly the story of one man, but out of the
story of television emerges a giant figure of Philo T. Farnsworth, guiding
genius, lonely experimenter, scoffed-at dreamer—history already has a
page reserved for this man who, convinced that mechanical principles were
wrong, held fast to his theories and made television a practical reality.
—FARNSWORTH TELEVISION AND RADIO BOOKLET

I n May 1930, a U.S. marshal served Sarnoff with papers: the Department
of Justice had accused RCA of abusing its power, restraining trade,
and taking kickbacks.

Sarnoff rallied GE and Westinghouse to his side—conducting two
and a half years of complex negotiations between the behemoths, then
with Washington, and then back again.

By the time FDR swept into office in 1932, Sarnoff had created NBC.

RCA and its child NBC now owned radio completely, and were perfectly poised to take over television.

There was only one player still in Sarnoff's way: Philo Farnsworth,
and the patents he had refused to sell.

———

In 1931, Farnsworth signed a deal with Philco of Philadelphia to produce and distribute TV sets based on his technology. Philco would provide space, engineers, and financing.

RCA responded by threatening to end Philco's access to its patents. Farnsworth and Philco were beaten before they began.

It got worse from there.

While Farnsworth was working at Philco, his fifteen-month-old son died suddenly. Heartbroken, the Farnsworths made plans to bury the baby in Utah. But Philco refused to give Philo time off.

Pem Farnsworth took the train home alone with the baby's body. Philo struggled with his loss at work. The marriage began to fall apart.

With RCA against him, Philco decided that Farnsworth was more trouble than he was worth. When their deal ended in 1933, they chose not to renew. On his own again, Farnsworth took his case to the public, with a new series of demonstrations unlike anything seen before.

In 1934, at the Franklin Institute in Philadelphia, Farnsworth hosted an exhibition of his television technology. The queue for the exhibit wrapped around the block.

Inside, a four-foot-high cabinet faced the audience. Then a strangely familiar image flickered onto the screen. It was the audience itself.

Thirteen years after his epiphany in the field, Philo T. Farnsworth gave the first successful demonstration of electronic television. Underfunded and under siege, he had beaten scientists from all over the world.

It was a stunning achievement, but it made little difference. Farnsworth didn't have the capital to manufacture his sets. And with Sarnoff and RCA out to destroy him, there were few places he could go.

So when John Logie Baird contacted Farnsworth for help in selling TV to the new British Broadcasting Company, Farnsworth packed up his lab and headed to England in 1934. Perhaps the BBC would give Farnsworth's vision a home.

Farnsworth demanded $50,000 and future royalties from Baird, who agreed.

In England, Farnsworth worked himself to exhaustion trying to get Baird's system ready for prime time. Then he returned to America. However, Baird attempted to combine the two systems, destroyed both in the process, and begged Farnsworth to return to England.

Philo hated the idea, but had little choice: by 1936, RCA was starving him out. The BBC was now his only way forward.

So he sailed back to England and ruined his health again, trying to repair the mess. Then Baird's lab burned to the ground.

In the rubble, Philo found the charred remains of his Image Dissector tube, and wept.

The Mormon teetotaler Philo began to drink heavily. He was prescribed a series of medications for anxiety, which made his health worse. One doctor advised him to take up smoking, which he did.

In 1936, RCA and NBC began experimental TV broadcasts. In 1937, Sarnoff began pushing the government to allow him to begin commercial broadcasts. He had a target date in mind: the 1939 New York World's Fair.

The Ruling

The Patent Office began grappling with the case of *Zworykin v. Farnsworth* on January 18, 1933. The process dragged on for over a year; both principals testified for hundreds of hours.

The litigation eventually cost Farnsworth $30,000—over $400,000 adjusted for inflation. It cost RCA much more.

RCA had filed patent interference claims, arguing that Zworykin's 1923 claim predated Farnsworth's patents. Zworykin had come first, they said, and Farnsworth was entitled to nothing.

It was up to the Patent Office to determine the truth.

A primary question was whose patent application had come first. Zworykin had applied for a patent on electronic television in 1923; Farnsworth had not filed until 1927.

But Zworykin produced no evidence of an actual working model of television from any time before the time that Farnsworth had created his. Nor could he produce witnesses who had ever seen him with one.

When questioned as to what exactly he'd done in 1923, Zworykin was not convincing. Had he ever actually *built* the tubes he had patented?

For once, Farnsworth had an ace in the hole. His patent attorney, Don Lippincott, had been an electrical engineer, and was happy to take on patent scourge RCA. He asked Farnsworth if he had told anyone else about his invention. Farnsworth thought about it, then said there was.

Lippincott went to Utah, and returned with Justin Tolman.

The teacher who'd looked after Philo when it all began told the officials about Philo's epiphany in the field. He detailed their many conversations in the classroom. He described the calculations the boy had drawn on his blackboard.

Then he pulled out an old piece of paper, a thirteen-year-old sketch.

It was the Image Dissector diagram Philo had drawn so many years ago.

———

In February 1935, the U.S. Patent Office delivered its decision in *Zworykin v. Farnsworth*. It found against Zworykin and RCA. It awarded Philo T. Farnsworth the patent for his invention of television.

RCA was ordered to pay Farnsworth a minimum of $1 million over ten years. It was the first time RCA ever paid for a patent. RCA's lead attorney wept.

Sarnoff had already moved on.

———

When the 1939 World's Fair began, there were fewer than 1,000 television sets in New York. It was enough.

The plan was set to have FDR deliver the first television address, but he was mildly upstaged.

The first recorded televised address was given on April 20, by David Sarnoff:

> It is with a feeling of humbleness that I come to this moment of announcing the birth in this country of a new art so important in its implications that it is bound to affect all society. Now, ladies and gentlemen, we add sight to sound![1]

All Worthwhile

> *Television? The word is half Greek and half Latin. No good will come of it.*
> —C. P. SCOTT, THE *MANCHESTER GUARDIAN*, 1928

Farnsworth went on to a series of ventures: running a sawmill, making bullet cases, and conducting experiments in nuclear fusion. As television spread, his contributions were generally unknown.

In 1957, Farnsworth appeared on television for the first and only time—as a mystery guest on a game show called *I've Got a Secret*. Three panelists tried to guess his profession, but none of them could.

When they ran out of guesses, he told them: "I invented electronic television."

He won $80 and a carton of cigarettes.

———

In July of 1969, Farnsworth watched Neil Armstrong walk on the moon. "They're using a miniature version of my Image Dissector tube," he told his wife, proudly. "Pem," he said, "this has made it all worthwhile."[2]

Farnsworth died on March 12, 1971, at age sixty-four.

David Sarnoff died exactly nine months later, on December 12, at eighty.

Their child had gone on to take over the world.

PART 2

COLUMBIA BROADCASTING SYSTEM

CHAPTER 10

WILLIAM PALEY

By the mid-1920s, David Sarnoff was a legend. He had come from nothing to build the radio hardware business, then the first network, and then the first media empire.

In 1928, Sarnoff would meet his match.

Sarnoff's nemesis would build the radio advertising business, the programming business, and the world's most prestigious network.

This new media mogul would be Sarnoff's opposite in almost every way: an exuberant, charming lover of the good life, marketing, show business, and high society.

Like Sarnoff, William Paley would begin his achievements by creating himself.

———

Between 1880 and 1924, nearly 2 million Jews emigrated from Eastern Europe to America. The Sarnoffs were among them. So were the Paleys, who came to America in 1888, and settled in Chicago's large Jewish ghetto.

But patriarch Isaac Paley simply did not want to work. In Russia, he'd been a successful lumber merchant; in Chicago, he was back at the bottom. He was a man accustomed to staying at the Ritz Carlton, now sentenced to life in a Motel 6.

Isaac tried to play the stock market and failed, took menial jobs but couldn't endure them. He had too much pride to start over. Deprived of the status he'd lost, Isaac resolved to become a man of leisure. The ghetto aristocrat relaxed at home, taking tea with his friends.

For Isaac's wife, Zelda, and their son, Sam, Isaac's indigence was a burden they'd have to endure.

But for Isaac's grandson Bill, who would dine with ambassadors and almost become one, it was an object lesson in refusing to settle. Bill would wonder later in life "whether something of my grandfather's feeling for the value of leisure and luxury did not brush off on me."[1]

In the 1890s, eight Paleys shared a four-room apartment. So young Sam Paley took on a variety of jobs, including peddling newspapers and making cigars. Sam liked the cigar business and set out to master it. In doing so, he inadvertently changed history.

In 1896, twenty-one-year-old Sam Paley took his minor savings and founded Samuel Paley and Company, cigar makers. In 1898, he married sixteen-year-old Goldie Drell. On September 28, 1901, their son William Paley was born in a small apartment behind their cigar shop.

Paley would later say that his father was a millionaire by that time. Like Sarnoff's *Titanic* stories, this was an embellishment. Thus began the parallel, invented narratives of Bill Paley and David Sarnoff, who arrived in America the year before Paley was born.

In 1904, Sam brought on his brother Jacob, and renamed his venture the Congress Cigar Company. Throughout Bill Paley's youth, the business improved, and the Paleys soon entered Chicago's middle class.

Sam began to focus on one cigar brand called La Palina, with a label bearing an image of Sam's wife, Goldie, a critical figure in Bill Paley's life. Though Bill adored his father, he was ambivalent about his mother, questioning her love for him. One associate countered that no woman alive could have given Bill what he needed.

When Bill joined the family business, some saw his eventual character begin to emerge: "charming but cold, enthusiastic but cautious, ruthless yet thoughtful, distracted as well as disciplined, sensitive and oblivious, shy but social, confident yet insecure, direct but devious."[2]

By the time Bill neared college age in 1919, the family business was thriving. Sam took Bill to look for potential new factory locations, starting in Manhattan. As the 1919 bull market raged, young Paley fell in love with Manhattan. Sam chose Philadelphia for the new factory, but Bill would return to New York as soon as he could.

In Philadelphia, Sam gave teenage Bill a larger role in the company. When the new plant got caught in an industry-wide strike, Bill successfully negotiated with union leaders, and discovered a new love: for making deals.

Bill enrolled at the Wharton School of Finance at his father's insistence. He hated it. After the drama on the front lines of the strike, he thought college was a waste of time.

Bill spent college chasing women and having fun, before taking over the cigar business.

He was fortunate: Congress Cigar was exploding. Between 1921 and 1926, net earnings grew from $75,000 to $1.7 million; production went from 55 million to 255 million cigars per year. By the end of 1926, the company had over 4,000 employees.

Bill never let work cut into his social life, which now included a smorgasbord of speakeasies, parties, hotels, and women.

It was the beginning of a lifetime of ambivalence for a man who would leave his company for months at a time, then return to seize the reins; in which the desire to be a man of leisure battled with a hunger to be at the center of the action. The battle would continue for the next sixty years.

In 1926, Goldman Sachs took Congress Cigar public, and the Paleys cleared nearly $3 million. Later that year they sold a large portion of the company to another tobacco company, netting another $4 million.

Bill's cut of the sale was $1 million. He was wealthy beyond his dreams.

Young Bill enjoyed his money to the hilt, staying out till the sun came up. Sam was angry with his son for aspiring to be like Isaac. He told Bill to clean up his act and start pulling his weight.

Bill most certainly would, but not in cigars.

Paley and Radio

Since 1921, America had been caught up in the wireless craze. By 1923, 2.5 million radios had been sold. By 1925, the Department of Commerce had issued over 1,400 broadcasting licenses. And in 1925, William Paley heard radio for the first time, on one of the small kit-based radio crystal sets that were sweeping the nation.

Bill couldn't figure out how music got into the crystal set's headphones without wires. He thought the gadget was a prank. When he saw that it wasn't, he was mesmerized.

Paley would reminisce about this period for the rest of his life. Like amateurs all over America, he stayed awake until the early morning hours trying to pick up distant signals. Like Sarnoff and Armstrong a decade earlier, he had found his passion. He just didn't know it yet.

As Bill fell in love with radio, America was discovering a new addiction: cigarettes. By mid-decade, production of cigarettes had grown from 16 billion to 82 billion. Unfortunately for the Paleys, cigar sales had begun to decline.

Congress Cigar launched a line of cigarettes, and put Bill in charge of marketing them. The problem was that they tasted terrible. Congress Cigar had used substandard paper that yielded a vile product, and the cigarette line had to be shut down.

In 1927, needing to increase cigar sales, Sam began sponsoring a radio show. It was named after the premier Paley product: *La Palina Smoker.*

In between songs and guests, the hosts promoted La Palina cigars relentlessly. The radio show brought Congress Cigar sales from 400,000 to 1,000,000 units per day. The show proved one of radio advertising's biggest brand successes.

The Birth of Radio Advertising

Radio ads were pioneered by an unlikely company: AT&T.

Although radio was a hardware business started by RCA, archrival AT&T saw another opportunity. In 1922, AT&T launched a station in New York, and started selling radio time to advertisers, nestled inside their programs. They helped turn radio into a dual-revenue-stream business, in which some companies made money selling radios, and other made money selling advertising on radio shows.

But listeners hated the ads. Regulators hated the ads. The objections came thick and fast, eventually from Secretary of Commerce Herbert Hoover at the National Radio Conference in 1922: "It is inconceivable that we should allow so great a possibility for service, for news, for entertainment, for education, to be drowned in advertising chatter."[3]

This period of radio's history offers a great case study in business model innovation. It illustrates the phases that recur throughout the history of business:

1. Inventors and entrepreneurs create something new.
2. Fans create a movement around it, making it the Next Big Thing.
3. Both the original inventors and larger players search for ways to own a piece of the Next Big Thing.
4. The winners take over the Next Big Thing, forcing or buying the others out.
5. If the spoils are large enough, government and industry begin to mud-wrestle over how the Next Big Thing will be regulated.

David Sarnoff had mastered all of these phases. He had been there when radio technology was the Next Big Thing. He had been successful at taking it over, monetizing it, fighting off competitors, and neutralizing government opposition.

Sarnoff was a mogul designed to master the Next Big Thing of radio, the aardvark to the ant of the radio business.

But incumbents in the Next Big Thing rarely own the next one. IBM owned the personal computer, but lost the operating system to Microsoft. Microsoft owned the operating system, but lost the smartphone/app economy to Apple.

Sarnoff had beaten AT&T and the government, wresting the radio network away from AT&T. While almost no executive dominates two Next Big Things in a row, David Sarnoff won the Next Big Thing of radio hardware, then the Next Big Thing of the radio network.

But David Sarnoff was not a master of advertising. Neither was the network that ran Paley's *La Palina Smoker* show.

La Palina's host network was a struggling enterprise called the Columbia Phonograph Broadcasting System, and it desperately needed help.

———

CBS was the awkward merger of a record company and a musicians' promotion company. The company was founded in New York in 1927, and its business model was a disaster. CBS sought to generate radio revenue by promoting musicians, thereby selling more records. It was too small a game and too late in the cycle—the wrong model at the wrong time.

So like others before it, CBS found itself in the path of a steamroller. It was being pummeled by the Death Star of radio, Sarnoff's NBC.

There was simply not enough money in musician promotion to keep CBS in business. The founders, Leon Levy and Jerome Louchheim, looked for someone to invest in the company. They needed cash to ride out the storm while they made the shift to an advertising-based world.

In 1927, Levy married Blanche Paley. He hoped his new father-in-law would be willing to help him out. So in 1928, shortly after the wedding, Levy asked Sam to invest $50,000 in CBS. Sam agreed.

CBS promptly burned through Sam's money. In August 1928, the partners agonized over whether to keep going, or to fold. They decided to give the business just ten more days.

Leon Levy and Jerome Louchheim were lucky. A few days later, Warner Bros. began buying ad time for its revolutionary movie, *The Jazz Singer*. Talkies had arrived, bringing CBS a big ad buy, and granting it a stay of execution.

Emboldened, the boys asked Sam to buy the company. After all, he had a cigar business: he could use radio to promote his brand. Sam reportedly put up $400,000; Bill may have put up some of his $1 million. On September 25, 1928, the Paleys took control of the company.

"I just bought the Columbia Broadcasting System for my son," Sam proudly told a friend.[4] It was unclear whether the network would survive, but it was worth a shot.

On September 26, 1928, Bill Paley was named president of CBS. He was twenty-six years old. Like a generation of pioneers before him, he was heading toward a collision with Sarnoff.

This time, the results would be different. Advertising had found its Marconi.

The King of Advertising

Bill Paley took on running CBS radio with the energy of someone who'd gotten the part he was born to play. His energy and charm battled with bouts of insecurity, hypochondria, and above all else, a love of the high life. But for now, he buckled down and did whatever he could to rescue CBS.

Paley got lucky in his first year at CBS. Presidential elections are the ATMs of media advertising, and Paley arrived just in time for one of the biggest of the radio age: Herbert Hoover and Alfred E. Smith. The election advertising covered the bills, allowing Paley to experiment with new things.

That's when the playboy turned out to be a visionary. In an industry in which everyone secretly believes they're a genius, Paley would be the first genius of radio advertising.

When Paley took over CBS, radio advertising was a local business. NBC and CBS sold advertising regionally, on an area-by-area basis. Paley saw an opportunity, and began the practice of national ad buys, giving sponsors steep discounts if they bought time on the full CBS network. Without knowing it, he was moving media toward the national network era.

Paley also forced the older, stodgier NBC to break multiple advertising taboos. He challenged NBC's custom of never mentioning prices of advertised products. He reduced the length of commercials, to fit more of them in less time. He provoked a scandal by accepting "bodily function" ads, running spots for deodorants and laxatives. Like smart, young, hungry media companies would do in the future, he forced the incumbent to bend.

At every turn, Sarnoff complained about and resisted but ultimately followed the advertising lead of his young rival.

Building the Network

As he came into power in 1928, Paley boasted that CBS was the largest radio network. He later admitted that this was "true, but only literally."[5] NBC was larger, with fifty-eight stations—they were just divided across its two networks. NBC was clearly number one, but Paley came out swinging.

He soon had a breakthrough that drastically altered the business. It came to him when he was in bed with one of his frequent hypochondriacal illnesses. It had to do with affiliates—the actual local stations that constituted the CBS network.

At the time, NBC charged its affiliates programming fees for many of its shows. This programming fee was up to $90 per hour. The affiliates hated paying the fee, but NBC countered that it had to charge them. Otherwise, it wouldn't have funds to produce the shows.

Paley saw a way to compete. NBC was focused on *revenue*, by making affiliates pay for programming. CBS, Paley decided, would focus on *reach*. It would build the maximum audience by harnessing its affiliates.

Paley's idea would make things better for the affiliates in the short run—but in the long run, it would shift the balance of power toward Paley, and away from the affiliate stations.

CBS started giving its affiliates programming for free—as much as fifteen to twenty hours per week. In exchange, CBS affiliates had to run CBS programming when asked. Having all the affiliates broadcast one show gave Paley the largest possible audience to sell to advertisers—and the ability to sell national network ads for the first time.

As the audiences of its affiliates grew, so did CBS's revenues. It was similar to the compound interest lesson every kid learns in school. NBC charged its affiliates more, which was effectively like NBC spending its money on payday. CBS, in contrast, was investing that money in its affiliates, to increase its eventual return.

As the number of CBS's affiliates grew, so did CBS's audience, and eventually its power over the stations, which became dependent on CBS for the programming its audience had grown used to.

Paley's innovation was a major step in the growth of national networks, and became a major part of the model that would power television.

Between July and December of 1928, CBS's revenues tripled.

———

In 1929, Paley hired Edward Bernays as his consigliere. Bernays was already famous as the father of public relations, an advertising innovator, and the nephew of Sigmund Freud. A master of audience psychology, Bernays helped Paley think through sales strategy and management style, as well as public relations and marketing.

Bernays later said that Paley had wanted to start a magazine about radio stars before there was one. Bernays didn't think anyone would want to read about radio stars, and talked Paley out of it. It was a decision they both regretted years later, when *TV Guide* sold for $3 billion.

Though NBC was far ahead, the tide began to turn. One group of affiliates soon left NBC for CBS. Sarnoff was furious, and NBC moved from ignoring Paley to meeting him in an all-out war. The battle would be bound only by what a growing radio audience would accept—almost anything—and what an occasionally interested government would prohibit—not much at first; then, later, enough to hobble them both.

For now, Sarnoff fought back with talent, signing former New York Philharmonic conductor Arturo Toscanini as leader of the NBC Orchestra. NBC would stand for *culture*, and leave the down-market twaddle for others. This was a poor decision by Sarnoff, and would come back to haunt him. The excitement in 1930s radio came from CBS, and everyone knew it.

The Big Leagues

Not surprisingly, Hollywood noticed too. The movie moguls saw a major threat in radio. They resolved to buy or bully their way in. William Fox at FOX and Adolph Zukor at Paramount both made Paley offers.

Paramount owned and operated a chain of a thousand theaters that Paley once said were "spread like a monster blanket over the country."[6] Paley took a $5 million investment from Zukor, at a valuation favorable to CBS. The deal gave Paramount a hedge in radio, and CBS cash from a formidable friend.

Paley had taken CBS from near insolvency to the number two network in America.

CHAPTER 11

SARNOFF VS. PALEY

The history of business is a tapestry of personalities, in which the most powerful industries are often driven by a dominant rivalry. So it was for radio and television.

Sarnoff and Paley were both Eastern European Jews, each driven by an insatiable need.

Sarnoff continued to avenge a childhood of abject poverty. He had come from the bottom to create an industry. He was going to build a second one, and he would not be stopped.

Paley was determined to be the very thing to which Sarnoff stood in contrast: the American aristocracy of the Wasp elite. Paley would do whatever it took to become one of them. And he would not be stopped.

Sarnoff's great loves were technology, intellectual property, and power. He wasn't interested in entertainment or pop culture. Above all, he needed to win. David Sarnoff was an archetypal technologist.

Paley didn't give a damn about technology. He cared about audiences, acclaim, and the spotlight. William Paley was an archetypal showman.

In a few ways the rivalry was similar to a more recent one: if Sarnoff was Bill Gates, Bill Paley was Steve Jobs.

Sarnoff was also ten years older than Paley. He'd seen radio coming, had wrestled it to the ground. His NBC was a monolith, dominating radio from Rockefeller Center. It was powerful, entrenched, and seemingly unstoppable.

Unlike most NBC competitors, Paley had no interest in copying Sarnoff.

CBS was young, playful, smart, and optimistic. It was comfortable in its own skin. CBS knew how to throw a party, and it knew how to *sell.* It enjoyed the ads, enjoyed the heat, enjoyed pushing the bounds of propriety.

CBS was Don Draper before *Mad Men* existed.

And Paley *was* CBS, creating its premium position as the "Tiffany Network." In one of his favorite stories, Paley told listeners of how he charmed a reluctant Pierre Matisse into selling him a prized painting called *Woman with a Veil.*

This was a lie, according to Paley's wife, Dorothy, who knew Matisse well and insisted that Paley had never even met him. According to Dorothy, Paley bought the painting at an art exhibition. Since Paley spoke no French and Matisse spoke no English, that seems likely.

But the stories worked, as always, to increase Bill's cache.

By now Sarnoff was an emperor, a remote figure with a small circle of functionaries. Executives would submit memos for feedback, but meetings were usually short. As the years went by, Sarnoff remained fascinated by technology, and was less interested in people.

In Paley's early years at CBS, NBC executives would not even meet with him, refusing to acknowledge the unsavory little upstart.

But as CBS became more and more successful, Sarnoff grew increasingly jealous. He wanted to know how Paley, a Russian Jew like himself, was doing so well in New York high society. "He couldn't understand why women were so attracted to Bill," CBS executive Frank Stanton said. "He couldn't understand why Bill spent so much time on social events. He didn't think Bill worked very hard, and he really resented the attention Bill got."[1] It didn't help that Paley's salary, as owner of a private company, was already double Sarnoff's.

When *Time* magazine ran a cover story on the radio boom in 1938, it was a grinning Paley they put on the cover. When Paley was referred to as "radio's restless conscience," Sarnoff exploded with rage.

As different as they were, Paley and Sarnoff shared one passion completely: situational ethics. In a politically correct age, it's not fashionable to call the deceased liars. But the most striking commonality between Paley and Sarnoff is how many lies they told, and how successfully.

The founders of NBC and CBS were both Olympian weavers of their own myths, masters of self-invention, escape artists who knew just how far to push the envelope of credulity.

How could *one* kid have covered the entire *Titanic* disaster, when it was the biggest story in the world? And why would Matisse sell a painting he wanted to keep, to a *radio executive*, of all people?

The obvious answer is that these things did not happen. The obvious answer is that these statements, like many other things the two men said, were lies.

The less obvious answer is that both statements are *possible*, but extremely unlikely. It's *ridiculous* for one telegraph operator to have worked alone, for seventy-two hours, the only link between the *Titanic* and the world. It's *ridiculous* that Matisse would have preferred Bill Paley to his friends and family, his neighbors and intimates.

Ridiculous, but possible.

The more one sees Sarnoff and Paley in historical context, the more significant this becomes: they were brothers in a particular art form, the art of the barely possible. They saw the world this way, looking both forward and backward—understanding what had already happened, and what was to come.

If the color blind can't see red and green, perhaps there are other permutations, in which not seeing is an advantage. Sarnoff and Paley lied so much, perhaps, because they didn't see the difference. In a brutal new business, that gave them an edge.

In any event, the marathon of their respective successes, the number of things they were right about, and the decades they lasted in an industry that measures jobs in months, bear witness to the depth of their influence. They were geniuses at a thing we don't have a name for. We can call it innovation, but that's too broad a term. They were geniuses at knowing where the world would have to go.

Reality was something they created as they went along. And given their power, that reality became a self-fulfilling prophecy. It was the beginning of the mogul's propensity to believe that consensus reality did not apply to them. This trend would continue, from the hubris of record company moguls who ignored the rise of digital technology to the magical thinking and odd parking behavior of Steve Jobs.

As their power increased, Sarnoff and Paley each focused on what he liked best, and delegated the rest. Sarnoff didn't care about programming, so NBC had an advisory council select its shows. It programmed shows on music appreciation, concerts, Shakespeare, and lectures. "If comedy is the center of NBC's activities, then maybe I had better quit," Sarnoff once said.[2] But his dismissiveness was a terrible mistake.

NBC's lack of focus on programming set the stage for the biggest disruption in radio history.

CHAPTER 12

INVENTING CBS

NBC was way ahead of us. Sarnoff was the visionary. He had the guts.
—FRANK STANTON, CBS

The Talent Raids

As the 1930s began, NBC was far and away the king of radio. As is generally the case with industry leaders, its dominance had grown out of a key competency. And that was technology. NBC was RCA; RCA sold radios, and controlled that patents that governed radio. It was a hardware business, selling devices, but not the content that ran on those devices.

Bill Paley's first burst of genius had been to sense that radio could be a huge advertising business.

Now, he saw something else Sarnoff did not: that radio was a business of programming original shows—and that in the long term, this part of the business would prove to be the key. The shows were what people loved, what would make them come back, and thereby build up a network's bottom line. The hit shows would get the audience to tune in, and keep them tuned in for the ads—and the more people tuned in, the more that CBS could charge for the ads.

For Paley, all of Sarnoff's endless labor in technology missed the point. The technology was simply a carrier.

To bring the point home, Paley asked his subordinates a question: what was a better business, an advanced movie theater with a movie no one wanted, or a mediocre movie theater with a movie everyone wanted to see? The answer was obvious.

Paley saw that the best programming would bring advertisers, affiliates, money, and power. Most of all, it would bring the audience, which would take care of everything else.

Sarnoff could have the fancy theater. Paley was going to go after what was on the screen. That meant that CBS needed stars, no matter what it took. And the stars were on NBC.

That had to change.

———

In the early '30s, CBS made some talent headway by signing Bing Crosby and Arthur Godfrey. But NBC still had the five top shows on radio.

To lure the stars away from NBC, Paley needed money. He got it in 1932, from one of the giants of society, Averill Harriman. An heir to a railroad baron with a $70 million fortune, Harriman was a future ambassador, presidential candidate, and one of the titans of New York society. Harriman and his colleague Prescott Bush (forebear of both Bush presidents) helped Paley execute a CBS stock buyback, then gave him $1 million of their own money.

Harriman also encouraged Paley to collect art, which Paley did with a vengeance, eventually sitting on the board of the Museum of Modern Art (MoMA), by invitation of the Rockefellers. Isaac Paley would have been proud.

———

Now that Paley had cash and deep-pocketed backers, he waited for an opening. It came in 1948, from the most powerful man in Hollywood, super-agent Lew Wasserman at mega-agency MCA.

Amos 'n' Andy was a juggernaut. It had been running for nineteen years on NBC. With 53 percent of the listening audience, the show was stronger than ever. Wasserman proposed an elaborate plan, a template for a new generation of Hollywood deals. To lure the stars from NBC, he and Paley would offer two great inducements: tax advantages and ego massage.

CBS and MCA would help each radio star incorporate, turning each NBC show into a new corporation. These corporations would then be bought by CBS—for much more cash than NBC was paying the stars, plus a huge tax break.

There was a less obvious benefit, Wasserman told Paley: once CBS owned the shows, the talent would no longer be able to leave, since CBS would be now be co-owner of the show itself.

Paley agreed.

———

In September 1948, Paley triumphantly announced that hit show *Amos 'n' Andy* was moving from NBC to CBS. The story quickly became national news. Surprisingly, Sarnoff did not complain; he stayed silent, which may have emboldened Wasserman for what came next.

The super-agent suggested to Paley they make the same offer—to the biggest star on radio, Jack Benny.

On NBC, Jack Benny's radio show was so big that the other stations barely programmed against it. Benny *owned* Sunday night; no one listened to anything else.

Benny was what NBC's "Must See TV" lineup would be in the 1990s: a roadblock on a signature night that proclaimed NBC's dominance.

Benny felt underappreciated at NBC, Wasserman told Paley. NBC was not sensitive to the needs of talent. And Benny's NBC contract was about to expire.

Paley knew this could be a game changer. A mutual friend convinced Benny to hear Bill Paley out. Paley called Benny at star George Burns' house and told Benny that talent was the most cherished asset at CBS, the most valuable part of the network.

A complex negotiation ensued, and Benny took the deal. To show his good will to CBS, Benny volunteered to recommend CBS to NBC's other stars.

The *New York Times* followed up with Paley. They'd heard from NBC that Benny's deal was a tax dodge. Paley was outraged and denied the charges.

Then Paley got another call, from David Sarnoff.

Sarnoff was horrified. This was an absolute betrayal. It would create a bidding war that would hurt them both. Why would you do this, Sarnoff asked. Paley paused and told Sarnoff that he did it because he needed to.

With Benny's encouragement, radio stars Burns and Allen, Edgar Bergen, and Red Skelton met with CBS. They soon abandoned NBC too.

There was speculation that Sarnoff had brought the defections on himself, by not working harder to please talent, not being more "Hollywood." George Burns denied this: "Jack left NBC because Paley offered him more money. It was as simple as that."[1]

Whatever the truth, the talent raids were national news, and a marketing triumph for CBS. On NBC, star Fred Allen joked, "I'll be back here next week same time, same network. No other comedian can make that claim."[2]

By the end of 1949, CBS Radio had twelve of the top fifteen radio shows. In both programming and profits, CBS was number one. Paley became the face of an empire.

As his success increased, Paley became a national figure, one of the country's rich and powerful. It was a role that took him away from work for months at a time. He began to love CBS the way he loved generally: in bursts of intensity, followed by disinterest.

Paley never really managed CBS again. The job of managing CBS would go to Paley's number two. His name was Frank Stanton.

Frank Stanton

Make people depend on you. The wise person would rather
see others needing him than thanking him.
—Baltasar Gracian

CBS was still young when Jack Benny came on its air in 1949. It needed to be retooled to handle the demands of success and growth. The young network needed process, management, and the structures of an ongoing business. None of these jobs were suited to Paley, a visionary owner and the face of CBS.

Paley hired well. PR legend Edward Bernays helped organize the network's divisions, set a crisp communications style, and helped grow the CBS brand. Former FCC man Sam Pickard helped expand CBS's stations group. VP Ed Klauber made the trains run on time. VP Paul Kesten had a great design sense and shared Paley's love of elegance.

As time went on, the demands of growth and managing the managers grew more complex. Overseeing all of it meant doing a bit of everything, or understanding enough of everything to be able to make the calls.

Bill Paley couldn't do everything, and he didn't want to try. The job of doing everything would go to Frank Stanton.

———

Born in 1908, Frank Stanton learned about hard work early. His father oversaw a school's industrial arts department; the home was filled with tools and construction projects. His father was always building something, and Frank started helping when he was five years old.

By elementary school, Frank was taking correspondence courses in cartooning. By high school, he was all about achievement: straight A's, class president, and yearbook editor.

Stanton began working at a local men's clothing store, and learned every aspect of the business, down to designing and lighting window displays. As Sarnoff had at American Marconi, Frank Stanton realized early that the key to longevity was to make himself necessary.

After high school, Stanton attended Ohio Wesleyan and was accepted to medical school. But the aesthetic side of his nature won out, and he decided not to go. Instead, he took a job in advertising, and was sent to a course at Germany's legendary Bauhaus studio. When the market crash of 1929 intervened, the ad job ended, and Stanton returned to college.

By now, he was convinced that his future was in advertising and media. When he tried to pursue a degree in radio, his dean ridiculed the idea, telling Stanton that radio was a waste of time.

So Stanton found another way: he became a psychology major. His 1932 master's thesis analyzed how magazine design affected readership. But it was his doctoral dissertation at Ohio State that would eventually shape an industry.

In "A Critique of Present Methods and a New Plan for Studying Radio Listening Behavior," Stanton argued that radio was much more powerful than print, and that new methods of data science were essential to growing the medium. As CBS was battling ratings in New York, Stanton proposed a completely new way of measuring audiences.

Stanton's findings were a gold mine: he reported that 78 percent of radios were turned on at some point each day. The average radio was in use 4.5 hours per day. Analyzing formats by popularity, he found that they were (in order from most to least popular) variety, comedy, popular music, classical music, and drama.

He also found that men listened to radio while eating, reading, or resting, while women listened while doing housework, cooking, or resting. It was a recipe for a new way of programming, and the most prescient document since Sarnoff's key memos.

Stanton wrote to both NBC and CBS with his findings. NBC ignored him.

But CBS was in the middle of a ratings problem. The first radio ratings service, called the Crossley Report, overwhelmingly favored NBC.

CBS executive Paul Kesten responded with a three-page letter, telling Stanton that CBS was interested in many of the same questions. He gave Stanton some more ideas to work on, and Stanton was thrilled.

The days of industrial arts with his father had served Stanton well. He designed and hand-built fifty boxes that connected to radios. These boxes printed out tapes of the radio stations that people had listened to, in one innovative, self-contained, accurate ratings collector.

Stanton went door to door and persuaded people to install the boxes in their homes. Then he went back every few days, to interview the families and collect the tapes.

Stanton presented his strategy to CBS in 1933. CBS's chief engineer looked at the homemade contraptions, and decided the effort was a complete waste of time.

But Kesten was smarter, and saw an opportunity. The Crossley system favored NBC dramatically, and the advertisers and affiliates knew it. CBS needed an alternative to Crossley. Kesten told Stanton to keep working on the project, and help CBS settle the score.

Stanton worked for two more years, and examined the Crossley reporting system. What he found was a revelation: what people *said* they listened to didn't match the data his boxes collected. It turned out that what was faulty was people's *memories.*

NBC was killing CBS in the ratings because people didn't remember what they'd listened to—and therefore their reporting to Crossley was all wrong.

In 1935, Paul Kesten hired Frank Stanton to head up CBS's two-person research department. Stanton was twenty-seven years old.

Stanton's Rise

For anyone stuck in a backwater job, Stanton's climb from the research department is inspirational. He used his research to win over advertisers and grow ad revenue. He then leveraged his success with advertisers to increase his department's budget, hire more staff, and expand his department.

In three years, he grew his team from two to 100.

Working eighty-hour weeks, Stanton compiled the first list of CBS ad rates. He developed a product called the program analyzer that let listeners push "like" or "dislike" buttons as they listened to radio shows—creating the testing that drives network TV to this day.

Beyond that, Stanton did what it took to get ahead. "Every time management would ask me a question, if I didn't know it, I would fake it to a certain extent, and then run like hell down the back stairs and get the *World Almanac.*"[3] It worked.

Stanton became an industry legend. He was offered jobs from new ratings king A. C. Nielsen and others in the late 1930s. He turned them all down.

Stanton was Paley's opposite in temperament: meticulous, analytical, and dogged. He eventually became a trustee of the RAND Corporation, the Stanford Research Institute, the Rockefeller Foundation, and the

Lincoln Center for the Performing Arts. He would get everything he'd hoped for, except the job he always wanted: Paley's.

Paley did not realize how lucky he was to have Stanton, but Paul Kesten did. In 1942, Kesten made Stanton vice president of research, advertising, sales promotion, public relations, building construction, operations, and maintenance.

For all his early triumphs, Stanton never had a direct meeting with the boss. Bill Paley had other things on his mind.

Inventing William Paley

What the 1920s had been for Sarnoff, the 1930s were for Paley: a meteoric climb to where he'd always wanted to be. His appetites were prodigious: for success, for status, for women, and for fun. He knew that the next step required the right woman.

To get where he wanted to go, he needed a woman like Dorothy Hart.

Dorothy Hart was a beautiful socialite with extensive cache. She was married to Jack Hearst, the son of newspaper magnate William Randolph Hearst, but that just made it more interesting. When the couple embarked on a cruise to Europe, Paley went too.

In London, Dorothy introduced Paley to Winston Churchill, and to Savile Row tailors. Finally, she gave in, divorced Hearst, and married Paley.

If Dorothy had any illusions about Paley, they ended in 1940. An aspiring actress who'd had a short affair with Bill checked into a hotel, wrote a love note to Paley, and jumped out a window to her death. The newspapers ran the story, and called CBS for comments. Paley's PR staff rushed to manage the fallout.

But again, Paley had other things on his mind.

Babe Cushing Mortimer was the apex of New York society, a beautiful relative of Roosevelts and Astors. She was a fashion icon, a model, and a perennial member of the Best Dressed list. Her friend Truman Capote summed up prevailing wisdom: "Babe Paley had only one fault. She was perfect. Otherwise, she was perfect."[4]

Paley's professional and personal lives were driven by the same force: he knew a star when he saw one. He met Babe in 1946, pursued her immediately, divorced Dorothy in 1947, and married Babe that same year.

The marriage attracted widespread media attention, including a major article in *Life*. It gave Paley access to the richest and most powerful cliques in the world. He had come a long way from Congress Cigar.

Eventually Paley's womanizing became a source of depression for Babe. When she considered divorce, Capote offered advice: being Mrs. Bill Paley was a wonderful job. She was great at it, and she should stay. She did. Bill Paley, they both knew, would be hard to replace. By then, he was one of the most respected men in America.

He was the man who had created broadcast news.

CHAPTER 13

BROADCAST NEWS

B y the mid-1930s, both Paley and Sarnoff faced governmental problems. Congress had been watching the growth of radio ads, and did not approve. Progressive Senator Burton Wheeler accused CBS and NBC of being merchants of filth, creating ads that polluted American life. The Federal Radio Commission considered limiting advertising, or moving radio to government ownership.

With the election of Franklin Roosevelt, the drumbeat grew louder. As Sarnoff maneuvered to avert disaster and retain control of RCA, the Wheeler bill was introduced in Congress. The bill threatened to revoke and redistribute all broadcast licenses, with 25 percent going to educational operators. The Wheeler bill was Sarnoff's and Paley's worst nightmare.

At this point, CBS had 100 affiliate stations and sixteen hours of daily programming. There was a lot to lose if the government ruled against them.

So in 1934, Paley appeared before the FCC, arguing that radio was a business, not a charity, and that someone had to pay for it. CBS's Kesten began a PR campaign, as Paley focused on the Beltway, hiring friends of Roosevelt as lobbyists to help fight the bill.

Meanwhile, NBC argued that it had always been a servant of the public trust, and emphasized its tradition of high-culture programming. Sarnoff's emphasis on educational programming was an NBC advantage, for now.

It was ultimately the political power of radio that saved them both. Roosevelt began his fireside chats, a series of talks that electrified the nation and allowed FDR to reach voters without going through the press. FDR knew a good thing when he saw it, and became the first media president. Deprived of FDR's support, the Wheeler bill died. But the drumbeat continued at the FCC.

Paley knew CBS had a problem. Though he rushed to add more educational programing, he knew it was a temporary solution. It would never disguise CBS's naked attempts to grow ad revenue through whatever programming people liked.

So Paley worked with Bernays to hash out a new PR strategy. CBS would become the home of *quality* news. Programming more news would mollify the government and increase the prestige of the network. News would give CBS a vital edge against NBC. News would distract from the lowbrow shows that brought CBS its revenue.

What began as a distraction would become one of the great forces of twentieth-century life. Broadcast news would shape public opinion, influence wars, and bring down a president.

What started as a ruse became Paley's greatest legacy.

―――――

In the early 1930s, radio news was an interloper, repeating and reskinning what the newspapers ran. Newspapers owned the news, and Sarnoff had never challenged them, obeying an unwritten rule that newspapers broke big stories, and radio followed afterward.

Sensing the moment, Paley broke Sarnoff's protocol, and scooped newspapers on coverage of the O. J. Simpson moment of its time: the kidnapping of aviation hero Charles Lindbergh's baby, which writer H. L. Mencken called "the biggest story since the Resurrection."[1]

The newspapers were furious, and wanted Paley's head.

Paley next created his own news organization, with funding from General Mills. The newspapers lobbied the government, which made Paley shut the news organization down. CBS would have to find another way into news.

It came from another world war, and from the most influential news-caster in history. In his battle for the veneer of public good, Paley found a massive weapon in Edward R. Murrow.

CHAPTER 14

EDWARD R. MURROW

Edward R. Murrow is the most revered figure in broadcast journalism. On radio, he was the voice of World War II for millions of Americans. He elevated the CBS brand to the "Tiffany Network," and moved radio news to the national spotlight.

Egbert Roscoe Murrow was born in North Carolina to a strict Quaker family in 1908. It was a stoic household, and Murrow was a serious boy. He grew up in a home with neither electricity nor plumbing, but he was president of his senior class and showed early gifts as a public speaker.

In college, Murrow studied drama and voice. After college, he joined the National Student Federation, then the Institute for International Education.

There he met one of Bill Paley's assistants, who recommended him to the boss. Paley wanted to expand the news programming, and Murrow's international experience was an asset. He looked good, dressed well, and carried himself like a star. Murrow, essentially, reminded Paley of Paley.

Murrow was hired in 1935. In his first year at CBS, he arranged over 300 talks from twenty-seven countries.

After setbacks from the newspapers and the government, Paley's prospects for news were beginning to improve. Paley was skating to where the puck was headed: Hitler's march through Europe increased the need for news. CBS would need someone to run news in London, someone who knew the terrain and could do CBS proud. In 1937, Murrow became director of CBS's European operations in London, helping CBS compete with NBC.

In 1939, Murrow became director of London-based *European News Roundup*. In a time when everyone got their news from newspapers, Murrow's radio team seized the day.

Murrow told his reporters not to repeat what the newspapers said. He encouraged them to speak to the audience as they would to a friend back home. He told them to think of seeing that friend in a bar, and filling him in on the day's events. He wanted original thoughts, in authentic language, from reporters the audience could relate to.

As the war closed in, the show became *World News Roundup*. Broadcast from cities throughout Europe, it reported on the gathering storm of World War II, with multiple voices from different perspectives.

When Hitler annexed Austria in 1938, Murrow shot to prominence. When London endured the Blitz and foreigners fled, Murrow stayed on. As bombs dropped over London, Murrow became America's window into the war.

In the past, announcers had delivered monotonous wire service copy. Murrow's *London after Dark* changed that; the drama and presence of his voice soon dominated every other news source. His broadcasts softened America's isolationism, and paved the way for its entrance into the war. A reporter summarized Murrow's strengths at the time:

1. He beats the newspapers by hours.
2. He reaches millions who otherwise have to depend on [local] newspapers for their foreign news.
3. He writes his own headlines.[1]

Paley had liked news as a PR tactic, but it had never made money; before the war, advertisers had simply not wanted to sponsor news. But now they did, and news became a profit center, as Sinclair Oil signed on to sponsor *World News Roundup*.

The British adored Murrow. And Murrow raised the perception of CBS, enabling Paley's greatest transformation: forevermore, the cigar man was the father of quality news. When Paley went to London, Murrow introduced his boss to everyone worth knowing. Though the moral crusader and the tycoon were in many ways polar opposites, for that part of their lives they were the closest of friends.

Paley and Murrow became mainstays of London society, socializing with Winston Churchill, his son Randolph, and his daughter-in-law, Pamela. Pamela and Murrow began an affair, which Murrow ended when he returned to America. Pamela divorced Randolph Churchill and married ambassador and CBS investor Averill Harriman, becoming the most influential woman in Washington society for the rest of the twentieth century.

Veneration for Murrow in England reached a fever pitch. He was seen, rightfully, as a catalyst for America coming to England's aid. Winston Churchill asked Murrow to be the joint director general of the BBC, but Murrow declined.

In 1941, Murrow returned to the United States, and was honored at a black tie dinner. FDR sent a telegram welcoming him home. One week later, Pearl Harbor was attacked, and Murrow returned to work.

Paley returned to London, and became good friends with General Eisenhower, the Supreme Commander of the Allied Forces in Europe and most powerful man in the world at the time. Eisenhower wanted help on radio, with propaganda, or whatever worked. He made Paley chief of radio broadcasting for the psychological war branch for the Allies. Paley's absences from CBS became longer. But fortunately Stanton was now running the network. In January 1946, Stanton was named president of CBS.

Always one to keep his options open, Eisenhower asked Sarnoff for help as well. Sarnoff leapt at the chance. He arrived in London in March of 1944, months later than Paley. When Sarnoff checked into his suite, he learned that the previous occupant had been Paley, who had just moved out and into a better room.

———

When the war ended in 1945, Murrow returned home. When he should have been happiest, he was filled with foreboding. As they were going home, he told his wife that they were going "to fight the same kind of things we've been fighting here."[2] He would be proven correct.

Paley would remember the war years as the best of his life. All of his bets had finally paid off. He had conquered news. He had conquered society. He would return home and drive the talent raids. Bill Paley had *won*. But that was not the best of it.

Without it knowing it, Paley's raids had positioned him for a windfall in a completely new medium.

Television was ready.

CHAPTER 15

TELEVISION TAKES OFF

World War II and Television

The battle for television had gone on longer than many lives. Sarnoff had seemed close to a coup at the 1939 World's Fair—but the threat of World War II put a halt to that. One day, Sarnoff received a call summoning him to the White House.

FDR had one major question. War was coming. Could he count on RCA? Sarnoff immediately turned his company to the war effort. He later wrote,

> By the summer of '41, I was convinced we could not avoid war and I knew RCA would be in the thick of it. Our technology would be indispensable for military communications. It was just too late in the game for television.[1]

On December 7, 1941, Sarnoff sent FDR a telegram: "All our facilities are ready and at your instant service. We await your commands."[2]

The war had been a setback, but it had ultimately been good to him. For advising Eisenhower and bending radio to Ike's needs, he was rewarded with an honorarium. Forevermore, the boy from the shtetl would be called General Sarnoff.

Sarnoff, Paley, and Television

Sarnoff had loved the idea of television for decades. He had fought for it, angled for it, and believed in its potential, long before any evidence that the medium could function. For twenty years before it existed, the General had delivered speeches on the power of TV.

Paley had shown absolutely no interest in the medium, regardless of how many times Stanton brought it up. When Paley saw that TV was inevitable, he still didn't understand it, thinking it would be used to beam events into theaters. He was dismissive of TV as a part of the living room, thinking that most people preferred to go out. Bill Paley made a classic business error: he assumed that his customers were similar to him.

By the '30s, Paley saw the writing on the wall, but resisted it. He wanted to delay TV, to postpone the threat to radio for as long as he could:

> "Bill did not want television," said Stanton. "He thought it would hurt radio. It was also a question of money. . . . He didn't see any profit in TV at all."[3]

Now it was Paley who was losing the plot. But Stanton carried on, with his own vision of the medium. He funded a lab for a CBS version of television, and approved a radically different concept: *color television.*

Meanwhile, Sarnoff brought his wartime cache to bear on the FCC, which had argued that RCA was a dangerous monopoly. If RCA was allowed to sell TV advertising, it would destroy all potential competitors, as it had done so successfully with Armstrong and others.

Sarnoff's friends in Congress pushed back. The FCC gave in later that year. The road to TV was down to one last battle.

Color TV and CBS

Like many media to come, from home recording to mobile phones, the last leg of TV's launch became a battle of conflicting formats. Manufacturers DuMont, RCA, Philco, and GE fought for VHF (very high frequency) broadcasting, a standard they'd been working with for years. The sole antagonist was CBS.

CBS fought for a UHF (ultra-high frequency) standard, and for its own color format, developed by CBS engineer Peter Goldmark. Color TV seemed much more attractive, and won many converts in a protracted legal scuffle.

The color TV battle went all the way to the Supreme Court—where CBS prevailed.

"We had taken on the great Sarnoff, the king of Radio City, and won," said CBS's Goldmark. "David had beaten the Goliath of industry. We trumpeted our victory from the pages of every important newspaper in the country."[4]

It was a stunning blow to Sarnoff. But it was short-lived. General Sarnoff told the FCC that RCA engineers would have a UHF color system ready in six months. A commissioner asked Sarnoff how he could be so very certain that his engineers could have a completely new TV system complete in only six months.

The General's response was simple: "I told them to."

Sarnoff was Sarnoff. The FCC accepted this, and the CBS standard was killed.

So in 1944, with one common standard for all, manufacturers finally got the green light to start building televisions.

With the race on to dominate the market, RCA and NBC multiplied their TV production efforts. In 1944, leading ad agency J. Walter Thompson predicted that television would be the biggest ad medium in history. Applications for TV stations exploded.

That year, NBC launched its first hit TV shows, *The Gillette Cavalcade of Sports* and *Kraft Television Theatre*, one of the most highly regarded anthologies of all time. Over the next fourteen years, *Kraft Theatre* would run more than 650 individual programs.

That same year, under antitrust pressure from the government, NBC sold the smaller of its two networks, called NBC Blue. Blue had been the place NBC ran experimental programs, while NBC Red was the commercial venture. Under duress, Sarnoff sold NBC Blue to the Lifesavers candy company. It would eventually be renamed the American Broadcasting Company.

In 1943, the Television Broadcasters Association gave David Sarnoff a title: "the Father of American Television."

Television Explodes

In 1946, the first big tranche of TVs hit retail. In the postwar glow, TV became the sign of a great new era, and sales went through the roof. In 1946, production grew from 225 to 3,242 sets. In 1947, it was 5,437. In 1948, it was 33,836. In 1949, it was 150,258. In 1950, it was 438,700—and by 1951 it was 650,700.

"The American household is on the threshold of a revolution. . . . The reason is television," said the *New York Times.*[5]

That same year, an editor named Syd Cassyd founded the Academy of Television Arts and Sciences. Its first meeting took place on November 14, 1946, with a handful of attendees. The organization was formalized in July 1947 with 147 charter members, and presented its first Emmy Awards on January 25, 1949.

In 1946, NBC broadcast its heavyweight championship. "Television looks good for a 1000-year run," reported the *Washington Post.* Advertisers began lining up. In 1947, TV stations covered the presidential conventions and Harry Truman's acceptance speech. Recognizing the need for new programming, Sarnoff made Robert "Pat" Weaver president of NBC in 1948. Weaver expanded NBC's stations from 25 to 189, and established new TV franchises in morning and late night. Nearly seventy years later, two of his creations, the *Today* show and *The Tonight Show,* are still on the air.

TV antennas became a sign of the times, sprouting like weeds, characterized by Norman Rockwell in his painting *New Television Antenna,* which appeared on the cover of *The Saturday Evening Post* on November 5, 1949.

The Effects of TV

No technology became ubiquitous as quickly as did television. It took eighty years for the telephone to reach 35 million households, fifty years for the automobile, and twenty-five years for radio. TV did it in less than ten.

TV became the major topic of conversation. Some thought it would support family life, creating a shared experience in the living room, a new lingua franca to bring people together. Others felt it would divide families into separate factions, watching separate programming. Both groups were correct.

What was clear early on was that television had the power to fundamentally alter life.

In the words of historian David Halberstam, "In the midst of extraordinary social change, television became the most important discursive medium in American culture."[6]

When people looked for something to talk about, they talked about what they'd seen on television. When people wanted to know how other people lived, or what other people thought, they were increasingly influenced by television. As the war years receded and the '50s commenced, the television age began.

The "First Turning"

After a depression and two world wars, America was leaving what historians William Strauss and Neil Howe call a "First Turning": a movement from a crisis to a boom. A First Turning takes a society from conflict and uncertainty into a time of civic and economic growth—in which war is replaced by social consensus, conformity, optimism, and prosperity.[7]

As America entered a new prosperous era, its talisman was television.

———

There are no precedents for the explosive growth of television in America. In 1946, there were 20,000 televisions, representing 0.02 percent of U.S. homes. By 1951, just five years later, there were 10.5 million, or 21.5 percent of homes. Seven years later, in 1953, there were 347 TV stations in America, and the average American viewer watched 3.5 hours of television.

As TVs proliferated, Bill Paley's hunch of years ago proved right. From then on, the battle would be over programming, and finding the shows that brought audiences in.

In 1947, one format began what would often be called the Golden Age of Television.

PART 3

TELEVISION AND THE 1950S

CHAPTER 16

THE ANTHOLOGIES

D
ramatic anthologies began in 1947, with the premiere of *Kraft Television Theatre* on NBC. *Kraft Television Theatre* pioneered the format of original and classic productions, and was sponsored by ad agency J. Walter Thompson.

Arriving in an era before TV commercials, anthologies generally had one sponsoring agency or brand, which paid for the show and called the shots on its content. Unlike modern series—with characters and stories that span seasons—drama anthologies were one-off episodes. Largely produced in New York, they grew out of Broadway's theater roots.

Kraft Television Theatre eventually spanned over 600 shows, many of which were as fine as the best Broadway productions. It featured performers including James Dean, Paul Newman, Grace Kelly, Jack Lemmon, George C. Scott, and Helen Hayes, and writers including Paddy Chayefsky and Gore Vidal—and a young writer named Rod Serling, whose Emmy-winning episode "Patterns" would be the precursor for a show called *The Twilight Zone*.

A host of anthologies followed in 1948 and 1949, including *Westinghouse Studio One, Chevrolet Tele-Theatre,* and *The Philco Television Playhouse.* The best teleplay to come out of the early anthologies was Chayefsky's *Marty,* later adapted into a film that would win three Oscars.

In addition to new content, anthologies often featured original performances of classics including *Cyrano de Bergerac,* and musical performances from luminaries Arturo Toscanini and Leonard Bernstein—a particular passion of David Sarnoff himself. *Westinghouse Studio One* adapted literary hits including George Orwell's *1984* and Reginald Rose's *Twelve Angry Men.*

The anthologies were the high water mark of television as a medium for traditional high art.

Anthology Production

Anthologies were originally shot live in front of an audience using multiple sets and cameras. Set and costume changes took place during commercials. As many as 10 million viewers were watching live for any one broadcast. Second takes were not an option: everything was live.

After the adoption of videotape in 1957, many dramas began shooting live to tape, still retaining a "live" television look and feel, but adding the ability to shoot retakes and rebroadcast programs.

The best-known anthology was *Playhouse 90.* It began in 1956, on CBS. *Playhouse 90* had two key differences: it was ninety minutes rather than sixty, and unlike the rest of the anthologies, was produced in Los Angeles.

Playhouse 90's 133 episodes are some of the finest TV of the era, including "The Miracle Worker," "Judgment at Nuremberg," and Rod Serling's breakout "Requiem for a Heavyweight," which swept the Emmys in 1958. The show's primary director, John Frankenheimer, became the most influential TV director of his time.

The anthologies were the great achievement of TV's initial period. It was the golden age for many New York–based artists, in the years before the industry began to move to Los Angeles. Additionally, TVs were expensive in the early years, skewing the total audience to a more educated demographic.

The anthology model was built around one single-paying sponsor. These sponsors got their name placed in the show, including Kraft, Westinghouse, and GE. But the anthologies faced pressure as TV's business model evolved. The single-payer model was gradually replaced by multiple sponsors, who bought TV commercials but did not control the show.

This meant less power for sponsors and agencies, and more power for networks and studios—so over time, the anthologies simply stopped making economic sense.

For decades, critics would bemoan the passing of the anthologies, which became less economically viable as the years went on. The genre was largely gone by 1960, but by then its progeny were prospering, including *The Alfred Hitchcock Show* and *The Twilight Zone*.

As anthologies did for drama, television comedy began by repurposing what it could find. This meant looking to radio and vaudeville, and to the antics of the man who would become "Mr. Television."

CHAPTER 17

MILTON BERLE

Mendel Berlinger was born in Harlem, New York, on July 12, 1908. He won a talent contest at age five, and began working in silent movies soon after, eventually acting with Charlie Chaplin. In 1924, he adopted the stage name "Milton Berle"; eventually his doting mother changed her name to Berle, too.

Berle became a major vaudeville star in the 1930s. But he became convinced that radio would beat live performance in the long term. So he decided to focus on where the audience was going, and spent more time on radio, turning down live work to increase his radio exposure.

He was right. By the 1940s, Berle had shows on both CBS and NBC, the culmination of which was 1947–48's *The Milton Berle Show*. It ran on NBC and cemented him as one of radio's biggest stars—just as TV was beginning to find its way.

Unlike many of his peers, Berle was sold on the promise of television, and decided to take his radio show and transition it to the new medium.

Berle became a rotating host of NBC's *Texaco Star Theatre*, alternating with other comedians. His over-the-top, manic bits made him the hit of the season, and soon NBC gave Berle the whole show.

Once he had the show, his rise was meteoric. He drew 5 million viewers that season, reaching 75 percent of the existing TV audience. As TVs continued to sell, he held his incredible lead, garnering 70 percent of the audience for the next two seasons. Berle was dubbed "Mr. Television," the medium's first legitimate star.

In 1951, NBC acknowledged his power, agreeing to pay him $200,000 a year for an unbelievable term of *thirty years*. Berle would get an NBC paycheck through 1981, the equivalent of a millennium in entertainment years.

Imitation, it's often said, is the sincerest form of television. That began early. Berle's success brought on a dozen knockoffs as NBC, CBS, and newcomer the DuMont network scrambled to cash in on the trend. Soon 30 percent of TV shows were vaudeville or variety.

CBS's best entry was *The Talk of the Town*, which had some fine guests but featured a stiff and vaguely disturbing host. It would take Ed Sullivan a few years to find his sea legs.

By the early '50s, TV had moved beyond being an urban phenomenon, and began to spread throughout the Midwest. One interesting by-product was the fall of Milton Berle. The data suggest a reason for Berle's ratings decline: more rural Americans were buying TVs, and loud, over-the-top Uncle Miltie was not for them. Berle's ratings plummeted and never came back.

TV moved into a series of new comedies. One was *Cavalcade of Stars* on the DuMont network. *Cavalcade of Stars* featured a neighborhood competitor of Berle's. Though it was a variety show, it featured a star so astonishingly watchable that he simply transcended the format.

His name was Jackie Gleason.

CHAPTER 18

JACKIE GLEASON

Jackie Gleason was perhaps the greatest comic actor ever to appear on television. He linked physical comedy to a knowledge of character with uncanny grace and timing. . . . He radiated a specific blend of urban guile and guilelessness that is simply no longer possible in our information-saturated times.

—PLAYWRIGHT ANDREW BERGMAN

Beginnings

The story of great television begins with a childhood so bleak that Dickens might have written it. Somehow, the protagonist would find, in his bleak beginnings, elements of humanity so universal that for decades, he would remind millions of their own families.

John Herbert Gleason was born in 1911 in Brooklyn. Herbert wanted his son named after him, but mother Mae said the name was too ugly to pass on. Herbert prevailed, but Mae ignored him, and called the boy "Jackie" from the beginning.

When Jackie was three, his fourteen-year-old brother Clement died. Jackie's father Herb began drinking heavily, and the marriage degenerated. Jackie soon started walking through Brooklyn in the middle of the night, beginning a lifetime of insomnia.

Two months before Jackie's tenth birthday, Herb Gleason left the family forever. The act was premeditated: he took or destroyed every family photo in which he appeared, so that Mae would not have a picture for the police.

Jackie never heard from his father again. Decades later, he would have J. Edgar Hoover trace the old man. The FBI found that Herb had died a few years earlier, at age seventy. Gleason never said a negative word about him. His stock comment: "He was the best father I'll ever know." It was whimsical, melancholy, and classic Gleason.

Mae tried to keep her son shut in, perhaps trying to keep safe the only person she had left. Gleason rebelled, joining local gangs, playing pool, and skipping school. He smoked by age ten, hustled pool at eleven, and drank bathtub gin at twelve.

Around this time, he visited the Halsey Theater. He would say it was his first memory: seeing the Halsey and deciding to be a star. It was the very theater in which he'd begin his career.

When he joined a school show and got his first laugh it was like "10 spoonfuls of cocaine. It was the greatest thing that could possibly happen to you."[1] Gleason soon left school and began appearing in small clubs. His mother, who surely objected, was already growing ill. In April 1935, Mae Gleason died. Jackie was nineteen. Everyone was gone.

After Mae's funeral, Gleason moved in with a fellow comedian. The timing was difficult: Gleason entered vaudeville as it was dying. He found roadwork in New Jersey and Pennsylvania. When he made money, he spent it immediately, as he would do for the rest of his life.

Gleason discovered that the edgier he was, the more people liked him, prompting him to dislike rehearsals, and to horrify his colleagues by banning them.

In the early '40s, Gleason headed to Hollywood. When he arrived, his new best friend, Jack Haley (the Tin Woodsman of *The Wizard of Oz*), said that Gleason was the most natural performer that he'd ever seen. But Gleason got a reputation for being dangerous to work with, did not set the town on fire, and soon returned home.

Back in the clubs, Gleason discovered in himself the performer that audiences found funniest. He would *become* that person, both on- and offstage. He would stay out for days, break into brilliant improvisations, then get so drunk that he would throw up on friends.

It culminated in a seminal friendship between Gleason and a New York legend.

Toots Shor was the owner of an iconic New York saloon, like Rick's in *Casablanca*. Everyone went to Toots Shor's: Joe DiMaggio, Harry Truman, Frank Sinatra, Charlie Chaplin, and Bob Hope.

To amuse that rarefied crowd, Gleason began developing the characters that would define his career. Soon he was calling himself "the world's great entertainer," though he still made far less than his nemesis, Milton Berle. When Berle exploded on TV, Gleason went to Broadway, and established himself as a star of the stage. Soon after, he returned to Hollywood and took over a role in the TV comedy *Life of Riley*.

Riley lasted a respectable twenty-six weeks, but it did not have good casting. Riley was a likable, dimwitted family man, the polar opposite of Gleason. But the show led to Gleason's big break: a call from the DuMont Television Network.

Cavalcade of Stars

It was the time of the talent raids, and DuMont had a problem. Its show *Cavalcade of Stars* had lost Jack Carter to NBC. Would Jackie fill in for two weeks? Unlike *Riley*, *Cavalcade* was shot live, allowing the host to mix it up with the audience. It was a format as close to the clubs as Gleason could get.

Gleason premiered on *Cavalcade* on July 8, 1950. There is no record of the show; like much of early television, the details have been lost with time. DuMont's primary business was manufacturing TVs, and its management style reflected that. The network spent as little as possible on programming, and Gleason felt badly treated from the start.

With the budget he had, Gleason made some fateful decisions, hiring writers Coleman Jacoby and Arnie Rosen, who would help shape the characters that dominated his career. When Gleason looked for another comedian, they suggested Art Carney, whom Gleason quickly hired.

Meanwhile, Gleason's marriage was falling apart. To settle out with his wife, Gleason asked DuMont for an advance of half a season's pay. If DuMont would front him the money, he said, he would extend his contract for another two years. DuMont said no, in a terrible decision that helped bury the network forever.

Gleason was furious, and resolved to look elsewhere. Soon Frank Stanton got a call from an employee who had Gleason in his office.

Stanton was told Gleason's ask was $50,000 a week and thirty-nine weeks on the air. It was exorbitant, but Stanton trusted his team and approved the deal. Stanton did not meet with Gleason that day—which was just as well, because Gleason was so drunk he could barely stand.

Paley would frequently refer to having seen Gleason on DuMont, and telling Stanton to sign him up. But according to Stanton, this was an outright lie; Paley didn't even know who Gleason was before they signed him.

According to another account, Stanton briefed Paley on Gleason when Paley returned from one of his trips. When Paley asked who the sponsor was, Stanton replied,

> "We haven't sold him yet." Paley responded, "I suppose if we don't sell him we can pay him off." "No," replied Stanton. "We have to play him even if we don't sell him." "Who was so stupid to make that deal?" Paley thundered back.[2]

Stanton had made the right call. Ed Sullivan would take a few more years to gather steam, and CBS needed someone who could compete with Milton Berle, the Brooklyn enemy from the clubs whom Gleason had been trying to surpass for a decade.

Gleason served out his DuMont contract for one more year, refining the characters that he would bring to CBS. Notable skits featured the Poor Soul, Gleason's bittersweet portrayal of a lovable dullard who always did the right thing and was usually punished for it.

Not everyone on DuMont's staff moved to CBS. But Gleason made sure Art Carney was on board. In the summer of 1952, the two men set out on a five-week vaudeville tour. Carney would recall it as the happiest time in their relationship. They performed a number of sketches, over and over, and discovered that one particular sketch was loved above all. It was called "The Honeymooners."

The Jackie Gleason Show

The Jackie Gleason Show debuted on CBS that September. Gleason exploded onto the small screen like nothing seen before. One critic called him "a gifted maniac," but he quickly became beloved by the public.

Gleason's days of befriending the press at Toots Shor's became a huge asset. Reporters relished revealing that Gleason had three identical wardrobes in different sizes, to accommodate his dieting and bingeing. His breakfasts, they reported, included five or six lobsters, or massive orders of Chinese takeout food. His drinking made news as well.

Gleason was rock before rock, hip hop before hip hop. In recognition of his extraordinary live talents, he acquired a new moniker, one he said was bestowed by Lucille Ball but which may have come from his friend Orson Welles. In either event, the name stuck, and Gleason became "The Great One."

Meanwhile, CBS was trying to sell the show to advertisers, and Paley was having a fit. He had learned the details of Gleason's rich deal, and bore down on Stanton to find a sponsor immediately.

This problem contributed to a major CBS innovation. It had begun trying to sell *partial* sponsorships: instead of having to pay for an entire show, a sponsor would only pay for a portion. This was a sea change in advertising, and to some extent, the commercial began as CBS scrambled to make good on its deal with the Great One.

Once CBS made the change, the Gleason show sold out in a week.

On CBS, Gleason expanded his astonishing variety of characters. In 1953 the show won an Emmy for Art Carney. Ratings rose, and CBS offered Gleason $100,000 a year for the next fifteen years. Soon he surpassed Milton Berle, and then stole Berle's sponsor, Buick. Revenge was sweet.

Gleason had come from behind to beat Jimmy Durante, Steve Allen, Mickey Rooney, and Perry Como. His only competition was Lucille Ball, who played one character for most of her career—while Gleason played a gallery of characters each week, live, without a net.

And Gleason was *always* in the news—celebrity biographies, stories of his excess, and a tabloid explosion when his wife confronted his new girlfriend.

In the 1950s, Gleason decided to produce records of "mood music," stringed arrangements of instrumentals for lovers. No record label would touch them so he paid for them himself. *Music for Lovers* became the first of more than forty Jackie Gleason albums. They would eventually sell over 120 million units, often netting Gleason over $1 million per quarter.

In his second season on CBS, Gleason was number two in the ratings, behind only *I Love Lucy*. *The Jackie Gleason Show* had hit its stride, and Gleason had found the formula that worked.

As usual, it wasn't enough. In 1955, Gleason shocked the business by ending his variety show. He would do a show based on one of his sketches. This was universally regarded as a terrible mistake.

The Honeymooners

Gleason likely moved to *The Honeymooners* for financial reasons. Like Lucy before him and Norman Lear after, he realized that variety shows had no afterlife, while comedies shot on film could generate revenue forever.

Whatever his reasons, it was a show he created almost single-handedly.

The conceit and the circumstances would be the same for all thirty-nine episodes. The show mixed live theater with the barest of elements. In the era of unprecedented American prosperity, the Kramdens would live in a tenement. There would be no phone, Gleason insisted; it would too easy for writers to distract from the three leads. There would be almost no sets, beyond the one room in which everything happened, and nothing happened. There would be limited rehearsals to keep everything fresh; Meadows and Carney would eventually develop hand signals to cue Gleason when he missed a line.

There would be no refrigerator, no kids, no job changes—no changes at all, really, just performances by one minor player, two outstanding actors, and one talent so raw that the human condition somehow blasted through him for thirty-nine episodes.

In some ways, it was an idyll to Gleason's sad past: the Kramdens' address and bleak apartment came directly from Gleason's childhood. In other ways, it was deeply ironic: Ralph believed that money would solve his problems, but his failures were always leavened by his wife and best friend, who loved him no matter what happened. Gleason, on the other hand, had all the money he could spend, but never had anyone that he really trusted.

What made *The Honeymooners* special would be debated for decades, in columns, books, and scholarly papers. Gleason would summarize it himself in a 1984 interview on *60 Minutes*:

The poor soul hasn't got a hell of a lot of ability but he keeps trying. He gets schemes. The schemes are all to make Alice happy, and he fails. And when he fails, she feels a great deal of affection. She knows why he did it.[3]

Upon Gleason's death in 1987, Andrew Bergman would summarize the show's impact:

It has never failed to reduce me to tears: Ralph and Alice Kramden exchange Christmas presents in "The Honeymooners" version of "The Gift of the Magi." Ralph has hocked his bowling ball in order to purchase a suitable gift for Alice; she, in turn, gives him a bowling bag. They stare at each other, in that mythic Brooklyn flat—the unadorned table and chairs, the bureau, the icebox, the sink, as imprinted on our memories as the particulars of our own first homes, maybe more so—and for a moment there is embarrassment. Ralph is broke. He has had to pawn his bowling ball. But then a beam of light appears—an epiphany, if you will—and Ralph launches into a paean to the Christmas season: "You know, Christmas is the greatest time of the year," he begins and proceeds to describe a holiday season of ringing church bells, friendly strangers, snow falling in the night—I begin to feel myself go—and finally the knowledge of walking home and of knowing that in that home "there's someone you're nuts about, someone you really love"—and I'm gone, a grown man crying at a 1950's sitcom for the 20th time.[4]

Gleason's gut calls would make *The Honeymooners* perhaps the most successful single TV season of all time.

Unfortunately, that would not happen for a decade; in its own time, the show was considered a failure. The great triumph of Gleason's career would occur during one of the saddest periods of his life. So as the show battled it out in the ratings, Gleason retreated more and more from the cast and crew.

CBS didn't like the show. They wanted Gleason back in variety, where he'd done them so much good in defeating NBC. After one season, Buick, which had left Milton Berle for Gleason, refused to sponsor *The Honeymooners* again.

Gleason's other CBS production, *Stage Show*, made everything worse. NBC's Perry Como trounced it in the ratings. Yet the show had a particular triumph: though rarely acknowledged, Jackie Gleason was the first person to put Elvis Presley on television, calling him "Brando with the guitar" and booking him six times in eight weeks. It was poetic: Presley and producer Sam Phillips had cut rock down to its most skeletal form in their masterful Sun Sessions, much as Gleason had done with *The Honeymooners*, at almost the same time. But the failure of *Stage Show* in the ratings brought even more pressure for *The Honeymooners* to end, which it did, after only thirty-nine episodes.

Another major factor contributed to the end of *The Honeymooners*: America had entered the age of Westerns, and the industry was generally skeptical of comedy's future. Actress Audrey Meadows would sum it up plaintively: "Whatever happened to *Easterns?*"[5]

After The Honeymooners

The postmortems on *The Honeymooners* were brutal. One reviewer wrote, "It has been inconceivable to us that a comedian carrying the towering impact of Jackie Gleason should have flopped so completely as he has."[6]

In 1956, Gleason returned to his variety show without Carney or Meadows. He quickly grew tired of the workload and repetition and, once more, looked for new mountains to climb. He guest hosted on Ed Murrow's *Person to Person*, where his skills as an interviewer proved to be outstanding.

He appeared on anthology *Playhouse 90* in William Saroyan's play *The Time of Your Life*, where he shocked the industry with his dramatic ability. Clark Gable, the idol he'd never met, called him to tell him how great he had been.

He appeared in a series of conversations with radio legend Arthur Godfrey. Again, his performances were a triumph. Columnists began to talk about Gleason as a talk show host, something Gleason would try to make happen for years.

Frustrated by CBS, Gleason returned to Broadway—and had yet another triumph, in *Take Me Along* by Eugene O'Neil. One colleague summed up the prevailing response: "He wasn't a trained dancer, but he danced beautifully. He wasn't a trained singer, but he sang beautifully."[7]

Laurence Olivier, the leading actor of his time, came to the show and loved the performance. He sent Gleason a note that began, "Dear Great One." Gleason threw it away.

During *The Honeymooners*, Gleason had been considered a has-been. Now, he was ascendant, a renaissance man. At last, Jackie Gleason would return to Hollywood.

The first film he made was from a concept he created: a sweet movie called *Gigot*, the story of a hapless bighearted mute, similar to the Poor Soul, and set in Paris. Originally Gleason's friend Orson Welles was set to direct and the great Paddy Chayefsky to write, but both eventually declined.

The Hustler paired Gleason with Paul Newman, with Gleason as Minnesota Fats, a pool shark Gleason transformed from a mastermind to a broken man. His next movie, *Requiem for a Heavyweight*, cemented his reputation as a dramatic actor. He played the merciless manager of a failing fighter (Anthony Quinn) with Gleason as a cold-hearted predator.

Eventually, Gleason agreed to return to CBS. But there was a catch: he would only shoot the show from Miami—so he could continue playing golf, his latest obsession. CBS would pay for a chartered train to bring down the cast and crew. CBS rolled its eyes, then agreed.

In 1964, the train became a PR machine. Stories of Gleason's booze-fueled party train of dancing girls and Dixieland bands became newspaper headlines. In the Miami period, Gleason's contempt for CBS escalated: "Any TV executive," he hooted, "must have one important attribute: *cologne.*"[8]

Through all the ups and downs, Gleason's final tally would be astounding: he was on CBS for eight years in the 1950s, then took a break, and returned to do eight more years in the '60s.

But by the end of the '60s, the world had changed too much. Gleason was a man of the '50s, and CBS decided to target the young. Gleason was canceled by CBS in 1970.

One last opportunity might have altered television history. In 1968, CBS executive Mike Dann had seen a British sitcom called *Till Death Us Do Part*. It featured a belligerent blue-collar worker; Dann thought Gleason might be perfect. When the part of Archie Bunker was offered to Gleason, he rejected *All in the Family* as a second-rate *Honeymooners*.

———

Gleason appeared in a series of specials and movies over the next seventeen years, including a 1983 pairing with Laurence Olivier called *Mr. Halpern and Mr. Johnson*. It was a nice coda for the lonely boy from Brooklyn.

Gleason's legacy includes performances of the broadest humor and the deepest pathos. His ability to create poignancy with flawed characters forged the way for Archie Bunker, Andy Sipowisz, Tony Soprano, and many others. For all of his flaws—or because of them—Gleason's Ralph Kramden would transcend his time to speak to generations. No one would touch his ability to express the bittersweet for fifty years, until another New York comedian named Louis CK.

Jackie Gleason died in 1987. That week, playwright Andrew Bergman would speak for millions:

> The passing of this intimate stranger, this neighbor, is so astonishingly painful that one realizes the nightly cycle of "Honeymooners" broadcasts repeated endlessly have become like mantras—half-hour prayers to the 50's, to our lost innocence, which is to say, the innocence of early television.

> Jackie Gleason reassured us of our humanity like no other television clown could because he used no visible artifice. He was pure television, pure instinct, pure talent. And away we go.[9]

CHAPTER 19

YOUR SHOW OF SHOWS AND ERNIE KOVACS

Gleason had taken the variety format from Berle and had transformed it into a riotous bar brawl of talent. As he did this on CBS, NBC met him with its own reinvention of the sketch show: *Your Show of Shows*, starring Sid Caesar.

Caesar was a generational jump from Berle, someone young families could relate to as America moved from World War II into the '50s. The show was overseen by NBC programming head Pat Weaver, the same exec who would create both *The Tonight Show* and *Today*.

Your Show of Shows was a ninety-minute variety show that brought an unprecedented stable of stars to television. Running from 1950 to 1954, it became one of TV's greatest sources of comic talent, with alumni including Mel Brooks, Neil Simon, Woody Allen, Larry Gelbart, and Carl Reiner.

Unlike Gleason's show, *Your Show of Shows* was not a one-man vehicle; it introduced a disciplined ensemble. In an age before the TelePrompTer, the stage-trained cast remembered every line. *Your Show of Shows* would provide inspiration to Reiner for another milestone, *The Dick Van Dyke Show*, which focused on the writing staff of a variety show, with Reiner in the Caesar role.

The success of the show prompted NBC to give Caesar and Imogene Coca their own shows in 1954, in an attempt to start the spin-off concept

Norman Lear would dominate later. But they were twenty years too early, and the Caesar era faded.

While Berle, Gleason, and Caesar dominated the postwar comedy airwaves, a lesser-known genius was creating television that was decades ahead of its time.

Ernie Kovacs

> Ernie Kovacs loved nothing more than to create his bizarre visions for the world to enjoy. We are fortunate that for a dozen years at the beginning of the most important medium of our time, he was able to do just that.
>
> —Diana Rico

Kovacs was his generation's great iconoclast. He was the only star to work on all four networks of the time, and the forerunner of a generation of TV comedy that would begin in the 1970s. His summation of his life captures his voice: "I was born in Trenton, New Jersey in 1919 to a Hungarian couple. I've been smoking cigars ever since."[1]

Kovacs developed an early interest in performing, and may have found inspiration in bucking the system from his father, who during Prohibition was both a policeman and a bootlegger.

Kovacs received a scholarship from the American Academy of Dramatic Arts, then became a radio DJ, and was picked up in 1949 by NBC's Philadelphia television affiliate. His first show was *Deadline for Dinner*, a cooking show for housewives. Kovacs quickly started calling it "Dead Lion for Breakfast," serving his trademark absurdity while guest chefs looked on.

By 1952 he was hosting *The Ernie Kovacs Show* on CBS. But Paley scheduled him against Milton Berle, and the show was soon canceled. In his final episode, Kovacs nailed a woman into a box and smashed up the set with the hammer.

Kovacs' next stop was the DuMont network in 1953. Here, he introduced many of his iconic sketches, including his most infamous, the Nairobi trio. The trio of silent, hat-wearing gorillas hit each other on the head to music, in a series of sketches that presaged *Monty Python* by decades. The DuMont show also began Kovacs's parodies of TV itself, with the first commercial parodies and fake celebrity interviews. New York audiences went wild.

Kovacs' DuMont success led to a million-dollar contract with NBC in 1955. *The Ernie Kovacs Show* ran mornings on NBC from December 1955 to July 1956. Always fearless, Kovacs followed a 1957 NBC special by superstar Jerry Lewis with a thirty-minute, completely silent performance by a Kovacs character named Eugene. Hollywood saw the brilliance of Eugene and started offering Kovacs movie roles. That same year, Kovacs published a bestselling novel titled *Zoomar*, a thinly veiled critique of television and many of its stars.

Kovacs moved to Hollywood in 1957, and appeared in the movies *Operation Mad Ball*, *Our Man in Havana*, *Bell Book and Candle*, and *It Happened to Jane*.

In Los Angeles, Kovacs became famous for his legendary parties, with a stable of guests including Frank Sinatra, Dean Martin, Milton Berle, Edward G. Robinson, and Billy Wilder. He was infamous for his spending and poker games, which eventually landed him in over $500,000 of debt.

Kovacs became a staple talk show guest and guest host. In 1959, his brilliant *Kovacs on Music* premiered on NBC, complete with a seventy-piece orchestra and dancers in gorilla suits. That same year, Dutch Masters Cigars signed him to host NBC game show *Take a Good Look*. Kovacs created commercials for Dutch Masters as well, leading to fruitful partnership.

In 1961, Kovacs began a series of summer specials for ABC and Dutch Masters. With cutting-edge special effects and extravagant budgets, they are often considered his finest work.

Unfortunately, the series of specials was never completed. On January 13, 1962, during a light rainstorm, Kovacs was driving home from a baby shower for Milton Berle's wife. He lost control of his car and crashed into a power pole, dying instantly.

Kovacs' singular blend of surrealism, absurdity, and harnessed insanity expanded the possibilities of the medium, influencing shows including *Saturday Night Live*, *Monty Python*, *Laugh-In*, and *Sesame Street*.

Kovacs' tombstone reads, appropriately: "Ernie Kovacs 1919–1962—Nothing in Moderation." He was inducted into the Television Academy's Hall of Fame in 1987.

———

By the mid-'50s, the medium needed something beyond variety and sketches. It needed something polished and heartfelt. It needed someone America would fall in love with.

CBS would find her in a fading B-movie actress, who gambled on television and changed it forever.

CHAPTER 20

LUCY AND DESI

I'm not funny. What I am is brave.
—LUCILLE BALL

There are different kinds of products, and different kinds of art. There are innovative products, popular products, beautifully designed products, and products that change the world.

I Love Lucy was all four. It was the prototype for sixty years of television comedy, and likely the highest-rated series of all time.

Like many of these stories, it's a miracle that it happened at all. This owes less to luck than to skill, to the complementary talents of two very different people who would become the most powerful couple in television history. And like many of these stories, it started with radio.

Lucille Desiree Ball was born in 1911. When she was four, a typhoid epidemic swept through town, killing her twenty-eight-year-old father. When he died, Lucy's mother was five months pregnant. She remarried in 1918, moved to Detroit to look for work, and left Lucy with her stepfather's parents.

Her stepfather redeemed himself when he took Lucille to Chautauqua, the legendary site of year-round performances. Chautauqua enchanted her, and inspired Lucy to pursue performing.

When her stepfather's Shriner group needed girls for a chorus line, Lucy got the part. At age twelve, she was hooked. She continued auditioning, fighting with her mother to wear makeup as she got older. At fourteen, she began dating a twenty-one-year-old. To distract her, the family enrolled her in a Manhattan drama school.

By seventeen, she'd moved to Manhattan, taking any job she could find. Eventually she hit bottom, and had to beg for a penny to make subway fare. "One well-dressed older man stopped to listen, then offered me a ten-dollar bill. 'Listen, mister,' I told him with a withering look, 'all I want is one penny.'"[1]

Things picked up in 1928, when she got a job as a model, with thirty costume changes a day. The job exhausted her; she caught pneumonia, then an unknown illness that sidelined her for two years.

When she returned to New York, the Depression was on, but she landed a series of minor chorus roles. Again, success came from modeling. She did a shoot as a Chesterfield girl, and was soon on a Times Square billboard. After the ad, an agent called, inviting her to California as a poster girl.

Lucy arrived in Los Angeles in 1933, and threw herself at every part she could find. Samuel Goldwyn didn't like her looks, but his people loved her work ethic—she simply would not stop trying. After booking small film roles with the Three Stooges and the Marx Brothers, she plowed on in film and on Broadway through the '30s. But stardom would not come.

By the late 1930s, Lucy was known as "the Queen of the B Movies." This was cemented when Ginger Rogers pulled ahead of her at RKO, and Lucy's career seemed to be on its last legs.

There was one more chance: RKO had licensed the musical *Too Many Girls*. Lucy was told to go see it on Broadway. It featured a song by a newcomer named Desi Arnaz.

Desi

Unlike Lucy, Desiderio Alberto Arnaz y de Acha III was born lucky. His father had been the mayor of Santiago, Chile, and an heir to the Bacardi Rum company. That had turned badly in the Batista coup, when Desi's father was imprisoned. Desi escaped to Florida and got a job with bandleader Xavier Cugat.

Desi's timing was perfect; he arrived during a Latin music craze. In 1933, he moved to New York, where Lorenz Hart, coauthor of *Too Many Girls*, saw him and loved him. Desi had never attended a Broadway show, but he opened in one in 1939. Lucy couldn't take her eyes off Desi. "A Cuban skyrocket," she later wrote, had "burst over my horizon."[2]

The next time Lucy saw Desi was at a studio commissary, while Lucy was shooting the part of a stripper. She thought he was beautiful. That night he saw her out of costume, and told a friend he felt the same way about her.

They were married on November 30, 1940. Desi toured constantly, and Lucy continued in small parts. They communicated by phone, and waited for a break. Lucy knew he was cheating, would accuse him, then would forgive him. She filed for divorce, then took him back. She wondered if working together could somehow help save the marriage. A show together would get Desi off the road, where she could keep an eye on him.

Things were rough on the career front too; by 1948, Lucy was nearing forty. Her glamour days were fading. So Lucy began doing some radio work.

This time her timing was perfect. In 1948, Paley began his talent raids, and sent executive Harry Ackerman to head CBS Radio's West Coast programming. Ackerman liked a book called *Mr. and Mrs. Cugat: The Record of a Happy Marriage*. CBS agreed to develop it. And an executive recommended Lucy.

She was interested in doing it—if Desi could do it with her. CBS refused, and cast another actor. They also brought in writer Jess Oppenheimer to rewrite the script. The tone became more slapstick, warmer and less highbrow. When Oppenheimer showed Lucy the final script, she refused to do it.

Oppenheimer had had enough of her attitude and quit. CBS chased him down, and Lucy apologized. The show went on the air, now called *My Favorite Husband*. Then Oppenheimer gave Lucy tickets to Jack Benny's radio show, and told her to study him, and to make his show her "school."

It was a revelation. The film actress saw the king of radio at work, and altered her approach to work a live room. When she went back to *My Favorite Husband*, she channeled Benny's approach; the crowd roared at her timing. After twenty-five years of nearly ceaseless work, Lucille Ball had finally found Lucy.

A reporter from the *Hollywood Reporter* was the first to note the spark: "It's too bad that Lucille Ball's funny grimaces and gestures aren't visible on the radio."[3] Soon Ackerman approached Lucy about a TV show on CBS. Lucy was interested, but only if she could do it with Desi. CBS was against having TV Lucy married to a Cuban bandleader. How would America react?

An advertising exec advised Lucy and Desi to produce an audition tape, and then shop it out for the highest bidder. Oppenheimer and his agent commissioned scripts from writers, and pitched the show to both networks. Then they leaked NBC's interest to CBS.

Ackerman looked for a way to meet Lucy halfway, and signed Desi as host of a radio game show. In the process, he canceled another show, starring a minor comic named Johnny Carson.

Lucy must have been torn. TV could be the end of her film career. She was getting old. How many years had she been doing this? TV was young; maybe it would work out. She took the leap.

Ball's demands were unprecedented: Jess Oppenheimer would be her producer and head writer. Her new company, called Desilu, would own 50 percent of the show. It would be produced in Hollywood so she could continue making movies. Desi *would* appear in the show. And CBS would pay for the demo reel.

Ackerman accepted her terms. CBS had a long series of meetings, trying to find the right concept. Eventually Oppenheimer wrote it up:

I LOVE LUCY

This is the title of an idea for a radio and/or television program incorporating characters named Lucy and Ricky Ricardo. He is a Latin-American bandleader and singer. She is his wife. They are happily married and very much in love. The only bone of contention between them is her desire to get into show business, and his equally strong desire to keep her out of it.[4]

His premise also involved a clown and a Hungarian immigrant. The pilot began shooting in March 1951. Lucy wore baggy clothes; she was finally pregnant, after years of trying.

Results were mixed. Lucy and Desi were very good. The clown and the Hungarian were not.

This was the age of direct sponsorship, so CBS shopped the show to ad agencies. No one wanted it. Lucy recorded her last radio show for *My Favorite Husband,* and bade a tearful goodbye to her audience. *I Love Lucy* looked dead.

Lucy and Desi were saved by their own tenacity. When CBS had rejected Desi, Lucy and Desi had set out to prove them wrong. As Gleason and Carney would do, they had gone on a vaudeville tour to prove out their act. They were right: *Variety* called the show "one of the best bills to play house in recent months." Some sponsors had seen the show and had been impressed.

One of these emerged, an agency repping Philip Morris, who bought thirty-nine episodes of *I Love Lucy* with an option to renew. As casting wrapped, the agent asked when the crew was moving to New York. Oppenheimer panicked. They weren't; they had agreed with Lucy to shoot in Los Angeles.

But Lucy did not understand television yet. In 1951, there was no national TV feed. And 85 percent of viewers were in the East or Midwest. Only 15 percent were in Pacific Time.

So if the show was shot in Los Angeles, 85 percent of viewers would have to watch a muddy recording, called a kinescope—and even then, not until the next day. Philip Morris wasn't willing to sponsor a show where only 15 percent of their audience would actually see the show with decent picture quality.

Innovation and I Love Lucy

Desi scrambled for a solution. There was only one: to shoot the show on film. Then copies could be sent to each station, which would air it at the right time. This had been done only once before, by *Amos 'n' Andy* (though without a live audience). Desi seized the lifeline. He told CBS he would shoot the show with three 35-millimeter cameras in front of a live audience. Nothing of the kind had ever been done. He quoted a price of $24,500.

CBS countered: film was too expensive. Lucy and Desi would each take a pay cut.

There's no way to know if Desi knew what he was doing next, whether he was just pushing the boundaries, or had a sense of the world to come. It doesn't really matter. What matters is what he said next.

Desi agreed to the pay cut for one small concession: he and Lucy would own 100 percent of the thirty-nine shows once they'd aired.

Desi was surprised when CBS agreed. But in 1951, TV was a live medium. Once a show had aired, it was over. Who cared who owned it then? It was as dead as yesterday's newspaper.

Later, Desi would say CBS went along because it thought the shoot would fail. Then he and Lucy would move back to New York, and CBS would get what it wanted.

That wasn't a bad guess, because Desi had a problem. He had absolutely no idea how to produce a three-camera TV show in front of a live audience. Neither did anyone else. But he knew they needed a live audience. The lack of audience feedback was why so many TV shows seemed stale.

One of their ad agency's execs, Eddie Feldman, gave Desi an answer: the TV game show *Truth or Consequences* was shot live, with three cameras and a studio audience. So Desi hired the man who'd created the technique, writer Al Simon.

Hiring Simon solved one problem, but another remained. Game shows don't have to look good, and Desi and Lucy wanted their show to look beautiful. They agreed on whom they needed: Karl Freund.

Karl Freund was a legendary Oscar winner, with credits including Fritz Lang's *Metropolis, All Quiet on the Western Front,* and *Dracula.* He was a master of technology, and he made women look great.

Desi called Freund and described what he wanted. He wanted to film a TV show as if it were a stage play, continuously, without any breaks. He wanted a big audience for plenty of laughs. He wanted to film it on three 35-millimeter cameras. The cameras would be synchronized so that the audio would be in sync, and the film could be edited seamlessly.

Freund replied no. This was impossible. Desi hadn't considered lighting: if one camera was wide shot and another was in close-up, the lighting would have to change. You couldn't do three angles with one lighting setup. And you couldn't reset lighting while a live audience sat there. Plus, Lucy was not young; lighting her well would be its own challenge.

But Arnaz knew Freund had plenty of money from his light meter invention. The way to motivate Freud was by targeting his pride:

> Desi turned on all the charm he possessed. "My God, Papa, you showed how to use a moving camera, you invented the light meter. . . . For such a genius, what I want you to do should be a pushover." Pointing out that "Lucy's no chicken," Freund said he would have to "use special lighting, put gauze on the lens." "I don't care what you have to do, Papa. I'll get you whatever you need." A bit more wrangling and Papa ventured, "Okay, I come out and we talk and we look."[5]

Freund signed on at union scale, joined *I Love Lucy*, and invented the art of sitcom lighting.

There was one more landmine. CBS had given Jess Oppenheimer 20 percent of the show for creating the concept and making it work. When Desi was reminded of this fact, he was furious. Lucy begged Oppenheimer to lower his number; if the show didn't happen, her career was over. He refused. Eventually Desi gave in, and the two men went on to cast the Mertzes together.

On set, Desi knew CBS did not want him, so he worked hard to make a good impression. Lucy, on the other hand, was often a nightmare— particularly to actress Vivian Vance. When Ball pulled off Vance's false eyelashes, a coworker asked Vance what she planned to do. Vance said, "Maury, if by any chance this thing actually becomes a hit and goes anywhere, I'm gonna learn to love that bitch."[6]

On October 15, 1951, *I Love Lucy* premiered on a Monday, avoiding the Tuesday nights then owned by Milton Berle. The reviews were mixed, but not for very long.

The American Research Bureau reported that *Lucy* was the first show to be seen in 10 million homes. Within a month, it had 14 million viewers a week. It was number three in its first season, then number one for four of the next five seasons. It garnered what is generally considered the highest season rating of all time: 67.3, which then meant it had 31 million viewers per episode, in a time when the television audience was still small.

To give Lucy rest during her pregnancy, Desi and Oppenheimer re-broadcast popular episodes. These too became rating winners, and led to the birth of the syndication market.

So *I Love Lucy* invented another first: the rerun.

Updates on Lucy's pregnancy became a sensation. CBS slated the birth episode to coincide with Lucy's actual due date. In January 1953, "Lucy Goes to the Hospital" was watched by 68.8 percent of viewers, on over 71 percent of American televisions—more than watched Dwight Eisenhower's presidential inauguration the next day.

In another first, viewers watched Little Ricky grow up on air. People liked Ike, but the Ricardos were America's First Family.

Lucy seemed unstoppable, until the House Un-American Activities Committee (HUAC) discovered she had been registered to vote as a Communist in 1936. One headline declared, "Lucille Ball a Red." Philip Morris and CBS were terrified.

Lucy told the committee she had done it at her grandfather's urging, and never intended to vote as a Communist. There was an avalanche of support among the press and the public. The chair of the HUAC was quoted: "We love Lucy too." She was left off the "Security List" that would destroy so many lives.

That night, Desi told the audience that "the only thing red about Lucy is her hair, and even that is not legitimate." The crowd roared; many wept. That meant little to Bill Paley and the men at Philip Morris. They held their breath till the ratings came in. The show remained number one. The next morning's *Los Angeles Times* read, "EVERYBODY STILL LOVES LUCY."

A middling performer on the big screen, Lucy now moved into a realm that had never existed in film. She was not worshipped; she was loved. She was not a goddess; she was a friend. She came into people's homes with her family. They knew her, or thought they did. When Eisenhower invited Lucy and Desi to the White House, he bluntly asked if Desi was the guy knocking him off of the front page.

If it seemed too good to last, it was. As the seasons went on, the pressure grew. Lucy took on more work, trying to finally create a great film career. Desi drove Desilu to new heights: in 1954, Desilu shot 229 half-hour shows, and Lucy and Desi joined the ranks of Hollywood moguls.

There was a price to the success. Desi began to age noticeably, burning the candle at both ends. Neither he nor Lucy spent much time with their children.

They began behaving like characters in a parody. Desi bought a country club, then spent almost $1 million renovating it. Lucy had furniture flown in from New York on a private plane. She liked to spend her little free time resting and playing with the kids. But Desi could not stop, whether it was golfing or gambling. The angrier she grew, the more he pulled away.

As all shows do eventually, *I Love Lucy* was running out of ideas. The *New York Times* summed up the critics' view: "Lucy has run its course and has no choice but to press too hard." So Lucy, Ricky, Fred, and Ethel went to Los Angeles, opening the show for a range of guest stars, including William Holden and Harpo Marx.

In 1956, both Oppenheimer and Freund left the show. According to his autobiography, Desi sat Lucy down. He asked her if they should end the show, enjoy their lives, and try to save their marriage. Lucy responded: how they could walk away from a number one show?

In 1957, Desi Arnaz won his greatest victory. In the beginning, no one had wanted him. In the beginning, TV had been disposable. No one could have guessed that their little show would be worth anything. But his foresight in getting full ownership was rewarded.

In 1957, CBS bought the rights to *I Love Lucy* from Desilu for an astounding $1 million—in 1957, an astronomical sum. Ball and Arnaz used the money for a down payment on the former RKO Studios, where Lucy had worked so long and so hard.

Desilu Studios

The legendary RKO lot became Desilu Studios. Lucy and Desi now controlled twenty-six sound stages. They would own hits including *The Untouchables*, *The Ann Sothern Show*, *The Walter Winchell File*, and *The Texan*—and eventually *Star Trek* and *Mission: Impossible*. Desilu would be the location for shows including *The Betty Hutton Show*, *The Danny Thomas Show*, *The Millionaire*, and *Wyatt Earp*.

Ten years earlier, television had barely existed. Now television had conquered a movie studio, and built a pipeline that dwarfed most movie lots.

Lucy had been wrong about one thing: doing the show together could not save her marriage. Magazines increasingly speculated about Desi's extramarital behavior. The more iconic Lucy became, the more Desi strayed.

In 1960, *I Love Lucy* finished its nine-year run, and Lucille Ball filed for divorce. The same day, in their final shot together, Lucy was dressed in a chauffeur costume:

> In the final scene, Desi was supposed to pull me into an embrace, mustache and all, and kiss me. When the scene arrived and the cameras closed in for that final embrace, we just looked at each other, and then Desi kissed me, and we both cried. It marked the end of so many things.[7]

Desi had always been the businessman. Lucy had always been the talent. But in 1962, Lucy shocked the world. She borrowed $3 million to buy Desi's 52 percent of Desilu stock.

And now wacky Lucille Ball from Jamestown, New York, became the first woman to own a major studio. She took an active role in the oversight, green lighting projects other studio heads might not have, including two of the most iconic series of the next decade: *Mission: Impossible* and *Star Trek*.

In 1967, Lucy sold Desilu to Paramount for $17 million—seventeen times what she had paid for RKO.

———

Desi Arnaz died in 1986.

Five days later, Lucy visited another aging B movie actor, in Washington, D.C.

"It's no secret that Nancy and I are friends of Lucy. And I think this redheaded bundle may be the finest comedienne ever."

"Like millions of Americans and people around the world, I still love Lucy," said the President of the United States.

As Reagan continued, Lucy began to cry. "I know Miss Ball would want us to pay tribute to the man who produced *I Love Lucy* and starred in it with her, the late Desi Arnaz." Then actor Robert Stack read a letter Desi had written on his deathbed that week.

It ended, "P.S. 'I Love Lucy' was never just a title."[8]

Weeping openly, Lucy nodded. Yes, that was true.

———

Lucille Ball died on April 26, 1989. The woman who struggled for decades in film received four Emmys, thirteen nominations, the Television Academy's Governor's and Hall of Fame Awards, the Women in Film Crystal Award, the Golden Globe Cecil B. DeMille Award, the Presidential Medal of Freedom, and the Women's International Center's Living Legacy Award. She was on the first cover of *TV Guide*, then on more of its covers than anyone else in its history.

Time magazine named Lucille Ball one of the 100 most important people of the century. On her ninetieth birthday, she was on a U.S. postage stamp. On her 100th birthday, Google put her on its homepage. That day, 915 Lucy imitators converged in Jamestown to celebrate.

Lucy often said that without Desi, none of it would have been possible. She often thought her life after Desi was nothing but a postscript.

It wasn't true, but it didn't matter. For generations to come, the two would always be together.

CHAPTER 21

QUIZ SHOW SCANDAL

As Lucy and Gleason soared, CBS basked in their success. But the problem for the networks then, as now, was that this level of talent was exceedingly rare. What would be more efficient would be a format that CBS could clone and repeat, one that didn't depend upon *talent*. That format came along in 1954, when the Supreme Court determined that television quiz shows did not constitute gambling. This freed up the networks to start turning the crank.

The first major quiz show was CBS's *The $64,000 Question*. The premise was to bring winning contestants back week after week. The longer the contestants won, the more cash they got. It was a quantum leap beyond the radio days: the consolation prize here was a new Cadillac.

It was promoted, not surprisingly, as the "biggest jackpot program in radio-TV history." The ratings were stupendous, and within months came the knockoffs: *High Finance, Treasure Hunt, Twenty-One, The Most Beautiful Girl in the World, Giant Step, Can Do,* and *Nothing but the Truth*.

The $64,000 Question was created by a producer named Lou Cowan. He was hired by CBS in 1955, and became its president of television in 1958. Before then, he added a spin-off, called *The $64,000 Challenge*. In the ratings, *The $64,000 Question* and *The $64,000 Challenge* would eventually be number one and number two, respectively, in the ratings.

The biggest quiz show, *Twenty-One*, premiered on NBC in 1956. Its early champion was Herbert Stempel. He was awkward, ill at ease, and generally unlikable. Stempel was challenged by Charles Van Doren, a handsome Columbia University instructor from a distinguished family.

The audience began rooting for Van Doren quickly. In December, he defeated Stempel, when Stempel missed a question, oddly, about his favorite film, *Marty*.

Van Doren prevailed for the next four months, before being defeated in 1957. By then, he was a national celebrity and got a job on the *Today Show*. Quiz show mania grew bigger than ever.

The next big show was *Dotto*, premiering on CBS in 1958. The show became so popular that NBC created a version as well. Soon *Dotto* was the number one show on TV. But there was a problem.

One night *Dotto* contestant Ed Hilgemeyer found a notebook with questions and answers—the very answers contestant Marie Winn was delivering at the time. It was clear to Hilgemeyer that the show had been rigged.

When CBS and NBC confronted the show's creator, he didn't argue: yes, the show was fixed. The show's producers had done it to improve the ratings, and it had worked.

CBS and NBC each canceled their versions of the show.

But the fire was spreading, because Herb Stempel had been talking. He alleged that *Twenty-One* had been fixed as well, that he had been told to lose by producer Dan Enright. The *Dotto* problems gave credibility to Stempel, and the *New York Journal–American* investigated the story.

Though the scandal began with *Dotto*, it was CBS's *Twenty-One* that took the heat of the scandal. Producers of the show claimed they had been pressured by the show's sponsor, Geritol. The first episode had gone so badly that Geritol had demanded that producers Enright and Jack Barry make changes. So as part of their plan, the producers of *Twenty-One* arranged the first Van Doren–Stempel face-off to end in three consecutive ties.

It was the model that professional wrestling would perfect: Van Doren was the hero, and Stempel was the heel. The rigging paid off, as millions of viewers tuned in to root for Van Doren.

Once the truth came to light, twenty quiz shows were canceled. The scandal threatened to take down the networks.

———

In September 1958, a New York grand jury was convened, and producers and contestants were asked to testify. Fearing public backlash, most of them lied, including Van Doren.

In 1959, a congressional investigation began. Herb Stempel and child star Patty Duke admitted they'd been given answers in advance.

On November 2, in a televised session, Charles Van Doren recanted his previous denials in a nationally televised session. "I was involved, deeply involved, in a deception." Van Doren pled guilty to second-degree perjury. Eisenhower called it "a terrible thing to do to the American people."

Most of those implicated, including Enright and Barry, eventually returned to television. At the time, fixing the shows was not illegal. TV was new, and the law had not caught up. Since no law had been broken, no one was sentenced.

But Van Doren was found guilty in the court of public opinion. He lost his job on the *Today Show*, and resigned from Columbia University. In 1959, he began working at Encyclopedia Britannica, for about 20 percent of his NBC salary. He stayed there for seventeen years, and repeatedly turned down interview requests.

When Robert Redford made the movie *Quiz Show*, Van Doren turned down a $100,000 fee to consult. Then, in 2008, he finally told his story:

> In the early fall of 1956 I was talking with a man named Albert Freedman. A man named Herb Stempel was winning week after week, but he wasn't popular and the ratings were suffering… [Freedman told me] "I've decided you should be the person to beat Stemple."[1]

In 1960, fixing of quiz shows was outlawed by Congress, and restrictions were placed on the monetary value of quiz show prizes.

Smart people would eventually find a way around the restrictions. Merv Griffin's wife suggested a show in which contestants were given the *answers*, but had to figure out the *questions*. Thus was the game show *Jeopardy* born.

Big prizes would return in the 1980s, and explode in the 1990s, with *Who Wants to Be a Millionaire*—another massively popular genre that would be overprogrammed until it collapsed.

Someone had to take the fall for the scandal. Paley and Stanton decided it would be Cowan. They badgered him to resign, which he did under duress.

One person saw the writing on the wall.

Ed Murrow's *See It Now* had one of the best time slots in television. And quiz shows were the opposite of everything he stood for. On June 7, 1955, he watched CBS, and saw *The $64,000 Question* as the new lead-in for his show, *See It Now*.

Murrow turned to his partner Fred Friendly and asked, "Any bets on how much longer we'll keep this time period? Not very long."[2]

CHAPTER 22

AMERICAN BROADCASTING COMPANY

Both Disney and Goldenson had a rare edge: they could see a little further into the future than the next fellow. They also possessed a business savvy that enabled them to keep meeting payrolls while nursing their visions toward reality.

—WARREN BUFFETT

For almost all of television's first three decades, ABC was number three of three. That had much to do with where it came from.

In the 1920s, an antitrust action had driven AT&T to sell its radio network. Once it sold its network to RCA, RCA had *two* networks, known as NBC Red and NBC Blue.

NBC Red was the King Kong of radio, the *real* NBC. Blue was the test zone, where the team tried new ideas.

But some cities had both Blue and Red, for a massive NBC advantage. And that advantage triggered *more* antitrust concerns.

The FCC investigated and ruled against RCA. RCA took the battle to the Supreme Court, but lost. So on July 30, 1943, NBC Blue was sold to Edward J. Noble of the Lifesaver candy corporation for $8 million. He renamed it the American Broadcasting Company.

ABC relaunched as a radio network in 1943, and as a TV network in 1948.

Soon the Mutual Broadcasting System (which had filed the initial complaint) was gone. The DuMont network soon was gone, too.

The next fifty years would be a three-way race.

United States v. Paramount Pictures

ABC was created by two antitrust actions. It was saved by a third one, five years later.

As the movie industry grew, the major studios (Paramount, Warner Bros, RKO, Universal, and Columbia) began controlling more and more movie distribution, via theaters. By 1945, they owned 17 percent of theaters, and 45 percent of box office revenue.

The more theaters the studios owned, the more they controlled what the public saw. They could crush anyone who tried to compete with their films, any nonstudio producers who tried to get in the game.

The 1948 *United States v. Paramount Pictures* decision ended this, forcing major studios to sell off their theaters. It was a boon to independent producers, and a first major blow to the studio system.

Between the Paramount decree and the birth of TV, the studios would never be the same.

Hollywood and Television

After the decision, the theaters formerly owned by Paramount were spun off as United Paramount Theatres. UPT had a well-respected lawyer who had started at Paramount after graduating from Harvard Business School in 1933. His name was Leonard Goldenson.

In 1939, Goldenson fell in love with a demo: David Sarnoff's miraculous television pavilion at the New York World's Fair. Goldenson became an early believer, and wanted in on TV.

As the antitrust ax fell on Paramount, Edward Noble was having major problems. He was fighting to compete with NBC and CBS while ABC hemorrhaged money. Noble got a $5 million bank loan, which kept the doors open for a while. But when the banks refused to extend his credit, he considered selling to CBS.

As Noble struggled with ABC, Goldenson was promoted to run United Paramount Theatres. But there was no way to grow theaters after the *Paramount* decree. He searched for a way to transform UPT. He found one, in ABC.

In 1951, Goldenson offered Noble $25 million to merge ABC with UPT. Noble leapt at the offer. The American Broadcasting–Paramount Theatres merger was approved by the FCC in 1953.

The pantheon was complete: first tech exec Sarnoff. Then ad exec Paley, with his genius for PR. Third came movie exec Goldenson, as smart but less liquid, who would have to compete on the cheap.

He turned it into the innovator's advantage: having less to lose, Goldenson took more risks.

Over time, Goldenson established a strategy: whatever NBC and CBS did, he would do the opposite. Working through his options, he came up with two brilliant ideas, which rewrote the rules of network television.

Sponsors and Control

First, Goldenson found a weakness common to both Sarnoff and Paley: production by sponsors. Both had come up in radio, where budgets were controlled by ad men. So CBS and NBC brought their radio model to TV, in which

1. broadcasters sold blocks of time to sponsors;
2. sponsors paid for the actual shows; and
3. sponsors were represented by advertising agencies, which produced the actual programming.

This gave the ad agencies a massive seat at the table. Why, Goldenson thought, give so much power away?

Rather than yield control to ad agencies, Goldenson looked for programming ABC could afford to pay for itself. This would increase ABC's power in the equation, and reduce the power of the ad agencies over time.

Goldenson picked new genres that ABC could afford, beginning with programming aimed at kids, then expanding into a wide range of Westerns. With Westerns, he hit pay dirt, as the new genre of programming put ABC on the map.

Advertisers, fearing that NBC and CBS would follow suit, lobbied the government to keep networks from owning programming. They lost. It was a huge win for networks, and for independent producers, who could now bypass ad agencies and go straight to networks.

Goldenson's next stroke of genius came from his background. Unlike Sarnoff and Paley, he knew Hollywood.

ABC and Disney

Even after the theater sell-off, movie studios wanted nothing to do with television. It was a down-budget medium that threatened box office revenue. But one studio had a different business model, and couldn't afford to be picky.

Walt Disney needed *cash*. And he needed it *now*. His massive dream project, Disneyland, was massively over budget. According to Goldenson,

> When I acquired ABC, everyone in the motion picture companies had refused to deal with television, but Walt Disney wanted to build Disneyland and he needed money. I made up my mind that I was going to do everything in our power to bring Disney into television. If I could crack Disney, then I could maybe crack the other motion picture companies.[1]

On April 2, 1954, ABC inked a deal with Disney. Walt agreed to produce a one-hour weekly series, *Disneyland*, for $2 million for one season, renewable for a total of seven years.

Goldenson threw in another $500,000 for 35 percent of Disneyland, and ABC guaranteed up to $4.5 million in loans, as needed for the park's construction.

In return, ABC got exclusive rights for all Disney's TV projects.

During its first season, *Disneyland* brought in nearly half of ABC's ad revenue. Goldenson programmed the show at 7:30 PM, giving ABC a jump on prime time at 8:00, and keeping viewers away from the other two networks.

Disneyland became ABC's first top ten show. It won three Emmys in 1954. ABC's first profitable year was 1955.

The catalyst was three *Davey Crockett* episodes, which made the character a national icon. Ninety million viewers watched those three episodes, with the audience *increasing* in reruns. One critic wrote, "The modern Crockett Craze, appearing in early 1955, is now considered to be one of the great popular culture events of the decade."[2]

Unlike NBC and CBS, which were all about adults, Goldenson's ABC targeted families with small children. He rightly saw that this was the demo with the most buying power: "We're after a specific audience: the young housewife—one cut above the teenager—with two to four kids, who has to buy the clothing, the food, the soaps, the home remedies."[3]

So ABC and Disney created a new series: *The Mickey Mouse Club.* Airing at 5 PM, it brought kids rushing home to watch.

The runaway success of *Davey Crockett* led ABC to expand Western programming. In 1957, it greenlit *Maverick. Maverick* was followed with a string of top ten Westerns including *The Rifleman* and *The Real McCoys.* It was the beginning of the Baby Boom media cycle that would move from Crockett to Kennedy to the Beatles.

In 1960, Westerns made ABC the number two network, ahead of NBC. It was largely due to Goldenson, who'd brought TV and Hollywood together. He had taken ABC from near bankruptcy to being the most innovative network of the '50s, increasing revenues by nearly 500 percent.

His next deal with Warner Bros. brought three series to the Tuesday night schedule: *King's Row, Casablanca,* and *Cheyenne.* Jack Warner got ten minutes an hour to promote Warner Bros.' current movies, and soon had the largest TV budget in Hollywood. Warner produced a third of ABC's 1959 schedule. Everyone won.

ABC followed Warner Bros. with an MGM block. CBS countered with 20th Century Fox and *The Twentieth Century Fox Hour.*

Soon, studios were designing shows specifically for ABC—especially Westerns.

CHAPTER 23

WESTERNS

*I was five years old when television entered the Martin
household. A plastic black box wired to a rooftop antenna sat
in our living room, and on it appeared what had to be the
world's longest continuous showing of B Westerns.*
—STEVE MARTIN, BORN STANDING UP: A COMIC'S LIFE

T he vacuum of the quiz shows was filled by another format, the
Western. It was logical: Westerns were popular in movies and radio. Like vaudeville, Westerns were easy to transplant to television. They could star young, inexpensive talent, freeing networks from
the costs of established stars. The genre began at NBC, but ABC jumped
in with both boots, as a cost-effective way to expand its young brand.

The year 1949 saw the premiere of the first TV Western, NBC's *The
Hopalong Cassidy Show,* targeted at kids. The show was a half-step, cut together from film footage. But it created a new business model: Hopalong
was the first image printed on a lunchbox.

Hopalong inspired a move from radio to television for *The Gene Autry
Show* and *The Roy Rogers Show.* By 1955, adult TV Westerns emerged as
a serious ratings winner, with *Gunsmoke* and *The Life and Legend of Wyatt
Earp.*

Gunsmoke may have begun when Bill Paley wanted a Western. The
creators strove to make something for adults rather than kids, to show
how hard life had been for America's pioneers. Compared to other
Westerns, *Gunsmoke* was darker and more realistic.

Executive Harry Ackerman, who also managed *I Love Lucy*, handled *Gunsmoke*'s transition from radio to TV. William Conrad had a great voice but was not a leading man. John Wayne suggested James Arness, who was cast in the role; Wayne introduced the first episode in 1955. Conrad would go on to narrate *The Fugitive* and *Rocky and Bullwinkle*, and star in *Cannon* and *Jake and the Fat Man*.

Gunsmoke would become television's longest-running live action show, running from 1955 to 1975. It was number one for many of those years, and in the top ten for most of them. It was eventually canceled in 1975 as CBS modernized its lineup; *The Mary Tyler Moore Show* and *Rhoda* took its place. The *Los Angeles Times* eulogized the show that week:

> Gunsmoke was the dramatization of the American epic legend of the west. Our own Iliad and Odyssey, created from standard elements of the dime novel and the pulp western. . . . It was ever the stuff of legend.[1]

CBS was not kind to *Gunsmoke*'s cast: like many actors before and since, they discovered their show was canceled when they read it in the newspaper.

ABC's *Maverick* ran from 1957 to 1962, and was a Western comedy about a traveling poker player. In its prime, the show beat both Steve Allen and Ed Sullivan, prompting the drive for more Westerns. It introduced TV star James Garner as Bret Maverick, who traveled America with his brother, looking for poker games and getting into trouble. The show won an Emmy for Best Series in 1959, before Garner left and was replaced by Roger Moore, the future James Bond.

Maverick was created by the prolific Roy Huggins, who went on to create both *The Fugitive* and *The Rockford Files*, with James Garner back as Jim Rockford. Garner said *Rockford* was a detective version of *Maverick*, but *Rockford* would be much-beloved in its own right—and would raise yet another generation of talent in the '70s—especially writer David Chase, who would go on to create *The Sopranos*.

NBC's *Bonanza* became the second-most-successful TV Western, running from 1959 to 1973. Rather than a lone gunman vehicle, *Bonanza* was an ensemble show, about a father and his three grown sons in 1860s Nevada. Lorne Greene, Pernell Roberts, Dan Blocker, and Michael

Landon became beloved performers, until the show was moved against *Maude* and then canceled. It had a massive resurgence in syndication, where a new generation grew up listening to its famed theme song.

By the late '50s, Westerns dominated television, and helped give ABC some of its first points on the board. In 1959, eight of the top ten TV programs were Westerns, with a total of twenty-six Westerns on the air. In the early '60s, Westerns were the most powerful genre block in TV, and then they quickly began to fade.

In some ways, the Western would return fifty years later, in a very different skin, in a show called *Breaking Bad*.

In the meantime, America was caught up in a different kind of showdown. It was the medium's finest hour to date, and would be Edward R. Murrow's last stand.

CHAPTER 24

MURROW VS. MCCARTHY

And if there are any historians . . . a hundred years from now and there
should be preserved the kinescopes for one week of all three networks, they
will find recorded, in black and white or color, evidence of decadence,
escapism and insulation from the realities of the world in which we live.
—EDWARD R. MURROW TO THE RADIO AND TELEVISION
NEWS DIRECTORS ASSOCIATION, 1958

Edward R. Murrow had returned from World War II as a national hero, the voice of quality news. And like most journalists, he was skeptical about television. But TV was the future, so he began doing pieces on TV's *CBS Evening News.*

In November 1951, radio's *Hear It Now* moved to television as *See It Now.* Murrow opened the show's first episodes by asking for patience: "This is an old team, trying to learn a new trade." The show moved to prime time in 1952, and averaged 3 million viewers, many more times than TV news gets now.

In 1952 the show made history with a special called *This Is Korea . . . Christmas 1952.* It sought "to try to portray the face of the war and the faces of the men who are fighting it." It did so magnificently, in a moving way *M*A*S*H* would work hard to emulate twenty years later. Murrow ended the show bluntly: "There is no conclusion to this report, because there is no end to the war."[1]

The *New York Times'* Jack Gould would call it "one of the finest programs ever seen on TV."[2]

In 1953, Murrow's celebrity led to a second show, *Person to Person*. It was one of the first of the celebrity interview genre, in which Murrow interviewed leading stars, politicians, and artists. It was a ratings hit, attracting 18 to 21 million viewers, and lasting through 1961. The two shows would be referred to as "High Murrow" and "Low Murrow," but even "Low Murrow" was classic in television terms. His guests included Jack and Jackie Kennedy, Elizabeth Taylor, Frank Sinatra, Marlon Brando, Humphrey Bogart, Margaret Mead, Harry Truman, Fidel Castro, and John Steinbeck.

In terms of influence, *Person to Person* was about to be dwarfed by one episode of *See It Now*, that would widely be regarded as television's finest hour.

McCarthy

The anti-Communist movement had begun in 1947, as the House Committee on Un-American Activities (HUAC) investigated hundreds of citizens, often making them unemployable for years. Lucille Ball was questioned by the HUAC, and eventually cleared.

Pert Kelton, the original Alice Kramden of *The Honeymooners*, did not fare as well. Like many, she was blacklisted, then fired by CBS.

A 1950 bill by the Subversive Activities Control Board proposed removal of citizenship and the detention of "subversives." It was vetoed by Truman, who called it a "mockery of the Bill of Rights" and a "long step toward totalitarianism." His veto was overridden by Congress.

Into the fray came Joseph McCarthy. He been a Wisconsin judge with an erratic track record, then had won his Senate seat in 1946. He shot to prominence in 1950 when he declared the State Department was "infested" with Communists, and quickly became the face of a virulent anti-Communist, anti-gay movement.

McCarthy went on a rampage as his fame increased—battling Truman, kneeing a journalist in the groin, and accusing the Democrats of "twenty years of treason." Truman called McCarthy "the best asset the Kremlin has," and fought him until his presidency ended in 1953.

Though Eisenhower disliked McCarthy, he was afraid to alienate his supporters, and campaigned with him in the 1952 election. In a 1953 televised speech, McCarthy praised Eisenhower for removing "1,456

Truman holdovers who were . . . gotten rid of because of Communist connections and activities or perversion." As their relationship soured, McCarthy amended his catchphrase to "twenty-one years of treason," to include Eisenhower's first year in office.

Many had hoped Eisenhower would clip fellow Republican McCarthy's wings when his presidency began. But again, Eisenhower worried about taking him on.

Ed Murrow watched McCarthy, and waited.

In 1953, McCarthy launched a variety of attacks, including reviewing books the State Department kept in its libraries. State caved in and ordered its staff to remove "material by any controversial persons, Communists, fellow travelers, etc." McCarthy became famous for announcing he had "documentation" that proved the guilt of hundreds, documentation he never revealed.

That same year, when McCarthy began an investigation of the Army, Murrow decided the time had come. He had his CBS staff collect all available footage of McCarthy. They worked on the show with Murrow for two months. Knowing he'd be attacked if he said anything negative about McCarthy, Murrow resolved to let McCarthy's actions do the talking.

In March of 1954, Murrow and colleague Fred Friendly let CBS know they were planning a show on McCarthy. Paley and Stanton did not watch the show beforehand.

The CBS logo did not appear, and the network refused to pay ad support. Murrow and Friendly paid for a *New York Times* ad themselves. As the airdate grew closer, a worried Murrow sent his family to Jamaica, to stay safely out of town until after the show aired.

On March 9, 1954, *See It Now* ran "A Report on Senator Joseph McCarthy." It revealed McCarthy in action, making a series of bullying, abusive, and contradictory statements. Individually, McCarthy's performances had always been eccentric. But edited into one show, they seemed much worse. The triumph of editing concluded with a statement from Murrow:

We proclaim ourselves—as indeed we are—the defenders of freedom, what's left of it, but we cannot defend freedom abroad by deserting it at home. The actions of the junior Senator from Wisconsin have caused alarm and dismay amongst our allies abroad and given considerable comfort to our enemies, and whose fault is that? Not really his. He didn't create this situation of fear; he merely exploited it, and rather successfully. Cassius was right: "The fault, dear Brutus, is not in our stars but in ourselves." Good night, and good luck.

CBS was deluged by letters, phone calls, and telegrams. They supported Murrow, 15 to 1. The next week, *See It Now* ran another criticism of McCarthy.

On April 6, 1954, McCarthy himself appeared on *See It Now*, and accused Murrow of supporting a "Russian espionage and propaganda organization."

Once again, public opinion overwhelmingly backed Murrow. Then on April 22, McCarthy's battle with the Army began.

ABC was the sole network to televise the hearings, greatly advancing the prestige of ABC News. The country watched McCarthy in unflattering close-up, as he accused the Army of harboring Communists. The hearings lasted for thirty-six days, and were watched by an estimated 20 million viewers.

On ABC's June 9 broadcast, McCarthy faced off against Army counsel Joseph Welch. Welch challenged McCarthy to actually *show* the new list of 130 Communists he was railing against. When McCarthy called a colleague of Welch's "the legal mouthpiece of the Communist Party," Welch was ready:

Let us not assassinate this lad further, Senator. You've done enough. Have you no sense of decency, sir, at long last? Have you left no sense of decency?

The gallery applauded.

A Wisconsin newspaper demanded McCarthy's recall as a senator. Soon the Senate drafted a resolution of censure, voting against McCarthy on two of forty-six counts. Republicans were split down the middle; the Democratic vote was unanimous, other than the abstaining Senator John Kennedy, whose brother Robert had worked for McCarthy.

McCarthy was senator for another two years, but he became a pariah. Eisenhower joked to his cabinet that McCarthyism was now "McCarthy-was-ism."

McCarthy died in 1957 at age forty-eight, from hepatitis combined with alcoholism.

———

It's impossible to know what would have happened had Murrow not entered the fray. On one hand, Paley was already furious at Murrow for criticizing General Douglas MacArthur in the *Korea* special, and Murrow's position was weakening. Murrow knew that McCarthy would take on the Army soon; it was the perfect time to strike.

On the other hand, Murrow could have easily done nothing. Taking on McCarthy put his career on the line.

The beauty was that his audience sensed this. The decades of rapport Murrow had developed with them were his real contribution to the battle. His voice tipped the scales, helping to end the witch-hunt that had ruined so many lives. It was a fight he could have ducked, but he chose to take it on.

It was a great final act, because his time was nearly done.

CBS had built its business on sponsorship. During the war, that had worked to the benefit of news. Once the war ended, the money went elsewhere. Sponsor Alcoa soon withdrew from *See It Now*, and the show lost its weekly spot. Paley scaled it back from a weekly show to a series of occasional specials. When the quiz show scandal broke, someone reported that *Person to Person* guests had received questions in advance. This exacerbated a long-brewing feud between Stanton and Murrow. Murrow made a statement to the *New York Times* ridiculing Stanton for comparing the two formats.

Paley continued granting equal time to those offended by Murrow. Murrow said he would need advance warning of these responses, or would not keep doing the show.

In a 1958 speech, Murrow spoke bluntly to a convention of news directors: "Television in the main insulates us from the realities of the world in which we live. If this state of affairs continues, we may alter an advertising slogan to read: Look now, pay later."[3]

Paley read the speech and hit the roof. He was finished with Murrow. Unlike most stars, Murrow was smart enough know he was done. He told a colleague: "You're only important around here as long as you're useful to them, and you will be for a time. And when they're finished they'll throw you out without another thought."[4]

Murrow took a sabbatical from CBS in 1959. When Friendly later asked if Murrow could coproduce with him, the request was denied.

In 1961, newly elected president John F. Kennedy asked Murrow to head the U.S. Information Agency. He'd considered Stanton, who was a better administrator, but wanted the halo of Murrow. Murrow accepted gratefully, telling the president it was "a timely gift." He resigned from CBS in 1961, and worked with the White House until 1964, when sickness forced him to resign.

———

When Murrow became ill, Bill Paley began to visit him, seeing him frequently for the rest of his life. According to some, he offered Murrow his job back. Murrow, too ill now, declined.

After a prolonged battle with lung cancer, he died in 1965.

Paley made a rare appearance on CBS network in tribute. He said that Murrow was "a resolute and uncompromising man of truth. His death ends the first golden age of broadcast journalism." For the rest of his life, Paley fought rumors that he'd cast Murrow to sea.

Murrow had invented much of the best of broadcast journalism. He had humanized a war and come home to bring down a tyrant.

But ultimately he was Moses: he could bring TV news toward the Promised Land, but he couldn't go there himself.

That role would go to a brighter star.

PART 4

TELEVISION AND THE 1960S

CHAPTER 25

KENNEDY AND TELEVISION

We wouldn't have a prayer without that gadget [television].
—JOHN F. KENNEDY, 1960

John Kennedy occupies a unique place in American history: its youngest elected president and most recently slain. In the half-century since his death, the mystique he so masterfully fostered has grown into a global affection without political parallel.

Though his presidential record is mixed, on another dimension, Kennedy is unequaled. No other politician managed media so well, so redefined the game for the media age. JFK was the first television president, and its most skillful to this day.

He had a great head start.

The Sons of Joseph P. Kennedy
Joe Kennedy was an early believer in the power of movies, a partner with Sarnoff in RKO, and an early financier of Hollywood. He was also an infamous market manipulator, a consummate Wall Street insider who sold before the crash.

He then used his influence to become FDR's head of the Securities and Exchange Commission, the very group whose job it is to keep Wall Street honest.

Joe Kennedy used the position as a PR machine, marketing his performance in newsreels and in the papers. As his fame and money grew, he had one overriding goal: to become the first Catholic president of the United States.

That goal seemed close at hand in 1938 when, under pressure, FDR made Kennedy the American ambassador to the Court of St. James. Kennedy swept through Europe with three photogenic Kennedy teens at his side. The English fell in love with Joe Jr., John (known as Jack), Kathleen, and even warmed to the old man himself.

But Joe's marketing was not enough. Hitler was on the march, throwing America's ambassador to Britain into the diplomatic spotlight. Kennedy could have furthered the bond between the two nations, as Murrow was doing. Instead, he did the opposite.

Ambassador Kennedy, reigning American diplomat in London, decided early on that England was doomed. He supported Neville Chamberlain's policies of appeasement, and opposed Winston Churchill's desire to fight Hitler head on.

Without FDR's approval, Kennedy sought a personal meeting with Hitler. Most of all, he loudly opposed FDR's plan to give the U.K. financial assistance. Both of these actions were the opposite of what an ambassador ought to do.

It came to a head in 1940. Kennedy continually questioned whether England could survive. On November 10, he told the *Boston Globe,* "Democracy is finished in England. It may be here [as well]."[1] They were words he'd regret for the rest of his life. Later that month, he was forced to resign.

Joe Kennedy's career in government ended there. After shaking off depression, he returned with a new ambition: his *son* Joseph P. Kennedy Jr. would be the first Catholic president.

In 1944, Joe Jr.'s plane exploded over the English Channel. And the burden of the father fell with force on the second son.

———

Jack Kennedy had been sickly since he was thirteen years old: back problems, colitis, and Addison's disease, a chronic failure of the adrenal gland. His jaundiced complexion, typical of Addison's, was blamed on contracting malaria during World War II.

As a boy, Jack Kennedy was often near death; he would have the last rites administered four times. For the rest of his life, he was in constant pain, plagued by a bad back and addictions to a variety of steroids, stimulants, and painkillers.

Unlike most people, Jack Kennedy knew in his bones that his time on Earth was limited. This awareness would fuel the best and worst aspects of his life.

Jack ended his Harvard years with a thesis that became the bestselling book *Why England Slept*. He became a war hero when his Navy patrol torpedo boat, PT-109, was rammed by the Japanese. For helping his men to safety, Kennedy won medals from both the Navy and the Marine Corps.

Then he returned home to carry out his father's plan, winning election to the House of Representatives in 1947, and the Senate in 1953. In 1952, he married the beautiful Jacqueline Bouvier; they were interviewed by Ed Murrow on *Person to Person* the next year. In 1956, Kennedy published *Profiles in Courage*, which won a Pulitzer Prize though the actual authorship was a subject of debate.

Like FDR, JFK worked fiercely to keep the truth of his health under wraps. Writer Gore Vidal later recalled a call from JFK:

> That friend of yours . . . is writing a piece for Esquire about "Kennedy's last chance" or something. Well, it's not true. Get to him. Tell him I don't have Addison's disease. If I did, how could I keep up the schedule I do?

Vidal complied, called the author, and told him Kennedy did not have the disease, noting later, "Thus one embraces, so painlessly, falsity."[2] The ongoing charade worked, as audiences warmed to the young senator with the beautiful smile.

At the Democratic National Convention of 1956, John Kennedy made a televised speech supporting Adlai Stevenson. It was a spectacular performance; on its back, the young senator came in number two in the vote for vice president. One thing was clear to everyone once he spoke on TV: Jack Kennedy was a star.

This was the turning point for JFK: in one night, the nomination speech rocketed the junior senator from complete unknown to star of the party, putting him on the short list for the next presidential run. The same tactic would yield the same result, forty-eight years later, for Barack Obama.

Joe Kennedy's disgrace had forced him out of the spotlight, but behind the scenes, he was managing it all. According to Speaker of the House Tip O'Neill, "Every time a Democrat ran for governor, he would go to see Joe, who would always send him home with a briefcase full of cash."[3] To grease the machine, Joe made massive contributions to Joseph McCarthy, to keep McCarthy's Catholic vote from turning on his son.

In 1957, *Fortune* magazine published its first list of the richest people in America. Joe Kennedy was in the top fifteen, with the equivalent in today's dollars of over $1.5 billion.

He used it to make history.

The Campaign That Invented Television Politics

> *We're going to sell Jack like soap flakes.*
> —JOSEPH P. KENNEDY

The 1960 presidential campaign was like nothing before. Richard Nixon was the two-time vice president of a beloved president, running against an undistinguished, Catholic junior senator. Nixon had the edge, but made a terrible mistake: he underestimated television. Jack Kennedy did the opposite.

Before Kennedy, newspapers were by far the main source of news. But by 1960, there were roughly 90 million U.S. televisions, one for every two Americans. Television was a sleeping giant. Jack Kennedy roused it.

The Kennedy campaign hired ad agency Guild, Bascom and Bonfigli to run television commercials, based on their work for Volkswagen cars. The ad team created TV commercials to address JFK's weak points: Catholicism, youth, and inexperience. While Nixon promised to speak in every state, JFK focused on television appearances and swing states—a crucial decision.

Then everything shifted, in what would be widely regarded as the day that American politics changed, the day that owning a TV became mandatory.

Nixon and Kennedy agreed to meet in four televised debates in September and October. They were the first debates of their kind, with the highest debate ratings to this day.

——

Nixon didn't think he needed to prepare for the debates, and rebuffed advice on his appearance. He wore a baggy suit and a loose-fitting shirt, and used something called Lazy Shave to cover his five-o'-clock shadow. He arrived at CBS slightly before airtime—leaving no time to dig out of the hole he'd made.

ABC president Leonard Goldenson contrasted the campaigns in his memoir:

> The Presidential election of 1960 was the first to use television in a significant way. . . . Nixon and Kennedy agreed to a series of four televised debates.
>
> . . . I sent word to each candidate that we would make our facilities available for three hours before each debate. Their respective adversary would not be present, and each would have free rein to look at anything in the studio and to do whatever he wished.
>
> Kennedy came with his brother, Robert, and with their own producer and director. They used virtually all three hours, carefully checking each rostrum and the lighting. Robert got up in the control booth and directed Jack, suggesting gestures, body language, and small movements around the rostrum.
>
> Nixon showed up twenty minutes before the debate. I said to myself then, "Here's a man trying for the most important office in the world, and he's giving it short shrift."[4]

Everything lined up for JFK that night. Constantly ill, he was in a rare moment of good health, partially brought on by the steroid cortisone. He had intentionally campaigned in an open car to get a good tan, and may have used a product called "Man Tan" as well. When CBS asked if the candidates wanted makeup, both Nixon and Kennedy said no; then Kennedy went to his dressing room and put on his own.

"On such decisions—Max Factor Creme Puff instead of Shavestick—rode the future leadership of the United States and the free world,"[5] David Halberstam would say.

Those who heard the debate on the radio thought Nixon had won. But those who saw it on TV thought Kennedy had won. And that's all that mattered: TV was now watched by 88 percent of Americans, and over 90 percent of all TVs had tuned in. Nielsen estimated the total audience at 74 million.

The next day, Kennedy crowds were larger than they'd ever been before.

———

After the debates, the impact of television became a national topic. Those who had argued it was a frivolous product were forced to take a second look.

Nixon's later debate performances were better, but never enough to recover from the first. The outcome was so devastating that despite public demand, there would not be another TV debate for sixteen years.

Kennedy's campaign spent millions on TV commercials. As the commercials ran, Kennedy blitzed the most popular shows on TV including Jack Paar's *Tonight Show* and *Person to Person*, as Nixon wearily crisscrossed the country pressing the flesh. Paley, a Nixon man, saw the writing on the wall: he urged Nixon to accept a fifth debate. Nixon refused.

In November, Joe Kennedy's second son won the presidency by a 0.2 percent margin, one of history's smallest. When asked what had made the most difference, Jack's answer was quick: "It was the TV more than anything else that turned the tide."[6]

There was breathless speculation at the time around how TV might undermine the presidency itself. The press watched carefully when, five days into his presidency, John F. Kennedy conducted his first press conference. His body language told the full tale: unlike anyone before, he ignored the 400 reporters in the room. He looked over all of their heads, and into the TV camera at the end of the room.

"Television," one reporter wrote, "has proven about as hazardous for Kennedy as water for a fish."[7]

Although Kennedy's record as president was uneven, his handling of television was not. In the White House, he perfected it; studying FDR's use of fireside chats, he decided to use TV sparingly rather than frequently, saving the medium for maximum effect.

The Presidency—"Camelot"

The presidency did not begin well. The attempted invasion of Cuba was designed to overthrow Fidel Castro, but became an unmitigated disaster. "How could we have been so stupid?" Kennedy later asked his aides.[8] But none of it had been televised, and so it was easier to manage. When Kennedy addressed the invasion on TV as a matter of national security, he appeared in control, and used direct access to the public to mitigate the damage. With no footage to damn him, the worst mistake of his presidency actually led to an uptick in his popularity.

The Space Program was a televised extension of the Kennedy brand, featuring brave, young, handsome astronauts, brand ambassadors of the boss himself. They were televised proof of his inaugural declaration: the torch had been passed to a new generation.

Mainly, Kennedy used television to define the tone of his presidency, rather than as a method of answering questions. Others had feared TV's power to reveal; Kennedy used it to conceal, to advance arguments, and to build rapport.

His genius was to see before any of his competitors that television was not a means of *reaching* the electorate. Television *was* the electorate.

His most important TV address came on October 22, 1962, when he informed the country that Soviet nuclear missiles had been placed in Cuba, ninety-three miles from the American coast.

> It shall be the policy of this nation to regard any nuclear missile launched from Cuba against any nation in the Western Hemisphere as an attack by the Soviet Union on the United States, requiring a full retaliatory response upon the Soviet Union.

It was the first time that television had been used for international diplomacy. His statement received wide support from Western Europe and from Pope John XXIII, and greatly improved the perception of Kennedy as a strong leader. In the televised address he appeared measured and strong. Americans were terrified, but they trusted him, and that was the objective; Kennedy's flagging poll numbers received another increase.

On December 16, reporters from CBS, NBC, and ABC met with Kennedy in what became known as the Rocking Chair speech. Kennedy knew the networks could air only thirty minutes of the long discussion, so he wisely gave crisp, telegenic responses to the questions he liked, and boring, rambling answers to the questions he did not like.

In 1963, powered by its greatest star, TV news surpassed print as the place most Americans got their news. That September 2 would be a triumphant day in television news, as CBS expanded its news program from fifteen to thirty minutes.

The other networks quickly followed suit, in what became a revolution. The newsroom became a place of drama, opening up the era of remote reports, and the hiring of news crews in different cities. And it had been made possible, to a large degree, by the first guest on the new CBS broadcast.

Cronkite opened his first thirty-minute show with the following words:

> Good evening from our CBS newsroom in New York, on this, the first broadcast of network television's first daily half-hour news program.

> At his summer White House in Hyannis Port on Massachusetts' Cape Cod, President Kennedy today talked with this reporter of many things.

Those comments would include thoughts on the new war, sparking fierce debates about what Kennedy might have done had things gone differently.

> In the final analysis, it's their war. They're the ones who have to win it or lose it. We can help them... But they have to win it—the people of Vietnam—against the Communists.

But Kennedy also said,

> I don't agree with those who say we should withdraw. That would be a great mistake. . . . This is a very important struggle even though it is far away.

Cronkite asked Kennedy if he was happy with the interview. The president replied as the expert he was, a TV star till the end:

> Yeah, that was fine. Maybe just a little long on the answer, so I don't mind if they decide to edit any of this stuff.

———

Eighty-one days later, Cronkite's thirty-minute show began,

> John Fitzgerald Kennedy was assassinated today in the forty-sixth year of his life and his third year as president of the United States.

TV had always been JFK's ally in life. It would prove to be an even greater friend in death. From November 22 through November 25, the networks pooled their coverage for four continuous commercial-free days, bringing kind words from even TV's sharpest critics.

Over 100 million Americans watched JFK's funeral, more human beings than had seen any one event in the history of the world.

Joe Kennedy had vowed to pay any price for the White House. Like Philo, he couldn't know how high that price could be.

CHAPTER 26

THE BEATLES

The impact of the Beatles – not only on rock & roll but on all of Western culture – is simply incalculable ... [A]s personalities, they defined and incarnated '60s style: smart, idealistic, playful, irreverent, eclectic.
— THE ROLLING STONE ENCYCLOPEDIA OF ROCK & ROLL

With Kennedy's assassination in 1963, America entered what Strauss and Howe call a "Second Turning." The First Turning had been the "high" that ushered in the broadcast age; a post–World War II era when institutions were strong and individualism was weak.

A Second Turning is an "Awakening": a time when the young accuse the old of moral bankruptcy; when institutions are distrusted and individualism trumps institutional loyalty. The idea of a Second Turning is what people mean when they say "the Sixties."

And the Sixties began in 1963, with the death of JFK.

Kennedy's death affected America profoundly. It particularly devastated the young, the massive "Baby Boom" generation born in 1946–64. They had identified with the young president, believed in his New Frontier; after his death, they had nothing to believe in.

That problem was solved four months later.

———

The postwar American boom in exports had sent American goods all over the world. These included the records of independent record labels, including Chess, Sun, and Stax.

One of the places these records came to shore was the old port city of Liverpool, England.

Postwar England was a difficult place. Germany had reduced many areas to rubble; the economy would take years to recover. Kids in England took to records during those bleak years as families in America had taken to radio during the Depression: as a source of magic in an unforgiving world.

Inspired by the energy of Little Richard, Muddy Waters, Elvis, and others, many of these kids formed bands of their own. One such band from Liverpool struggled for acclaim locally, then shipped off to become the house band at a series of filthy red-light clubs in Germany—ironically, the country that had bombed their hometown.

It was perhaps the finest training a band could have gotten, forcing them to play for twelve hours at a clip mixing rock and roll, blues, standards, comedy, German songs, impressions, and insults—anything to amuse the motley audience of sailors, thugs, and prostitutes.

Playing marathon sets to the rowdiest of crowds, the band had to be innovative just to survive. Over the months of long nights, something clicked. When the youngest of them, George Harrison, got deported, they returned to England a different band.

England had seen nothing like the new Beatles. They sounded like no one else, looked like no one else, behaved like no one else.

Because they wrote their own songs, they attracted major label interest, and were lucky to be signed by EMI and producer George Martin. With Martin's help, they soon dominated the charts, toured Europe, and made plans to visit the United States.

By the time they arrived, Ed Sullivan had perfected the show that Gleason had beaten back in its early years. *The Ed Sullivan Show* was now a Sunday night institution, the show every family in America watched.

The Beatles first appeared on *Sullivan* on February 9, 1964, and were watched by 74 million viewers in 23.2 million homes—a full *38 percent* of the U.S. population.

Not even JFK had generated ratings like this, or adulation like this. Nothing had. The streets around the theater were shut down, as screaming girls fainted and mobbed the police. Whenever the Beatles appeared on TV, crime rates in America plummeted.

Given the brilliance of the records and their revolutionary appearances on television, the Beatles became a cultural force, the lightning rod for seismic changes in culture, fashion, politics, and art. John Lennon's comments about Christ sparked a frenzy in America, and Paul's casual comments about drug use did the same around the world.

Some TV and radio commentators denounced the Beatles as heretics, while others lauded them as the geniuses of their time. They would speak out against Vietnam, appear on the first global satellite TV broadcast, and create an early instance of independent production, for the BBC with *The Magical Mystery Tour* in 1967.

Requests for a televised Beatles reunion would be the most requested popular programming idea for ten years.

In the '70s, John Lennon's cultural gravitas would grow so vast that Nixon would personally work to deport him. The '60s era would end with Nixon's resignation, but the nail in the coffin was John Lennon's murder in 1980.

The aftermath of the '60s raised a generation who would grow up to reinvent television in the cable age.

CHAPTER 27

CIVIL RIGHTS

In 1954, the Supreme Court ruled against segregation in public schools, prompting Rosa Parks to refuse to surrender her bus seat in Birmingham, Alabama. The struggle for civil rights became a defining story of the 1960s.

Kennedy distinguished himself with several speeches on civil rights. When Alabama governor George Wallace attempted to prevent two black students from registering for school, Kennedy mobilized the National Guard and took to television to address the problem:

> One hundred years of delay have passed since President Lincoln freed the slaves, yet their heirs, their grandsons are not fully free. We preach freedom around the world and we mean it. And we cherish our freedom here at home. But are we to say to the world—and much more importantly to each other— that this is the land of the free, except for Negroes? Now the time has come for this nation to fulfill its promise.

Martin Luther King, Jr., called the speech "a masterpiece." Kennedy's approval with white southerners plummeted, as his numbers with black Americans soared. His actions helped mobilize TV news crews, to cover the struggle as a national story.

Bobby Kennedy, now attorney general, would force Wallace to integrate the University of Alabama, one of the last all-white public colleges in the United States.

On August 28, 1963, Martin Luther King, Jr., brought civil rights to the national forefront, delivering his "I Have a Dream" speech to a crowd of 300,000 in Washington, and to a national audience on CBS.

Mississippi governor Ross Barnett would blame TV for spreading civil disobedience—and in a way, he was right. Before then, people read about police dogs ripping at the flesh of protesters, but now people were *seeing* it, firsthand. Television news brought injustice into the living room. White America began to understand. It felt as if progress might be on the way.

———

In a flash, everything shifted. Kennedy was gone, and Lyndon Johnson inherited the presidency.

Johnson resolved to build his own legacy, while simultaneously displaying public love for JFK. He did it by passing legislation that Kennedy could not. In his first 100 days, Johnson pushed through a staggering body of legislation: the Civil Rights Act of 1964, the Economic Opportunity Act, the Voting Rights Act of 1965, and the Civil Rights Act of 1968—all planks of the program Johnson called "the Great Society."

It was one of the greatest legislative triumphs in American history. Johnson used his prodigious political skill to build a bridge from the final works of FDR to the unrealized promises of JFK. Kennedy had talked about it, but Johnson was the one who got the bills through.

Had it ended there, Johnson would have been remembered as one of the greatest presidents of the century. It did not. Along with the presidency, LBJ inherited from Kennedy a skirmish in a small country named Vietnam.

As television news grew ever stronger, the Vietnam conflict escalated into a full-blown war.

Television had captured the best of JFK's presidency. Now it would bring the worst of LBJ's into America's living room.

CHAPTER 28

LBJ AND VIETNAM

What television did in the 1960s was to show the
American people to the American people.
—DAVID BRINKLEY

Before Kennedy, TV had had a minor role in presidential politics. When the cameras blew around Ike's comb-over when he spoke in a rainstorm, making him look old, the General gave in to his staff and hired a TV consultant. But politically, television was an afterthought.

After Kennedy, television *defined* the presidency.

TV had made JFK. It would break LBJ.

LBJ

Lyndon Johnson was born in abject poverty, in a Texas farmhouse that had neither power nor running water. At one point he dragged a plow with his back, substituting for the horse his family could not afford. "Poverty was so common, we didn't know it had a name," Johnson would say.

While Joe Kennedy had orchestrated his son's ascent from House to Senate to White House, Johnson had clawed his way there over two long decades, culminating in his legendary reign as Senate majority leader. Referred to by biographer Robert Caro as "Master of the Senate," he was likely the most effective congressional leader of the century: a brutal, brilliant giant who bullied, charmed, and manipulated to get legislation done. The presumptive next president, LBJ foolishly delayed entering the race, opening himself to a convention defeat by "the boy," as he called Kennedy then.

The Kennedys hated Johnson, and the feeling was mutual. Kennedy's legislative achievements were minor. He was viewed by much of Congress as a dilettante rich kid. But when Johnson had hesitated to join the presidential race, Kennedy jumped into the breach; his charm, and Joe's money, gave the young star the nomination.

But JFK needed Johnson to be competitive in the South, so his campaign offered Johnson the VP slot. It was a marriage of necessity, and an uneasy peace. Johnson took it, and gave up his seat in the Senate.

Once Johnson was vice president, all of his power evaporated, as the Kennedys iced him out of their Ivy League inner circle. He was mortified.

Then on November 22, 1963, it all became his.

———

Johnson's domestic triumphs did what Kennedy had not: advancing civil rights, the social safety net, and voting rights, in a stunning series of wins.

But Johnson refused to be the first American president to lose a war. So he expanded U.S. presence in Vietnam. Unfortunately for him, the expanded network news departments now sent reporters to Vietnam.

Network news was now America's most powerful platform, an express lane to the living room that no politician could override. One reporter in particular would vex LBJ, a young correspondent named Dan Rather. CBS wanted someone with a Texas accent to cover the Texan president. Rather soon became a thorn in Johnson's side, prompting him to ask a staffer, "Why is that boy so hard on me?"

In 1964, the United States announced that North Vietnam had attacked two U.S. Navy vessels. Congress approved the Gulf of Tonkin Resolution, allowing military action in the region. In 1965, there were 200,000 U.S. troops in Vietnam. Complaints about the war began to mount.

In 1965, CBS's Morley Safer aired footage of Marines setting fire to a Vietnamese village. The footage led to public outrage. This opened the door for other reporters to expose the brutal side of the war, making the

White House version look deeply corrupt. As LBJ raged, the body counts became part of the news, in a graphic way unthinkable fifty years later.

By 1967, there were 500,000 U.S. soldiers in the region. Polls showed most Americans thought the war was a mistake. Many in Johnson's cabinet began to suggest that the war was unwinnable. But Johnson was simply afraid to back down.

He explained his dilemma to biographer Doris Kearns Goodwin later:

> If I left the woman I really loved—the Great Society—in order to get involved in that bitch of a war on the other side of the world, then I would lose everything at home. . . . But if I left that war and let the Communists take over South Vietnam, then I would be seen as a coward.[1]

So Johnson pressed on, with increasingly erratic decisions, becoming combative and surly with the press. When one reporter annoyed him, Johnson erupted: "Why do you come and ask me, the leader of the Western World, a chicken-shit question like that?"[2]

As antipathy for Johnson morphed into violence, the antiwar movement found one TV show to take him on. In September 1967, folk singer Pete Seeger appeared on *The Smothers Brothers Comedy Hour*. He sang "Waist Deep in the Big Muddy," a protest allegory for LBJ and Vietnam.

The song told the story of an arrogant captain who takes his ship into dangerous waters against the advice of his crew: "Every time I read the paper, those old feelings come on / We are waist deep in the Big Muddy and the big fool says to push on."

CBS cut the song from the show. The Smothers Brothers mounted a protest campaign, but their show was soon canceled.

Johnson's greatest fear was not Vietnam. More than anything, he feared the ascension of Robert F. Kennedy.

Bobby Kennedy

Bobby Kennedy was Joe Kennedy's third son. He was not a member of the World War II Generation that produced (a record-breaking) seven presidents. He was part of the Silent Generation of 1925–1940, the only generation so far to produce none.

Bobby adored his brother Jack. He was bad cop, protector, and enforcer of his brother's will. Joe Kennedy proudly noted that "you can trample all over [Jack], and the next day he's there for you with loving arms. But Bobby's my boy. When Bobby hates you, you *stay* hated."[3]

And Robert Kennedy hated Lyndon Johnson with biblical intensity, spawning one of the most bitter feuds in White House history. As attorney general, RFK cut Johnson out of the loop, ridiculing the big man as "Rufus T. Cornpone." Bobby was the gatekeeper, Jack's only real confidant, until the day Jack was gone.

Then it was over, and Bobby's life fell apart.

RFK withdrew from public life for a bit, then returned—as a senatorial candidate from New York. He won.

1968

At first, Kennedy had not wanted the 1968 presidential nomination. Johnson was the incumbent president of his party. And the wounds were still fresh.

But as antiwar nominee candidate Eugene McCarthy gained traction in the polls, the drumbeat increased for the return of the Kennedys, whom many still viewed as America's first family.

LBJ watched the return of RFK with mounting horror. It was a rebroadcast of a nightmare he could not escape. Jack Kennedy's campaign song, "High Hopes," had been sung by no less than Frank Sinatra. Johnson's song was now being sung by protesters: "Hey, hey, LBJ: how many kids did you kill today?"

Johnson believed that RFK would run for president against him in 1968, and win. He would be a hayseed footnote in history, between the great Kennedy brothers. His presidency would be an accident of history, remedied once Bobby took back the White House for the Kennedys.

But Johnson was put out of his misery by a different star.

Anchorman Walter Cronkite of CBS News was the most trusted man in America. He had been since the withdrawal of Murrow. In February 1968, he made a rare trip to report from the field, and met the commander of all U.S. troops in Vietnam. General Creighton Abrams did not mince words: "We cannot win this goddamned war, and we ought to find a dignified way out." After years of reporting the Vietnam news, Cronkite came off of the sidelines.

On February 27, 1968, Cronkite aired "Report from Vietnam: Who, What, When, Where, Why?" His closing told the story: "We have been too often disappointed by the optimism of the American leaders. . . . It seems now more certain than ever that the bloody experience of Vietnam is to end in a stalemate."

As Johnson watched in Texas, aides saw him reel. The Master of the Senate knew the truth immediately. There was no being president with Walter Cronkite against you. "If I've lost Cronkite, I've lost middle America," Johnson told an aide.

On March 31, 1968, Johnson appeared on television to talk about Vietnam, and added an unannounced postscript: "I shall not seek, and I will not accept, the nomination of my party for another term as your president."

The next day he appeared before the industry itself, at the National Association of Broadcasters:

> As I sat in my office last evening, waiting to speak, I thought of the many times each week when television brings the war into the American home. No one can say exactly what effect those vivid scenes have on American opinion.[4]

Johnson blamed his downfall on television.

Ten weeks later, Robert Kennedy was assassinated.

CHAPTER 29

Nixon and Ailes

Television and I grew up together.
— Roger Ailes

The assassinations of Martin Luther King, Jr., and Robert Kennedy shattered whatever unity remained in America. Riots spread through major cities, powered by the despair and rage at the failures of civil rights and in Vietnam.

The Democratic Party was in shambles. Fearing a rout by Robert Kennedy, Johnson had withdrawn from the election, only for Kennedy to be murdered. At the Democratic convention in Chicago, anti-war candidate Eugene McCarthy lost the nomination to Johnson VP Hubert Humphrey. Outside the convention, policemen beat protesters with billy clubs. The crowd chanted, "The whole world's watching," which it was, as the beatings were televised. On ABC's convention coverage, William Buckley and Gore Vidal tore at each other's throats, arguing whether the left or the right was responsible for the decline of America.

Conflicts loomed for Republicans as well. Richard Nixon had been out of office for eight years, following his agonizing loss to Kennedy in 1960, and a humiliating defeat in the 1962 California governor's race. In the interim, he relentlessly dissected his every misstep, determined to never lose an election again.

Nixon knew he'd made two principal mistakes. First, he had underestimated television. He'd watched Kennedy's 1956 convention speech, and thought it revealed him to be a callow, inexperienced rich kid. Nixon assumed that TV would help Nixon in the debates, and show Kennedy to be a lightweight.

But TV had *loved* Kennedy, and helped him steal the election. Now, Nixon saw he needed his own plan to conquer TV.

Second, Nixon had played it clean. He campaigned by the rules, and it had cost him everything. Underneath the facade, Kennedy had proven to be a master of dirty politics. Suspect voting results from Chicago (from dead voters in some cases) and Johnson's Texas tipped the scales, giving Kennedy a lead of fewer than 100,000 votes, from a total of 68 million cast. Kennedy won fewer states, but took the Electoral College, in the tightest election of the century.

Being honest had cost Nixon the presidency. Next time, he would learn from Kennedy, and do whatever it took to win.

Thus, with the election of 1960, did Watergate begin.

Early Life

Richard Milhous Nixon was born in California in 1913, to hardworking Quaker parents who farmed and then ran a general store. His childhood in the town of Whittier was punishing: one older brother died when Richard was twelve, and a second ten years later.

Dick Nixon was a serious student and an indefatigable worker, rising at 4 AM, driving the long road to Los Angeles to buy vegetables for the family store, then returning home and heading to school.

His father had been born unlucky, had never caught a break; he brooded and had violent moods. His mother, Hannah, was the opposite, withholding and distant.

Caught between fire and ice, Nixon yearned for their approval, excelling at school in a lonely childhood. Decades later, Henry Kissinger would ask, "Can you imagine what this man would have been like if somebody had loved him?"[1]

Nixon performed in the school play, wrote excellent papers, became high school class president, and was accepted to Harvard. Unfortunately, he could not afford to attend, beginning a lifelong bitterness toward the Ivy League, and "Harvard bastards" in particular.

Nixon attended Whittier College in 1930, and experienced another of the rejections that seemed to plague him, when campus club the Franklins declined to accept him. Nixon responded by creating a new group called the Orthogonians, a bigger club for the "have nots."

When Nixon ran for class president, his victory seemed assured—until the Franklins submitted a candidate at the eleventh hour. Nixon pounced, proposing that the campus allow dances, and submitted a plan to the administration. He won the election.

In 1934, Nixon won a scholarship to Duke Law School, after which he returned to Whittier, took a job at a small law firm, and met a beautiful USC girl named Pat Ryan. Pat had grown up in poverty, and like Nixon, worked nonstop to improve her future prospects. Nixon asked Pat out for two years before she said yes. They were married in 1940.

When war broke out, Nixon joined the Navy. He was already an anti-Roosevelt Republican. In 1945, with the end of the war at hand, he was asked if he wanted to run for Congress.

Nixon was selected to take on five-term Democrat Jerry Voorhis in the 1946 race.

Never a natural public speaker, he worked tirelessly to improve his style, and hired a campaign manager named Murray Chotiner, who began schooling Nixon in the art of negative campaigning.

Nixon implied that Voorhis was a socialist, while Nixon positioned himself as a man of the people. Nixon crushed Voorhis and headed to Washington, where he met another new congressman, also fresh from the Navy, on the Labor and Education Committee. The colleagues traveled to Pennsylvania, where they discussed labor policy in a mock debate. Nixon said his new friend, Jack Kennedy, and he were "like a pair of unmatched bookends."[2]

———

In 1948, the Red Scare was in full effect, and the viciousness of the House Un-American Activities Committee was making Republicans look bad. The leadership thought a younger voice might help their party's image, so Nixon was recruited. He soon began building a case against a Democrat named Alger Hiss, a suspected Communist.

Alger Hiss had gone to Harvard Law, clerked at the Supreme Court, and been involved in the creation of the United Nations. He was handsome, from a good family, and in almost all ways the opposite of Richard Nixon. When Nixon questioned him, Hiss pushed back: "I am familiar with the law. I attended Harvard Law School. I believe yours was Whittier?"[3] The class mockery was not a wise move by Hiss.

Over a period of months, Nixon bore down on Hiss, found evidence against him, and had him indicted for perjury. When Hiss was convicted, Nixon became both a hero and a villain. The right saw him as a natural foe of communism; the left saw him as a political opportunist, exploiting fear of communism for his own ends. Both were correct.

The left dropped the Nixons from the guest lists of Georgetown's inner circle, even as his stock rose, and he prepared for a Senate run. When he announced his intentions, one Democrat came to commend him: "Dick, I know you're in for a pretty rough campaign, and my father wanted to help out."[4] Then Jack Kennedy handed Nixon a check for $1,000, for which Nixon was grateful.

But the Kennedys underestimated Nixon. His opponent, actress Helen Gahagan Douglas, was an easy target for Nixon's anti-red techniques. Nixon beat her easily, and took his Senate seat in 1950.

Rumors began that the young anti-Communist senator was being considered as the running mate for war hero General Dwight Eisenhower. Nixon was formally selected at the 1956 Republican Convention. The boy from Whittier had gone from nowhere to the top in one remarkable decade. Trouble was coming, but a new device would help.

Checkers

Soon after Eisenhower chose him as his 1952 running mate, Nixon was accused of accepting bribes. A headline appeared in the New York Post: "Secret Rich Men's Trust Fund Keeps Nixon in Style Far Beyond His Salary." Republicans smelled a scandal, and urged Ike to dump Nixon.

The drumbeats of Nixon's enemies grew louder. Already on the campaign trail, the Eisenhower camp stopped communicating with Nixon. A lifelong insomniac, Nixon paced the floor and suspected the worst.

Then Eisenhower called Nixon with a piece of advice: Nixon should take his story to the people. He should go on television. Nixon pushed for his support, but that's the only option Ike gave him: go on TV, and then we'll decide.

The pressure was tremendous. Nixon worked on the speech for days, rewriting it over and over. The Republican campaign bought Nixon a prime-time slot from NBC immediately following *Texaco Star Theatre* starring Milton Berle. The slot was a massive live window, with no safety net.

Nixon figured he was finished, but would not go down without a fight. He appeared on NBC on September 23, 1952, at 9:30 PM Eastern time. He sat behind a cheap cardboard desk on a flimsy talk show set, with Pat beside him. Nixon confronted the accusation that he had taken bribes, as 60 million Americans watched.

Nixon disclosed the couple's rent, a loan from his parents, and how much they paid for life insurance. "That's what we have, and that's what we owe. It isn't very much." Pat did not have a mink coat, he said, but a "respectable Republican cloth coat." Without saying it explicitly, he positioned himself as a victim.

He wasn't done. In a final flourish, he disclosed one gift that he *had* received: for his two young daughters, a cocker spaniel named Checkers. The girls, he said, loved the dog, and Nixon was drawing the line: "I want to say right now that regardless of what they say, we're going to keep it."

Nixon encouraged voters to contact the Republican National Committee, and then was cut off. He had run out of time.

After the speech, Nixon thought he was doomed. And indeed, most journalists who'd watched were disgusted. Nixon was vile, they thought, an obvious fraud.

But in the studio a few cameramen were weeping. They knew a working man when they saw one. In Eisenhower's suite, his advisors were skeptical. But his wife, Mamie, was not. She was crying, too.

NBC was flooded with calls supporting Nixon. So was the Republican National Committee, by telegrams saying the same thing.

Nixon received over 4 million letters and telegrams. Checkers was flooded with collars, dog food, and toys. When Eisenhower appeared for a stump speech that night, the crowd chanted Nixon's name. Television, everyone said, had saved Nixon's career.

He had used television to go over the heads of the chattering class, the ones who never liked him anyway.

If it hadn't been for that speech, he often said, he never would have been around to run for president.

In January, at age thirty-nine, Richard Nixon became the thirty-seventh vice president of the United States.

The Kitchen Debate

The most important challenge of Nixon's vice presidency would be an international one, around the Cold War. It took place on television.

Soviet leader Nikita Khrushchev was on a roll. He had pushed to modernize Russia, dismantle Stalinism, and advance the space program. In 1956, he famously told a group of Western ambassadors that "we will bury you."

Khrushchev was the face of the Cold War and boogey man of 1950s America. Eisenhower needed to meet with him, but decided to send his subordinate first.

So Nixon traveled to Moscow in 1959, where he and Khrushchev went to an RCA-built studio for a broadcast on Russian TV. Nixon proudly demonstrated RCA's color TV: "This is one of the most advanced developments in communication that we have in our country—it is color television. . . . It is one of the best means of communication that has been developed."[5] Khrushchev was unimpressed.

Next, they moved to a set designed to show Russian viewers what an American kitchen looked like, and began a broadcast for both Americans and Soviets. In it, Nixon stood toe to toe with Khrushchev, seeming to win his respect:

Khrushchev. I hope I have not insulted you.

Nixon. I have been insulted by experts. Everything we say [on the other hand] is in good humor. Always speak frankly.

––––

Khrushchev. You're a lawyer of Capitalism, I'm a lawyer for Communism. Let's kiss.

Nixon. All that I can say, from the way you talk and the way you dominate the conversation, you would have made a good lawyer yourself. What I mean is this: Here you can see the type of tape which will transmit this very conversation immediately, and this indicates the possibilities of increasing communication. And this increase in communication, will teach us some things, and you some things, too. Because, after all, you don't know everything.[6]

The Kitchen Debate was broadcast by all three American networks, and was a huge boost to Nixon's presidential aspirations. By standing up to Khrushchev, Richard Nixon had shown that he was ready to lead.

Kennedy

By the time Dick Nixon and Jack Kennedy ran against each other, they'd known each other for thirteen years. Nixon had gone to Kennedy's 1953 wedding, and to his hospital bed one year later, after Kennedy had nearly fatal surgery. Nixon wept, praying by the unconscious Kennedy: "Oh God, don't let him die!" Perhaps this led Nixon to underestimate Kennedy. It probably influenced Nixon's hunch about television: it would show Kennedy to be the sickly man he was.

———

As the 1960 campaign commenced, Kennedy focused on TV appearances, blanketing popular shows with his family and his smile. Meanwhile, Nixon foolishly announced he'd appear in all fifty states, with over 15,000 miles of travel quickly wearing him down.

Nixon was exhausted on September 25, the day of the first debate. He'd wasted his morning speaking to a hostile labor union, and arrived at the studio only twenty minutes before the debate. He was still suffering from banging his knee on a car door, and had lost ten pounds due to an illness. Kennedy was well rested and completely prepared.

The first debate was produced by Don Hewitt of CBS News, who would go on to create and oversee *60 Minutes*. Hewitt knew Nixon looked bad, and worried Nixon would blame him later. He was right; it was the beginning of a long-running enmity between Nixon and CBS News.

The speech was the most watched political event since the Checkers Speech, with 80 million viewers. Nixon's advisors had warned him to go easy, to moderate his voice, to avoid his frequently belligerent tone. The caution left him looking ill at ease.

When the debate ended, one audience member yelled up to Nixon: "That's all right. You'll do better next time." The microphones picked her up. They were supposed to; she worked for the Kennedy campaign.

Before the debate, many questioned Kennedy's fitness for the presidency. He was young, inexperienced, and simply not ready. After the debate, that issue was defanged. On the heels of a post-debate surge in the polls, Bobby Kennedy exploited another media gift.

Nixon had always polled higher in the black community than Kennedy. The poor man from Whittier had more sympathy for the disenfranchised, and had shown more interest in civil rights than the millionaire's son. Nixon had stood up against segregated hotels on behalf of black reporters covering his campaign. So when Martin Luther King was arrested that October, Nixon wanted to act, and asked the White House to intervene.

Ike refused.

So Bobby Kennedy went into action and got Dr. King released. A great photo opp ensued. The black vote began to move from Nixon to Kennedy, where it helped tip the scales and cemented Nixon's fate.

———

Nixon came to believe that the press had been in the bag for JFK all long. Kennedy dined and drank with leading reporters. He gave exclusives to the ones who were good to him. He played the game.

Nixon later summarized what he'd learned for the future: "I vowed that I would never again enter an election at a disadvantage by being vulnerable to them—or anyone—on the level of political tactics."[7] Nixon would be on the offensive for the rest of his career.

Tricky Dick

Nixon next ran in the 1962 gubernatorial race, in which he was beaten badly. After staying up all night and drinking too much, he made one of his greatest blunders before the TV cameras:

> Good morning, gentlemen. Now that all the members of the press are delighted that I have lost, I'd like to make a statement of my own. . . . Just think of how much you're going to be missing. You won't have Nixon to kick around anymore, because, gentlemen, this is my last press conference.

It would have been the end of almost anyone else.

Nixon returned to private life to dissect every mistake he had made, and to wait for another chance. By the end of 1967, evidence was growing that—provided he could win on TV—America might be ready for Nixon in '68.

Then on January 9, 1968, Richard Nixon met the future of TV news.

Roger Ailes

Nixon was appearing on the popular *Mike Douglas Show* when he was approached by the show's twenty-seven-year-old producer. The producer promptly diagnosed Nixon's problem in the '68 campaign: he needed a media advisor, for television.

"What's a media advisor?" asked the candidate.

"*I* am," said Roger Ailes.

"It's a shame a man has to use gimmicks like this to get elected," Nixon told Ailes.

Ailes's rebuke was quick: "Television is *not* a gimmick. And if you think it is, you'll lose again."[8]

Nixon knew that television would make or break his campaign, and Ailes seemed to know what he was doing. So Nixon hired him, and Ailes went to work, producing a series of TV segments called "Man in the Arena." They showed Nixon as a thoughtful, responsive, measured leader, complete with Hollywood lighting and makeup.

Nixon did as he was told, even appearing on *Laugh-In*. At one campaign appearance, he poked fun at himself: "Gentlemen, this is *not* my last press conference."

It worked. Richard Nixon was ready for prime time. And unlike the increasingly erratic LBJ, on TV Nixon was measured, calm, and statesmanlike. With Ailes's help, in November of 1968, he became the thirty-seventh president of the United States.

While working for Nixon's White House, Ailes wrote "A Plan for Putting the GOP on TV News." The 15-page memo argued that the White House and the Republican Party needed to create their own production arm for television. The new organization would take on "prejudices of network news," providing pro-Republican stories pre-rendered for television news.

Ailes's argument was prescient:

> Today, television news is watched more often than people read newspapers, than people listen to the radio, than people read or gather any other form of communication. The reason: People are lazy. With television you just sit—watch—listen. The thinking is done for you.[9]

The White House, Ailes said, needed to produce TV that would do the thinking for America.

It was one of the smartest documents since the memos of Sarnoff, but Nixon's interest in reaching out was at an end. Ailes was terminated by the White House in 1971.

Ailes returned to the White House for Nixon's ally, George H. W. Bush, who had been Nixon's chairman at the Republican National Committee and his ambassador to the United Nations. Ailes would advise Bush on wardrobe, staged briefings (to "heighten the drama for the news media") and choice of activities ("Do a little more fishing and less golfing"), until the world was ready for his bigger vision.

In 1996, Roger Ailes launched the Fox News channel.

CHAPTER 30

ALLEGORY

Television in the 1960s was the best of times and the worst of times. News continued to expand and improve, covering the huge issues of the time with dedication and authority. The same could not be said of scripted television, which was dominated by a crop of escapist, simplistic fare.

This was not a coincidence. The reigning execs now had a captive audience; in search of the largest possible audience, they decided to let the bar sink. NBC executive Paul Klein even gave it a name: "Least Objectionable Programming." Shows were chosen not for any inherent sign of quality, but because they were the ones least likely to make viewers get up to change the channel.

In an era of war, riots, and murder, scripted television entered its most dismal period, dominated by series like *Mister Ed, The Beverly Hillbillies,* and *I Dream of Jeannie.* Norman Lear, the man who would end this, once mused that in an era of massive upheaval, the biggest problem on television was that mom had dented the car.

There were exceptions: *The Dick Van Dyke Show* was a new kind of naturalistic comedy, where smart and funny scripts were enacted by a talented cast. *The Dick Van Dyke Show* mirrored the optimism of the Kennedy era, but began running out of steam as the decade grew darker. Dramas of the 1960s would have to find another way.

And they did. The most important dramas of the '60s were allegories. Because war, intolerance, and assassination were so jarring, the best TV of the time took these issues on in a new way. *The Fugitive* (ABC,

1963–67) followed the flight of an innocent man, sentenced to death for murdering his wife. A story of injustice, it chronicled his journey to find his wife's murderer while evading the police.

The Prisoner (ITV, 1967–68) was the story of a British secret agent (called "Number Six") who was drugged, kidnapped, and sent to a mysterious village. The village turned out to be a prison, in which people were held for the rest of their lives unless they supplied information to an evil agent named "Number Two." The surreal show's themes included fascism, mind control, and government corruption, as Number Two tried to crack the spirits of those who resisted him.

Two other '60s allegories rank with TV's most innovative dramas: *The Twilight Zone* and *Star Trek*.

CHAPTER 31

THE TWILIGHT ZONE

Nothing ever troubles me. And yet I am troubled.
—SAMUEL BECKETT, "THE UNNAMABLE"

*T*he *Twilight Zone* spoke to a fundamental need of Americans moving from the '50s to the '60s.

When World War II ended, soldiers came home, married their sweethearts, and bought homes to raise their families. On the surface, it was a time of tranquil prosperity. But underneath, there was trauma.

Thousands of soldiers were dead. Life had changed completely. People had moved away from their extended families, beginning the compartmentalized life that continues today: from house to car to office and back, with large chunks of downtime in front of the television. The dark side of the 1950s was a creeping sense of dislocation.

One show would address this more than any before or since. *The Twilight Zone* pushed TV's boundaries to reveal the anxiety of American life.

Rod Serling

Rod Serling was a successful but frustrated TV writer. He had earned his stripes on anthologies including *The US Steel Hour, Appointment with Adventure,* and *Hallmark Hall of Fame.* In 1955 he had a major hit on *Kraft Television Theatre,* the story "Patterns" earned Serling the first of his six Emmys. His next seminal work was *Playhouse 90*'s *Requiem for a Heavyweight*, the poignant story of a boxer in decline.

Serling became one of the most respected writers in television, but he hated the incessant interference from sponsors. It particularly annoyed him when the line "Got a match?" was deleted from *Requiem* by sponsor Ronson Lighters.

The censorship reached a new extreme with "Noon on Doomsday," for *The US Steel Hour*. It was a fictional version of the 1955 lynching of Emmett Till, a fourteen-year-old African American boy. Network censors ground the script down until it featured a white foreigner in New England. In a *Playhouse 90* production of *Judgment at Nuremburg*, the network cut a line about gas chambers because the sponsor worried about an association between Nazis and the sponsor's appliances. That was Serling's breaking point.

With anthologies on their last legs, Serling decided to create a show format that could evade network censorship. As a child, he'd loved pulp fiction's ability to obscure real messages in fictional worlds.

Serling decided to do the same for television.

He rewrote an earlier script, expanding it to create an hour-long format. He called it *The Twilight Zone*—"The Time Element," and sent it to CBS.

CBS bought the script based on Serling's reputation, but was reluctant to produce a fantasy show. They shelved it. The script collected dust until Bert Granet, a producer for the *Westinghouse Desilu Playhouse* anthology, discovered it while looking for a script to add gravitas to *Westinghouse.*

Granet bought the script from CBS for $10,000.

The script met resistance from McCann-Erickson, *Westinghouse*'s ad agency, who didn't like its ambiguous ending. So Granet recruited Desi Arnaz to go to bat for the episode, and *Westinghouse* backed off. When it aired on November 24, 1958, it received more positive feedback than any other *Westinghouse* episode. CBS took notice, and commissioned a pilot for *The Twilight Zone.*

Bill Paley watched it and loved it. He offered Serling a 50 percent stake in the show, with an agreement that Serling would write 80 percent of the scripts in the first season. On October 2, 1959, *The Twilight Zone* premiered on CBS.

The Twilight Zone Premieres

> *You unlock this door with the key of imagination. Beyond it is another*
> *dimension: a dimension of sound, a dimension of sight, a dimension*
> *of mind. You're moving into a land of both shadow and substance, of*
> *things and ideas. You've just crossed over into . . . the Twilight Zone.*
>
> —ROD SERLING

On his own show, Serling was able to outwit censors, hiding social and political issues behind supernatural forces. In "Judgment Night" and "Deaths-Head Revisited," Serling addressed the horror of the Holocaust and how the human race could allow it to happen again. "Third from the Sun" and "The Old Man in the Cave" exposed the anxieties of the Cold War and the consequences of nuclear war.

In "The Eye of the Beholder," Serling focused on the power of the state, and societal prejudices inherent in "acceptable" standards. The episode opens in a fictional society, where ugliness is threatening to the totalitarian regime. A woman is shown receiving her eleventh surgery. The goal is to make her look "normal." The actors' faces (both patient and doctor) are hidden from the audience. When the bandages are removed, the doctor and nurses are horrified. The procedure has failed. Then the camera pulls back to show that the patient is attractive, and that the doctor and nurses are hideous.

The Twilight Zone's most popular episode may be "Time Enough at Last." It featured Burgess Meredith as Henry Bemis, a man who wants to isolate himself from humanity, and simply read books. When the rest of humanity is wiped out in a nuclear attack, Meredith becomes the last man on Earth. Even better, he discovers a library where he can read alone for the rest of his life. As Bemis cracks open his first book, he breaks his glasses, rendering him virtually blind. Alone, with all the time in the world to read, Bemis ends up trapped in his own worst nightmare.

In "The Monsters Are Due on Maple Street," residents panic when they face an alien invasion. But instead of banding together to battle their extraterrestrial enemies, they become paranoid and regress into a violent mob. This leads the alien invaders to conclude they can easily end mankind, by letting it destroy itself.

Serling eventually wrote or cowrote 92 of 156 episodes, with a variety of premises unmatched by anyone before or since.

In 1964, CBS's James Aubrey canceled *The Twilight Zone*. Though Aubrey blamed low ratings, others said he just disliked the show.

Like many before him, Serling sold the rights to his show to CBS—assuming it would never recoup its production costs. He died in 1975.

Legacy

Today, *Twilight Zone* plots are widely viewed as having inspired more movies than any property in history, including films *The Truman Show*, *The Sixth Sense*, *Poltergeist*, *Midnight in Paris*, *Meet Joe Black*, *Liar Liar*, *The Village*, *Ruby Sparks*, *The Cobbler*, and *Child's Play*. In 2013, *TV Guide* ranked the show the fifth greatest drama of all time. Many still consider it the finest.

Serling, the master of televised surrealism, once noted that "it is difficult to produce [television] that is both incisive and probing, when every twelve minutes one is interrupted by twelve dancing rabbits singing about toilet paper."[1] More than anyone in his time, Rod Serling found a way.

CHAPTER 32

STAR TREK

After Lucy and Desi's divorce in 1960, Desilu had begun losing steam. Desi had been the primary driver of business development, while Lucy had generally focused on Desilu's cash cows: *I Love Lucy*, then *The Lucy Show*.

Once Desi was gone, Lucy increased her efforts to stay involved. She listened to pitches when she could, when her own show allowed. One of the pitches she liked went on to change the world.

———

In 1964, out-of-work TV writer Gene Roddenberry came to see Desilu's director of production, Herb Solow, with an idea.

Roddenberry had a colorful past: an introverted kid from El Paso, then a World War II Army pilot, then a pilot for Pan Am, then a Los Angeles motorcycle cop. From there, he used his cop uniform to get the attention of legendary agent Swifty Lazar.

When Roddenberry hunted him down—in full motorcycle uniform—Lazar assumed he was in trouble with the law. He opened the envelope Roddenberry left, expecting a summons.

But it was a television script. Impressed by the writing, Lazar signed Roddenberry, and got him his first jobs as a TV writer.

Roddenberry wrote for a variety of shows in the early '60s, most notably on hit Western *Have Gun—Will Travel*. From there, he pitched and ran his own show, a military drama called *The Lieutenant*. It was canceled after one year, leaving Roddenberry frustrated and unemployed.

Like Rod Serling, Roddenberry wanted to run his own show. Like Serling, he chafed at the constraints of sponsors and networks, and looked for a way to tell stories of consequence.

A project he'd worked on, inspired by 1961 movie *Master of the World*, gave him a concept for an ensemble show, with a difference.

Though science fiction had been a no man's land on TV, Roddenberry thought he knew why—and geared his new script to overcome these problems. He pitched his new concept as "Wagon Train to the Stars." Like *Wagon Train*, the show would be a series of self-contained episodes, each of which was part of an ongoing "mission."

But set in the future, on a space ship.

To avoid the expense of science fiction sets, Roddenberry added cost savings to his pitch: the main location would be the spaceship itself. Planets would be limited to Earth-like environments, so that sets could be simple, with no '60s-era spacesuits required. Since that meant aliens would be humanoid, it also would make alien costumes cheaper: they could be done with make-up, wigs, and simple prosthetics.

Unlike other science fiction on TV (and unlike *The Twilight Zone*), this show would not be an anthology; it would have an ongoing cast, simplifying casting, costumes, and other tasks from week to week.

Most of all, this show would expand the palette of topics that TV could address. As in *The Twilight Zone*, Roddenberry's fantasy world would let him cover serious topics from a safe distance.

In 1964, Roddenberry pitched the show to the staff at Desilu, who desperately needed to prove that it was still in the game. Sometime later, Lucy asked Solow how the "South Seas series" was doing. Solow had no idea what Lucy was talking about, and asked her what she meant. Lucy repeated it: she liked the pitch about the USO entertainers who traveled by ship during World War II . . . the one called *Star Trek*.

Thus did Lucille Ball green light the most lucrative TV franchise of all time.

Star Trek and NBC

TV is a game of buyers and sellers, in which studios like Desilu are sellers, and networks like NBC are buyers. Desilu's job was to pitch shows that networks would put on the air. NBC's job was to buy shows that people would watch.

Then as now, the odds for a new show being bought were long. First, Roddenberry would need to write a final script to Desilu's approval. Then, Desilu would have to convince CBS, NBC, or ABC to buy it. So Roddenberry's original script went through extensive revisions.

Then Desilu approached CBS, with whom Lucy had been in business for her entire career. CBS already had a space show in development called *Lost in Space*, so they passed—but not until they had heard the pitch, and sucked up as many of Roddenberry's ideas as they could. Roddenberry would rail against *Lost in Space* for years.

Solow had more luck at NBC, where he had worked prior to Desilu and knew several ranking executives. In May 1964, he met with NBC's vice president of the West Coast programming department, Grant Tinker. Tinker liked the idea and commissioned a pilot, eventually called "The Cage." It was commissioned as a ninety-minute feature, giving NBC the option to run it as a movie if it later chose not to go forward with the series.

"The Cage" featured Captain Chris Pike, an emotional Mr. Spock, and other elements not familiar to later fans. NBC rejected "The Cage" for being too intellectual and having a subpar cast. Tinker advised that they cast the *Enterprise* crew more as a family. But NBC still liked the idea, and agreed to pay for a second pilot.

This time, Desilu hit pay dirt: Roddenberry had added James Kirk, Scotty, and Sulu. The iconic "star date" opening voiceover was added as well, and *Star Trek* went on NBC's schedule for fall of 1966.

Season One

The first episode of *Star Trek* was aired on September 8, 1966. It was striking in both style and production complexity. Because the show was so expensive to produce, Roddenberry's focus on "Earth-like" sets was a godsend. The "Earth-like" stipulation allowed the crew to shoot on other

Desilu sets: in episodes "Miri" and "The City on the Edge of Forever," you can see Floyd's Barber Shop and the Mayberry Courthouse from *The Andy Griffith Show*.

Visual effects were particularly problematic. Desilu had hired an effects company to produce the show's critical array of effects shots. At the eleventh hour, approaching the premiere date, Roddenberry and Desilu discovered the effects house had completed almost none of the needed sequences. When they confronted the owner of the company, he burst into tears and said they were doomed.

Star Trek had no choice but to bring its effects work in-house. In an era before computer effects, they pioneered a range of modeling and camera effects techniques, in which one small mistake could ruin an entire day's work. The end results were stellar for the time, but burnout and exhaustion plagued the team.

Most notably, the crew had to assemble the now famous opening sequence from spare bits of footage. If you watch the show, you can see it: instead of an elaborate flight through space, the *Enterprise* simply makes several short passes by the camera. It's a remarkable testament to *Star Trek*'s team that this opening was re-created in movies nearly fifty years later.

Another huge asset of *Star Trek* was Art Director Matt Jefferies, who brought *Star Trek* a level of design thinking rarely seen on TV. Jefferies designed the bridge, most ship interiors, and the *Enterprise* itself, one of the iconic designs of the television age.

Unfortunately, the hard work wasn't helping the bottom line. *Star Trek*'s ratings were mediocre; it ranked number thirty-three of ninety-four shows in week two, and then fell to fifty-one. The reviews were mixed as well. *Variety* called *Star Trek* "an incredible and dreary mess of confusion and complexities."

Given its ratings, any other show probably would have been canceled. But *Star Trek* was saved by an unlikely development: in the early 1960s, NBC had begun looking at viewer demographics: meaning *who* was watching a particular show, instead of *how many viewers* were watching.

The objective was to gather high-value viewers: those who were young, well educated, affluent, and likely to buy products from advertisers. These viewers, it turned out, were exactly who was watching *Star Trek*.

So NBC ordered ten more episodes, and *Star Trek* made it through its first season.

Season Two

In spite of its many innovations, *Star Trek* was in many ways a digital show in a pre-digital world; the show was geared toward a tech-savvy audience during a time when consumer technology was in its infancy. There was no way for people to catch up on missed episodes, and nothing like the Internet to help spread the word. *Star Trek*'s second season premiered on September 15, 1967. Despite its quality, the ratings declined. And in 1967, Lucy sold Desilu to Gulf+Western, which eventually renamed it Paramount Television.

Morale became a problem. The cast and crew tried to ignore cancellation rumors, and to focus on their grueling schedule. William Shatner became so convinced the show would be canceled that he began looking for his next job. Once again, *Star Trek*'s savior was its demographic, this time in the form of direct response.

Star Trek's audience had always been vocal. During the first season, the network received over 29,000 fan letters praising the show. When the likelihood of cancellation increased, Roddenberry reached out to uber-fan Bjo Trimble for help.

Bjo Trimble is one of the forerunners of the modern ComiCon fan. She was instrumental in building the Los Angeles Science Fiction Society and the World Science Fiction Convention. Not surprisingly, she loved *Star Trek*. Starting with 4,000 names from a sci-fi convention mailing list, she and her husband, John, asked fans to write to NBC, and then ask ten others to do so.

She and Roddenberry also contacted newspaper columnists, some of whom implored readers to save the best science fiction show on TV.

Demonstrators picketed NBC's Burbank studio. Over 200 Caltech students marched with signs reading "Draft Spock" and "Vulcan Power." There were similar demonstrations at Berkeley and MIT.

Between December 1967 and March 1968, NBC admitted to receiving 116,000 letters demanding the return of *Star Trek* for a third season. Even New York governor Nelson Rockefeller joined the letter-writing campaign. One NBC executive went off the record to peg the actual number at over 1 million letters, a staggering total in the days before email. The Smithsonian Institution requested prints of the show, the first time it had ever done so.

NBC caved, and renewed *Star Trek* for a third season. There was even better news. In an era where time slots meant life or death, *Star Trek* would now appear on a perfect slot for a show aimed at teenagers, college students, and young professionals. Its third season would air on Mondays at 7:30 PM.

Season Three

Exultant, Gene Roddenberry traveled to Palm Springs. He brought a stack of scripts to work on, and resolved that this would be *Star Trek*'s best season to date. Two days later, he got another call from NBC.

NBC hit *Rowan & Martin's Laugh-In* was currently on Monday, and its producer, George Schlatter, had hit the roof at the idea of moving to accomodate *Star Trek*. If NBC moved *Laugh-In*, Schlatter said he would quit.

So instead, NBC was moving *Star Trek* to Fridays, at 10 PM.

For a show with a young demo, this was a death sentence. In the era before the Internet, DVR, and VOD, *Star Trek*'s young audience would be out for the night.

"If the network wants to kill us, it couldn't have made a better move," Roddenberry said.[1] He told NBC he would quit if they didn't back down. NBC did not budge. Neither did Roddenberry. So *Star Trek* entered its third season without its creator.

To twist the knife, NBC also reduced the show's budget. Actress Nichelle Nichols, who played the role of Lieutenant Uhura, viewed the cuts as a way kill the show: "While NBC paid lip service to expanding *Star Trek*'s audience, it slashed our production budget until it was actually 10% lower than it had been in our first season. . . . This is why the third season you saw fewer outdoor location shots, for example. *Star Trek*'s demise became a self-fulfilling prophecy."[2]

Despite another torrential letter-writing campaign, after two and a half seasons, *Star Trek* was canceled in 1969.

Star Trek and Allegory

Ultimately, Roddenberry was right: science fiction gave the show a chance to take on issues TV would not have tolerated otherwise: "[By creating] a new world with new rules, I could make statements about sex, religion, Vietnam, politics, and intercontinental missiles."[3]

For example, in "Let That Be Your Last Battlefield," the crew meets two aliens, one of whom is a police commissioner. He accuses the other of being a traitor and rabble-rouser from an inferior race. When Kirk responds that they look exactly the same, the commissioner is indignant: He is white on the left side of his face, and black on the right side. His prisoner is black on the left, and right on the white. Isn't his inferiority obvious? This seems absurd to the crew of the *Enterprise*, and to the audience.

In "Plato's Stepchildren," Nichols and William Shatner made history with the first interracial kiss on U.S. television. NBC worried the kiss would anger affiliates in the Deep South and ordered two versions of the scene: one with the kiss, and one without. The two actors deliberately flubbed every take of the kiss-less version, forcing the episode to air with the kiss intact. It aired and received a largely positive response.

And in "A Private Little War," the crew members of the *Enterprise* discover a planet on which their enemies, the Klingons, are arming one side of a war. Kirk grimly decides to arm the other side. The episode was an obvious reference to U.S. involvement in Vietnam.

Star Trek and Technology

Star Trek anticipated and paved the way for a range of new technology. For decades of cell phone pioneers, *Star Trek*'s communicator was the Holy Grail. This culminated in a device named after the show: Motorola's StarTAC, which debuted thirty years later. Versions of the universal translator (Google Translate) and the phaser (taser) now exist as well.

Star Trek advanced interest in the space program and in science generally, sparking a passion for technology in a generation of children who would grow up to build the first websites. Most importantly, *Star Trek* modeled a human-computer interaction in a way that transformed public perception of computers and contributed to the adoption of PCs.

Star Trek's Characters

Star Trek's characters were more nuanced than those of most dramas of its time. The interaction of its leads demonstrated one such dynamic: Spock was intellectual, McCoy was emotional, and Kirk was instinctive. Kirk led the *Enterprise* by drawing from both Spock and McCoy, weighing their arguments and keeping their perspectives in balance. In the process, the trio inspired decades of academic papers on leadership, and an explosion in the relatively new medium of fan fiction. This was due to the fact that *Star Trek* and Roddenberry did not discourage fan fiction, fan art, and character dress-ups. The fan culture of *Star Trek* launched its huge convention business, which itself was the forerunner of the era of Comic-Con.

The major phenom of *Star Trek* in its own time was Spock himself. The alien who had to be logical, the half-breed who struggled to keep his emotions under wrap, triggered an outpouring of affection that made actor Leonard Nimoy a national celebrity. Nimoy's response was ambivalent. His 1975 autobiography was defiantly titled *I Am Not Spock*. The public didn't buy it; he never got another major role, but he seems to have made his peace with that. His 1995 autobiography is titled *I Am Spock*.

Star Trek also showed a future in which racism was extinct, in which the people of Earth had moved past discrimination. The part of Lieutenant Uhura was the first place in American media in which an African American woman was the equal of white men.

At one point, actress Nichelle Nichols became discouraged, as her parts seem to grow smaller as each week's shooting script evolved. One day, she told Roddenberry she was leaving the show, and headed out for the weekend.

She attended an NAACP fundraiser that evening. There, she was summoned to the table of a fan—Dr. Martin Luther King, Jr., who told her how much he loved *Star Trek*. When Nichols told King she was planning to leave the show, his opposition was fierce:

> Don't do this, Nichelle, you can't do this. Don't you know that the world, for the first time, is beginning to see us as equals? Your character has gone into space on a five-year mission. She is intelligent, strong, capable and a wonderful

role model, not just for black people, but for all people. What you're doing is very, very important, and I'd hate to see you just walk away from such a noble task.[4]

Nichols stayed.

Afterlife

Star Trek's future was quietly cemented eighteen months before the series was canceled. An innovative station group owner named Dick Block saw the potential for the series in syndication. Block's Kaiser Broadcasting owned five local stations, and had previously passed on the syndication rights to *The Twilight Zone*. Block was not going to let another monster get away. He put *Star Trek* reruns at 6 PM, directly against the *Evening News*, knowing the target audience of kids and teens would be looking for something to watch then. He also announced he'd run each of the episodes, uncut, on the exact time and date of the initial NBC broadcast.

Block's foresight ignited a new *Star Trek* mania, which could now be seen every day at a convenient time by its intended target market. His repeated airings spawned generations of *Star Trek* fans.

Though *Star Trek*'s maiden voyage lasted only seventy-nine episodes, it went on to spawn—as of this writing—five additional television series (*The Animated Series, The Next Generation, Deep Space Nine, Voyager,* and *Enterprise*); thirteen feature films (*Star Trek: The Motion Picture, The Wrath of Khan, The Search for Spock, The Voyage Home, The Final Frontier, The Undiscovered Country, Generations, First Contact, Insurrection, Nemesis, Star Trek (2009), Star Trek into Darkness,* and *Star Trek Beyond*) and an array of books, games, and merchandise too wide to catalog.

When *Star Trek* was canceled, Paramount offered Gene Roddenberry the option to buy the rights to *Star Trek* for $150,000. He was unable to come up with the money.

By 1994, Paramount estimated *Star Trek* had brought them over $1.4 billion.

These rights are now valued at over $4 billion.

CHAPTER 33

AUBREY'S WASTELAND

The American public is something I fly over.
—JAMES AUBREY

In 1960, JFK's FCC commissioner, Newton Minow, became famous for calling television a "vast wasteland."

But the famous quote was an abridgement; what he actually had said was:

When television is good, nothing—not the theater, not the magazines or newspapers—nothing is better.

But when television is bad, nothing is worse. I invite each of you to sit down in front of your own television set . . . until the station signs off. I can assure you that what you will observe is a vast wasteland . . . a procession of game shows, formula comedies about totally unbelievable families, blood and thunder, mayhem, violence, sadism, murder, western bad men, western good men, private eyes, gangsters, more violence, and cartoons. And endlessly commercials.[1]

The walking definition of that wasteland was James Aubrey.

James Thomas Steven Aubrey was the privileged son of an advertising executive. He attended Phillips Exeter and Princeton. He was a Paley kind of man: not the kind Paley had been, but the kind he liked to hire. "My father insisted on accomplishment,"[2] said Aubrey. He delivered: a football star, he graduated with honors and joined the Air Force, where he became a major.

Aubrey had begun his career at CBS but had moved to ABC. In 1957, he became ABC's vice president of programming, where he shepherded *77 Sunset Strip, Maverick, The Rifleman,* and *The Donna Reed Show* to air. In the wake of the quiz show scandals, Frank Stanton got a call from an agent who said there was someone who wanted to come back to CBS. Aubrey was hired.

By 1959, the quiz show scandal had broken, and former president Lou Cowan was forced to resign. In Lou Cowan's wake, Aubrey became CBS's new network president.

Aubrey was handsome, charismatic, and well bred. He rose at 5 AM, worked twelve-hour days, and threw legendary parties in between.

Like Paul Klein's "Least Objectionable Programming" at NBC, Aubrey's prime-time tactic was to cast the widest net possible. Under Aubrey, the network of Murrow became the "Country Broadcasting System" of *The Beverly Hillbillies, The Andy Griffith Show, Mister Ed, Green Acres,* and *Petticoat Junction.*

Aubrey also ushered in an era of fantasy shows: *My Favorite Martian, The Munsters,* and *Gilligan's Island,* the latter of which would tweak FCC commissioner Minow by naming Gilligan's ship the "S.S. *Minnow.*"

Aubrey was both a populist and an elitist. He programmed what he thought people would want, but his contempt for the audience—and CBS talent—was palpable. The only opinion he valued was his own:

> I'd gone to CBS, and I'd become convinced Beverly Hillbillies was going to work. Bill Paley wasn't convinced. . . . He genuinely disliked Beverly Hillbillies. I put it on the schedule anyway.[3]

Aubrey's formula would be referred to as "broads, bosoms, and fun." *Life* magazine described it as, "Feed the public little more than rural comedies, fast-moving detective dramas and, later, sexy dolls. No old people."[4] When JFK was assassinated, Aubrey told a CBS newsman, "Just play the assassination footage over and over again—that's all they want to see."[5]

Writer David Halberstam called Aubrey "the hucksters' huckster, whose greatest legacy to television was a program called *The Beverly Hillbillies*, a series so demented and tasteless that it boggles the mind."[6]

The public overruled the critics; 57 million Americans watched the show regularly. Aubrey won. His priority was making advertisers happy:

> A breakfast food advertiser may, for example, wish to make sure the programs do not contain elements that make breakfast distasteful. A cigarette manufacturer would not wish to have cigarette smoking depicted in an unattractive manner.[7]

Though Aubrey's arrogance was legendary, so was his success. His line-ups were so successful that NBC and ABC waited for CBS's schedule before they announced their own.

Though suspicious of the high costs of sports, it was Aubrey who paid the NFL $28.2 million, for a two-year deal of seventeen games a year. It was a visionary gamble that flouted conventional thinking, and generated many more millions in ad revenue and brand equity for CBS.

By the 1963–64 season, Aubrey's CBS had fourteen of the fifteen top prime-time shows, and most of the top daytime shows as well. The *New York Times Magazine* declared that CBS was the best TV network for the tenth year in a row. One analyst said CBS was comparable in its dominance to General Motors or General Electric.

Aubrey was brutal. When he didn't like a pitch, he would walk out of the room, leaving writers wondering what to do next. Once a CBS producer advised a writer, "This has nothing to do with a good script or a bad script. It has to do with pleasing one man, Jim Aubrey. Don't ever forget it."[8]

As Aubrey's success grew, so did his bad behavior. When '50s host Garry Moore tried to return to TV, Aubrey refused him. "No man in TV history made bigger profits or more enemies,"[9] the *Los Angeles Times* would say.

Aubrey fired John Frankenheimer, the most respected director of 1950s TV. Frankenheimer would go on to a stellar career in movies and called Aubrey "a barbarian." Aubrey also fought with CBS mainstays Red

Skelton, Danny Thomas, and Arthur Godfrey. Lucille Ball detested him, and told Stanton she would not deal with him.

The coup de grâce came when Aubrey confronted the onetime king of CBS Radio, Jack Benny. Benny had been the turning point for CBS, the key talent who had come aboard when the chips were down.

Aubrey himself delivered the news to Benny: "You're through, old man."[10]

Not surprisingly, Aubrey also fought with Fred Friendly, who stayed on as head of CBS News when Murrow left. Aubrey complained that news was a huge capital drain, and moved to cut its budget. In this one case, Paley intervened.

In 1964, a tabloid alleged Aubrey was taking kickbacks from producers. The FCC investigated and discovered it was true. Aubrey's Central Park South apartment was owned by the head of Filmways, producer of the *Beverly Hillbillies, Petticoat Junction,* and *Mister Ed.* They were all shows that Aubrey had bought for CBS.

And though Aubrey had a chauffeured car from CBS, he had a second one paid for by another production company. Apparently the second car was to keep Aubrey's meetings secret from CBS. It looked bad because it was bad.

In 1964, Aubrey made a proposal to Stanton. Aubrey had investors who would buy CBS, he said; once they took control, they would fire Paley. Stanton would get Paley's job, and Aubrey would get Stanton's job.

Paley got word, and quickly called Stanton. Stanton fired Aubrey in 1965.

According to the *New York Times Magazine,* "Aubrey was torpedoed at last by a combination of his imperiousness, the ratings drop, and a vivid afterhours life culminating in a raucous Miami Beach party—details of which no one ever agrees on—the weekend he was fired."

Aubrey had been with Jackie Gleason, whose absurd circular house he had bought as part of Gleason's new deal. Gleason distrusted most executives, but hated Aubrey in particular, and was delighted to have had a part in bringing him down.

"I don't pretend to be a saint. If anyone wants to indict me for liking pretty girls, I'm guilty," Aubrey would say, consistent to the end.[11]

When he was gone, critic Murray Kempton wrote the eulogy: Aubrey "was the fourth president of CBS-TV as Caligula was the fourth of the twelve Caesars. Each carried the logic of his imperial authority as far as it could go. Each was deposed and disappeared suddenly leaving bad press behind him."[12]

The wasteland would continue for a few more years, but the post-Aubrey regime would change television forever.

The revolution would be driven by a writer named Norman Lear.

PART 5

TELEVISION AND THE 1970S

CHAPTER 34

NORMAN LEAR AND AMERICAN LIFE

As the 1960s came to a close, America neared a breaking point. The country had descended from the Summer of Love into an abyss of war, riot, and despair. Television news brought it all home every weeknight.

But if you didn't watch the news, you would never have known. Outside of news, TV was a parade of inane sitcoms, stranded millionaires, magic powers, and talking horses. While TV news was powerful, much of the rest of television was infantile, as the networks took advantage of the limited choice viewers had.

Klein's "Least Objectionable Programming" still reigned at all three networks. The goal was not to be good. The goal was to suck a little less than the other two.

One writer thought differently. Critics and fans would lionize him for turning television comedy into an art form. What they didn't know was that it started with a small boy and his dad.

H.K.

Norman Milton Lear was born to Herman (H.K.) and Jeanette Lear of New Haven, Connecticut, in 1922. The household was tense; Norman would later say his parents lived "at the ends of their nerves and the tops of their lungs."[1]

Jeannette was a narcissist. H.K. was an inveterate runner of get-rich-quick schemes, who claimed he could "sell shit on a stick for lollipops."[2]

H.K. was always a few days away from being a millionaire, Ralph Kramden without the soft heart. He loved his kids the way he loved his favorite show, *The Lone Ranger*—no less and no more, with equal intensity. When asked if this took a long time to get over, Norman thought about it, and said, "Yes—my whole life."[3]

When Norman was nine, H.K. was arrested for selling fraudulent bonds. He was sentenced to three years in prison.

After H.K.'s sentencing, the family returned to the house, to sell off his furniture for much-needed cash. For reasons Norman does not understand, his mother and sister Claire prepared to move away without him. Norman would stay with a revolving door of relatives for two long, sad years.

As his mother and a stranger haggled over the price of his father's beloved chair, the boy began to weep. A relative gripped his shoulder in reprimand: "Remember, Norman, you're the man of the house now. . . . A man of the house doesn't cry."[4]

The words struck the boy like a fist. He was barely nine years old. His father was off to prison. His mother and sister were abandoning him. And he was being told not to cry.

Lear says the moment revealed to him the absurdity of the human condition. Whatever he took from it, the moment would change both Norman and America.

While H.K. was in prison, Norman had a few potential father figures. Uncle Jack was his favorite, a press agent who would often flip Norman a quarter. A quarter was *a lot*. A man who could give away quarters was big. Norman decided he would be a press agent, too.

H.K. eventually came home and the family reunited. The constant arguments between his parents resumed, with H.K. telling his mother to "stifle" herself, while telling Norman he was "the laziest white kid he ever met."[5]

Norman was torn. He knew his dad loved the family, and though H.K. could be horrible, Norman saw his problem wasn't hate. It was *fear*. It was an understanding of human nature Norman would use to re-create television.

For now, Norman was off to college, then to war. He flew fifty-two combat missions for the Air Force in World War II, and then came home to work in public relations, like Uncle Jack. Norman's first job as a press agent lasted less than a year. Then he worked for his father in a new venture named Lear, Incorporated—until the old man went bankrupt. In May of 1949, Norman headed west with his new wife and young daughter, to restart his PR career in California.

Los Angeles

In Los Angeles, Norman and his family moved into a tiny one-room guesthouse. They spent much of their time with his cousin Elaine and her husband, Ed Simmons. The couple had moved to Los Angeles from Boston so that Simmons could become a comedy writer. In the meantime, Lear and Simmons sold baby pictures door-to-door.

One night the wives went to the movies while the men stayed home to watch the kids. Simmons asked Lear to help him out on a comedy sketch he was writing. The two cranked out a parody called "The Sheik of Araby." When the women returned, the always-enterprising Lear suggested he and Simmons go out and sell their new sketch.

The pair walked to a nightclub, and promptly sold the sketch to a performer. They made $40—more than Lear made in two full days of selling baby pictures. He was hooked. So Simmons and Lear sold baby pictures by day and sketches by night, until Lear hatched a scheme that ignited their careers.

———

Danny Thomas was an enormous star, a comedian with a legendary style. Lear and Simmons had an idea for him. So Lear called Thomas's agent, impersonating a reporter from the *New York Times*. He told the agent that he was boarding a plane, and needed to fact-check a story, *quickly*. If he couldn't check with Thomas before the flight, the story wouldn't run.

The agent believed Lear, and gave him Thomas's personal number. When Lear called to pitch a sketch, Thomas asked how he'd found him.

Lear told him about the ploy, and Thomas laughed. In fact, he had a gig tomorrow. How soon could Lear get him something to look at?

Lear said it would take him a few hours. Then he and Simmons quickly wrote a sketch and raced it over to Thomas. Thomas paid them $500 and performed the routine for years.

Norman began writing in the earliest days of television, for Jack Haley's variety show. When superstar Jerry Lewis saw one of their skits, he told his producers to find its writers. Soon Simmons and Lear were writers for Dean Martin and Jerry Lewis, on *The Colgate Comedy Hour*. Their first sketch for *Colgate* foreshadowed Lear's ability to make news.

By 1950, TV was becoming a threat to the movies, eating into box office revenue as viewers stayed home to watch TV. In response, a theater trade group created a PR campaign, titled "Movies Are Better than Ever."

On *Colgate*, Lear and Simmons poked fun at the campaign, with a sketch in which Jerry Lewis played a young boy passing a movie theater. Dean Martin played the manager of the movie theater; he tried to hustle Lewis into buying a ticket. Martin smacked Lewis on the head every time Lewis's character said "television." Though Lewis wanted to go home and watch TV, he agreed to go into the theater—which turned out to be empty.

The next day, the studios and theaters were furious. Martin and Lewis took out full-page ads, apologizing in the trades. And Lear learned a valuable lesson about the power of television.

After three years with Lewis, Lear went on to write for several other shows. In 1958, he founded Tandem Productions with his new partner, director Bud Yorkin. The two created films throughout the '60s, including *Come Blow Your Horn* (starring Frank Sinatra), *Divorce American Style*, *The Night They Raided Minsky's*, and *Cold Turkey*.

Everyone in show business preferred film to television. But well before most, Lear saw an implication of TV's rise. It came from a friend's divorce:

> What prompted me to think about doing a situation comedy was when Simmons and I were living in New York, and [a friend] came to visit me, and he had five kids and was getting divorced. I was in the process of being divorced with one kid. I asked him how it was going for him, because I was having a real rough

fuckin' time, and he said, "Oh, easy. All she wanted was my Joan Davis reruns, my rights to [the TV show] I Married Joan." And the deal was, he gave her the Joan Davis Show, and he was free. And I said, "Son of a gun. We don't own anything in live television. I gotta do that." So that was on my mind a few weeks later—when I heard about Till Death Us Do Part. And I thought of my father.[6]

Like Lucy and Desi, Norman saw a future in reinventing TV comedy. Variety shows were ephemeral; they aired once or twice and were dead forever. Good sitcoms, on the other hand, made money in reruns and syndication. They provided regular payouts and could be an annuity that kept on giving.

So Lear decided his next show would be a scripted comedy, and he began to look for an idea. The right one showed up quickly.

All in the Family (1971–1979)

> You being colored, well, I know you had no choice in
> that. But whatever made you turn Jew?
> —ARCHIE BUNKER TO SAMMY DAVIS, JR.

In 1968, at age forty-six, Norman Lear was reading *TV Guide* and saw a piece about a British show called *Till Death Us Do Part*. It featured a bigoted father and his liberal son who fought constantly. Lear immediately thought about his relationship with his dad.

He secured the rights for a remake, beating out CBS—which wanted to retool the show for Jackie Gleason, who didn't like the idea of playing a bigot. When Lear pitched the role to actor Mickey Rooney, Rooney's response was typical: "If you make that show they're gonna shoot you in the streets."[7]

Lear's great insight was that the most topical shows had failed by being preachy and pedantic. Neither the left nor the right in America were bad; they were each trying to make sense of the ambiguity and absurdity of the times.

All in the Family would not work unless its lead was sympathetic. At a casting call, Lear loved Carroll O'Connor's face immediately—he had a blustering but vulnerable quality that made him sympathetic. When O'Connor began to read as Archie, Lear wanted to jump for joy.

With Carroll O'Connor as Archie and Jean Stapleton as Archie's wife, Edith, Lear and Yorkin sold the show as a pilot to ABC.

When ABC tested the show, the results were mediocre. So Lear went to watch the focus group tests himself. He saw the problem quickly: the audience was howling with laughter, but they were too embarrassed to admit that they liked to watch a bigot.

ABC suggested to Lear that Archie's daughter and son-in-law needed to be recast. So Lear shot a second pilot in 1970, with different actors as Mike and Gloria. ABC still did not air it, and Lear knew why: they were scared. CBS had canceled *The Smothers Brothers Comedy Hour* two months earlier over Pete Seeger's jab at LBJ. And *All in the Family* made *The Smothers Brothers* look quaint.

ABC surrendered its option and turned *All in the Family* loose. After two years of work, it seemed to be dead.

Then Yorkin called Lear with incredible news: he had shown the pilot to CBS, who loved it.

New CBS president Robert Wood had a controversial strategy: he planned to move away from "The Country Broadcasting System" shows of James Aubrey toward a younger, more valuable demographic. That meant edgier programming, like the pilot Lear had produced for ABC.

Wood asked Lear to reshoot the pilot. Lear refused; the show had consumed two years of his life, and he didn't want to waste more time. Wood countered: it wouldn't just be a pilot. It would be thirteen episodes, on the air—*guaranteed.*

Lear relented, and changed the show's title to *All in the Family.* Sally Struthers and Rob Reiner joined the cast as Gloria and Mike. Rob Reiner had auditioned for the pilot on ABC a few years ago. Then, he was too young. Now, he was perfect.

Casting director Marion Dougherty had captured lightning in a bottle. The interminable pilot shooting turned out to be an asset, leading to a cast that would weather nine seasons at the forefront of the American conversation. In Lear's view, they had gotten lucky:

When that kind of magic happens, some other entity has to take credit—for everybody being alive at the same time, available at the same time . . . magically, chemically connected when they finally get together.[8]

But *All in the Family* wasn't out of the woods yet. Before the pilot aired, Wood asked Lear to remove one mildly suggestive line from the show. Lear refused. Partially, this was due to *Cold Turkey*; the success of that film brought Lear a three-picture offer. Everyone Lear knew told him to take the movie deal and run. Lear thought of his dad, and couldn't walk away.

But he would not change the line. If he changed one line this week, it would be two the following. He wouldn't do the show as a watered-down compromise. Wood was shocked, but eventually relented.

CBS tried another way the night of the premiere. What if they showed the second episode *first*, and aired the pilot untouched in a week? It was the perfect compromise; Lear would keep his line, but it wouldn't open the series.

Lear refused. That wasn't how he'd written the show. CBS needed to commit all the way, or there was no point going forward.

Then he hung up, and wondered if he had just made a terrible mistake.

The first show aired intact that night, on January 12, 1971.

Ratings were mediocre; reviews were tepid or negative. Some viewers were shocked by America's first on-air toilet flush, but most just didn't know the show existed.

Some of that was due to its time slot. Though he'd given in to Wood, Paley hated *All in the Family*. So he buried it in a graveyard time slot between *Hee Haw* and *The CBS News*. Paley figured he'd give Wood the promised thirteen weeks on the air, and that by then the disagreeable show would be dead in the ratings.

All in the Family was saved by three forces: timing, the Television Academy, and Johnny Carson.

———

If *All in the Family* had started in the fall as most shows did, Bill Paley's assessment might well have been correct. But because it had premiered on

January 12, it went into reruns when viewers had already seen everything NBC and ABC had in the time slot. So when repeats began, viewers tried *All in the Family*, and it began to climb in the ratings.

Then, as he often did, Carson changed everything.

In 1971, Johnny Carson was a TV star so big that there was simply no one to compare him to. From his desk at NBC's *The Tonight Show*, he made and broke careers. Carson had the best curatorial ear in TV, and he loved *All in the Family*. And Carson was hosting the Emmys that year.

He called with an idea: he wanted to open the Emmys with *All in the Family*. Edith would be excited to be on the show; Archie would be angry. They'd open the show with a skit, then go into the Awards. Which was timely: it turned out the Academy had been watching, too.

That night, *All in the Family* won Emmys for Outstanding New Series, Outstanding Comedy Series, and Best Actress in a Comedy. It would eventually become the first show in which all lead performers won Emmys.

After the Emmys, *All in the Family* went through the roof, becoming the most-talked-about show of the year. Following the Awards, Wood and Silverman moved *All in the Family* to Saturday nights, where it became the backbone of the most powerful lineup in television history. *All in the Family* dominated television as America's number one show for five consecutive seasons, from October 1971 to April 1976.

The show went on to tackle an unprecedented number of social issues, including racism, sexism, homophobia, menopause, and rape. Archie railed against minorities, but found he liked the *people*; that cognitive dissonance made him easier to love. When a swastika mistakenly was sprayed on Archie's door, Archie met and liked the Jew who'd been targeted by a hate group. At the end of the episode, Archie's new friend was blown up in his car.

Although it dealt with many issues, Lear's show was rooted in the reality of the changes that had left many people feeling shaken and confused. The world seemed to Archie, as it did to many people, to have gone absolutely *mad*. As the show's theme song, "Those Were the Days," suggested, Archie just wanted things to go back to the way they had been. Like H.K., Archie wasn't bad; he was terrified.

And his son-in-law, Mike, was as stubborn and scared as he was. Over time they grew to love each other and the audience grew to love them both. But first, the audience had to see Archie as sympathetic, and that job was all on actor Carroll O'Connor.

The burden made Carroll O'Connor difficult to work with from the beginning. He started rewriting the pilot script as soon as he was cast. Lear put his foot down early: O'Connor would play the script that Lear delivered. But the tension continued. As the show grew, O'Connor knew that his actions as Archie would be judged by over 30 million Americans, for better or worse.

O'Connor would rail against the scripts, demand rewrites, and skip rehearsals—until Lear confronted him with his contract. Then each week, O'Connor would cross some inner threshold, and from the other side, Archie Bunker would emerge.

Though he would not live to see it, Carroll O'Connor opened the door for a new era of television, one that portrayed *authentic* people on television for the first time. In an era before which every hero was "good," O'Connor and Lear paved the way for real people, and real subjects. They so did by winning the audience over, by confronting them and bringing them further along as they went. For five of its eight seasons, *All in the Family* was watched by an average of about 30 million Americans a week.

Sanford and Son (1972–1977)

For their next show, Lear and Yorkin retooled a second British program. *Steptoe and Son* was another bittersweet tale about a father and son at odds who worked together in the family's salvage business.

But Lear and Yorkin took this one in a different direction. They had seen volatile comic Redd Foxx in Las Vegas, and loved him. Foxx was a beloved icon of African American culture. He was also prolific, with over fifty albums to his name (such as *You Gotta Wash Your* Ass). The idea of Foxx on TV was hard to believe, until you saw him in the role of Fred Sanford, where he was an absolute riot. The cast of *All in the Family* attended a rehearsal, and agreed.

Exhilarated, Lear called CBS, to offer them Tandem's second show. But Wood's number two, Fred Silverman, never showed up. Lear scheduled a second performance—still no Silverman. So Lear and Yorkin showed it to NBC, who bought it on the spot.

Sanford and Son reached an emotional high when Fred Sanford—who often spoke to his dead wife, Elizabeth—finally found love again. Plaintively, he looked up at the sky, and told Elizabeth that no one could ever take her place... he was just looking for someone to fill the space.

Powered by Foxx, the show became an instant top ten show in 1972, eventually reaching number two, behind *All in the Family*.

Maude (1972–1978)

> *Archie, you can either get up and eat breakfast,*
> *or lie there, feeding off your own fat.*
> *And if you choose the latter, you could*
> *probably lie there for months.*
> —MAUDE FINDLAY, TO ARCHIE BUNKER

As *All in the Family* took off like a rocket, a potential plot twist occurred to Lear. Since Archie *never* backed down from an argument, why not create a character who could fight him to a draw? That would be comedy gold.

Lear remembered the family fights he had witnessed in his childhood, when his cousins would have epic arguments and refuse to let go of grudges. Lear decided to introduce a cousin of Edith's—who had never wanted sweet Edith to marry "that Nixon slob" Archie.

Lear thought of Bea Arthur, with whom he'd worked years ago, and Maude Findlay was born. Bold, big, gravel-voiced, and stridently liberal, Bea Arthur would be Lear's alter ego for the next six years.

Maude first appeared on the second season of *All in the Family*, and moved through Archie and Edith's house like a hurricane. She was smarter than Archie, and had hated him from first sight. Her appearance was a heavyweight bout in which Archie didn't stand a chance. Fred Silverman called Lear the night the episode aired, and suggested they give Maude her own show.

Maude premiered in September 1972, and quickly entered the top ten. In an era still dominated by demure women, Maude took guff from no one. When a phone caller asked if she was Mr. Findlay, she responded, "This is Mrs. Findlay. Mr. Findlay has a much higher voice."

A three-time divorcee and a bleeding-heart liberal, Maude became the most polarizing of Lear's characters, adored by the left and reviled by the right. The show took on issues that *All in the Family* could not touch, including women's liberation, alcoholism, plastic surgery, divorce, and abortion.

Roe v. Wade was passed in 1973. Abortion was a topic that divided America. Five months later, in a landmark episode, Maude discovered that she was pregnant. Nearing fifty, Maude agonized over what to do. A friend of the same age begged her to have the child. But after much soul searching, at the end of the second episode, Maude decided to have an abortion.

CBS begged Lear to change the episodes. But his success with *All in the Family* and *Sanford and Son* gave him unprecedented power, and CBS backed down.

For the first time in history, many local stations would not air a show from their network; when the show repeated, thirty-nine markets refused. Many of those that did air it were picketed. The story sparked a national discussion about the rightful role of TV in society, and whether the media had finally gone too far. CBS received 17 million letters. Protesters even went as far as lying down in front of Bill Paley's car as he tried to go home.

Good Times (1974–1979)

You may be looking at a brand new face,
but you'll still be hearing the same old mouth.
—FLORIDA EVANS, AFTER MAUDE'S FACELIFT

As *All in the Family*, *Sanford and Son*, and *Maude* dominated the ratings, they spawned two more hit shows, the first to center on African American families.

Maude's maid Florida, played by Esther Rolle, was a scene-stealer. Lear thought that she warranted a show of her own. So a new show began, focusing on Florida and her family, called *Good Times*.

The Evans family scraped by in Chicago's Cabrini Green projects, struggling with the economic hard times of the mid-'70s. James (John Amos) worked two jobs at a time, taking whatever work he could get. Oldest son J.J. (Jimmy Walker) was a talented artist; siblings Thelma and Michael were ages sixteen and eleven when the show began.

Both Rolle and Amos were eventually eclipsed by Walker, with his '70s catchphrase "Dy-no-mite!" Soon, audiences burst into applause whenever Walker entered a scene.

Rolle thought Walker was a terrible role model for black kids, and voiced her opinion: "He's 18 and he doesn't work. He can't read or write. . . . They have made J.J. more stupid and enlarged the role."[9] Amos was unhappy as well, and blamed the writers for dumbing down the show.

Amos grew so unhappy that he was eventually written out, sparking a massive outcry when beloved James died. Rolle left after the fourth season. In the sixth season, a new breakout character emerged, played by a young Janet Jackson.

The Jeffersons (1975–1985)

As *Good Times* grew more popular, a frequent criticism emerged. It came to a head when the Black Panthers came to Lear's office to confront him. The show, they said, was a white man's patronizing view of a black family. Lear and colleague Al Burton resolved to fix this, and *The Jeffersons* was born.

George Jefferson had been Archie Bunker's next-door neighbor and nemesis. He was louder, cockier, and more successful than Archie. George ran a dry-cleaning operation, then was rear-ended, won a court case, and made enough money to buy his own store.

When *The Jeffersons* began in 1975, George owned five stores. He and his wife moved into an opulent apartment building populated by wealthy neighbors, on the Upper East Side of Manhattan.

The Jeffersons was less confrontational than Lear's other series, with a few exceptions. When George and Louise moved in, they found that their neighbors included an interracial couple. George was appalled and called their children "zebras."

In its first season, *The Jeffersons* was the number four series of the year, and fluctuated from number three to number twenty-four over the course of the decade. It ran for eleven seasons, becoming Lear's longest-running show, and one of the longest-running sitcoms in history.

By the end of the 1974–75 season, Lear's success was beyond precedent. *All in the Family* was number one. *Sanford and Son* was number two. *The Jeffersons* was number four. *Good Times* was number seven. *Maude* was number nine.

One Day at a Time (1975–1984)

By 1975, divorce had gone from taboo to a central fact of American life. Lear's next show, *One Day at a Time*, was the story of a divorced mother, Ann Romano, raising two daughters, Julie and Barbara. It arrived as a pitch from Whitney Blake and Allan Manings, based on Blake's own life as a single mother.

But by the time *One Day at a Time* aired, the cultural pendulum had begun to swing. The exploration of social issues was now facing resistance. It came to a head before the show went on the air, over a minor line that CBS demanded be cut.

Lear considered his options. His company had *paid* for the pilot. CBS had not. So it was still his property. He locked the tapes securely in his garage, and headed on a vacation to Maui.

It took Fred Silverman days to track down Lear. CBS wanted the pilot—*immediately.*

Lear told Silverman that CBS hadn't paid for the pilot. If the network wanted it, it would have to pay up, and agree to leave the line intact. CBS eventually agreed.

One Day at a Time eventually became a pillar of the early '80s CBS Sunday lineup, along with *The Jeffersons* and *Archie Bunker's Place.*

Hot L Baltimore (1975)

The edgiest of Lear's dynasty, *Hot L Baltimore* focused on prostitutes and eccentric characters in a rundown Baltimore hotel. It found a surprising champion: ABC's Michael Eisner, who loved the show and went to every taping. He had bad news, however: the sales department hated it. It was the kiss of death, he said; the show would never stay on the air.

Eisner went on to run the Walt Disney Company as the most famous entertainment executive of his time. *Hot L Baltimore* was canceled in its first season.

Mary Hartman, Mary Hartman (1976–1977)

Before *All in the Family*, Lear had been obsessed with the idea of a late-night soap opera, a dark comedy that satirized the growing strangeness of American life.

When the networks passed on the pilot, Lear invited local station managers from across the country to dinner *at his home*—to hear about the show directly from the creator.

The day after the dinner, offers rolled in. For a time, stations that carried the show referred to themselves as part of "the Mary Hartman Network." The show became another national sensation, garnering the covers of *Newsweek*, *TV Guide*, *People*, and *Rolling Stone*. It created a completely new TV business model, carving out a first-run syndication market that had never existed before. *Mary Hartman* foreshadowed the weakening of the broadcast networks: twenty years before the Internet, it bypassed the big three networks completely.

But more immediately, it telegraphed Tandem's frustration with the broadcast business.

Television and America

In 1974, as religious groups' protests increased, CBS decided to respond by sanctioning producers and shows. They proposed a concept called "Family Viewing Hour," which would push "offensive" content out of a new "safe zone" between 8 and 9 PM.

Congress and the FCC soon got into the act, extending the zone to 7 PM.

The ramifications were grim. *All in the Family* was forced out of its Saturday 8 PM slot, where it had reigned as TV's number one show for five seasons. *Maude* was moved from 8 PM to 9 PM. Its ratings were damaged and never recovered.

Lear mounted a First Amendment lawsuit against "Family Hour." In his deposition, he told the networks, "In search of ratings, excess violence is coaxed out of writers and production companies by the very networks that bring on from another direction a Family Viewing Hour to lessen it." In November 1976, the judge found against the networks, and "Family Hour" was overturned.

Out on Top

When the ninth and final season of *All in the Family* approached, Carroll O'Connor made a surprising pitch. He wanted to stay on the air as Archie, even if he had to do it alone. Lear was ambivalent; he thought it was time to say goodbye.

Then Lear heard, for the first time, from William Paley.

Paley told Lear that Archie Bunker belonged to the American public; they should have the right to extend this irreplaceable national treasure. That may have been true, but they both knew it was all about the money.

Archie Bunker's Place went on the air, without Norman Lear.

When he decided to step away from his day-to-day role, Lear reached out to friends who might step into his shoes, including Carl Reiner, and Larry Gelbart, who had just stopped running *M*A*S*H*.

They looked at the workload Lear carried—*six simultaneous shows*—and respectfully declined.

In 1985, Lear sold his company to Coca-Cola. His end of the deal was $200 million, after tax.

Television and Innovation

Norman Lear is broadcast television's most influential producer. He finished one season with three of the top four shows, and another with five of the top nine—prompting Carson to open the Emmys by saying, "Welcome to the Norman Lear show." When he flew over the country, Lear could imagine that for every home with a light on, he had made someone in that home laugh.

Lear's dedication to depicting the human condition brought television the most authentic collection of characters that it had seen to date.

When asked his opinion on the importance of television, Lear remarked that television is America in microcosm. In the early days, he says, networks made thirty-nine episodes and used the thirteen weeks of summer for experimentation. With the advent of tape, that was cut to twenty-six episodes and twenty-six repeats. Then that was cut to thirteen, and eventually lower still, with shows routinely being canceled after only two episodes had aired. This is counter to innovation, counter to quality, and part of the reason broadcast TV began its decline:

Television [is] just another group of American conglomerates . . . [in which] the need for a profit statement this quarter larger than the last is the predominating, controlling force.

You can see clearly in television all of American business, by looking at the tube in your own home, and seeing how this has evolved.[10]

Lear arrived in time to sense the artistic opportunities for comedy on broadcast television. He transformed it, revolutionized it, and turned it into an art form. He knew when to sell, and when to walk away.

As of this writing, he was creating a remake of *One Day at a Time*—for Netflix.

CHAPTER 35

MARY, GRANT, AND MTM

You can't be brave if you've only had wonderful things happen to you.

—MARY TYLER MOORE

The Dick Van Dyke Show

In the 1950s, Lucy and Gleason had set the bar for comedy. In the 1960s, that bar was raised by the Dick Van Dyke show. Van Dyke and Carl Reiner created a more naturalistic comedy, in which gags and pratfalls were secondary to the humor of everyday life. To keep it real, they based the show on what Reiner knew best. He played a fictionalized version of Sid Caesar, while Van Dyke played a fictionalized version of Reiner, on a fictionalized version of *Your Shows of Shows*.

The "TV show within a TV show" concept was a great source of comedy, but *Van Dyke*'s heart was the living room. While most sitcom couples squabbled, Rob and Laura Petrie clearly loved each other, in plots based on the realities of 1960s life.

As Laura Petrie, Mary Tyler Moore had been a national treasure: a sitcom wife who was beautiful, vulnerable, and funny. Her greatest compliment came from the show's studio landlord, when Lucille Ball came by the set to tell Moore, "You're very good."[1] Mary Tyler Moore soon won two Emmys for the show.

Van Dyke and Moore became the TV analog of the Kennedys. Not only did the show echo Jack and Jackie; it was partially financed by Kennedy money. When seeking seed money for the pilot, Reiner had gone to actor Peter Lawford, who was the husband of Jack Kennedy's sister Patricia. Lawford agreed to put up the money, but only if Joe Kennedy approved. Joe did, propelling another brand extension of the Kennedy era.

Moore found her own JFK on the set of *The Dick Van Dyke Show*. Grant Tinker was an advertising exec who worked with the sponsors of the show, and attended nearly every taping. Handsome, polished, and charismatic, Tinker married Moore shortly before the second-season premiere.

The assassination of JFK may have taken some sheen off of television's Camelot. In any event, the world was changing quickly. Reiner and Van Dyke decided to leave at the top of their game, and the show wrapped in 1966. When Tinker took a new job at NBC in New York, Moore decided to reignite her theater career.

Unfortunately, the vehicle she chose was a gritty dramatic musical based on *Breakfast at Tiffany's*. Moving from sweet Laura Petrie to a musical about a prostitute was not, on balance, the right career move. The show closed quickly. Devastated, Moore withdrew from sight, wondering if her career was over.

Then in 1969, Van Dyke invited Moore to appear on a reunion TV special. It was a massive hit; CBS soon offered Moore a series of her own.

Moore and Tinker weighed their options. Mary had starred in one of the most beloved series of all time. She did not want to fall into a typical insipid sitcom. Tinker agreed, and had a thesis: unlike other TV execs, he believed that television was fundamentally a writer's medium. "From my earliest days around and about television," he said later, "it's been clear to me that good shows could only be made by good writers."[2]

Moore and Tinker made a counterproposal. It was a modified version of Lucy and Desi's gambit. They wanted full creative control of Moore's new show, and an agreement that it would be produced by Moore and Tinker's new company. CBS agreed.

Though they had absolutely no idea what that show would be, Tinker and Moore created a new company to house it. It was called Mary Tyler Moore Enterprises, eventually MTM.

Brooks and Burns

Moore and Tinker wanted a show for the changing times, something fresh. Beyond that, they were open to ideas. Tinker had moved from NBC to 20th Century Fox, and in 1969, Fox had a series called *Room 222*. Well before *All in the Family*, it was a half-hour comedy set in an integrated Los Angeles high school, and dealt with issues like prejudice and drug abuse—in a *comedy*. This was completely new.

Tinker loved *Room 222*'s ability to mix comedy with issues. He approached creator Jim Brooks and producer Jim Burns, two relative unknowns. Would they be interested in working on his wife's new show?

At first, the two were ecstatic; both adored *The Dick Van Dyke Show*. Burns had even applied for a job there. But then they became concerned. Clearly, it couldn't be a domestic comedy—no one would want to follow *Dick Van Dyke* with a similar show starring Mary herself.

Also, they loved taking on real topics. They did not want to give that up. As Norman Lear would decide around the same time, the world was changing, and TV should, too.

The process by which Brooks and Burns came up with their concept was made possible by a revolutionary act of Tinker's: he left his writers *alone* to work through their process.

Brooks and Burns came back to the things they knew: since Mary could not play another housewife, they decided that the show should be a workplace comedy. Originally, the show was set at a gossip magazine, but over time, Brooks and Burns refined this: they wanted to signify that Mary was a modern, independent woman. Brooks had previously worked at CBS News in New York. And *Dick Van Dyke* had proven that TV itself worked as a setting.

They found their high concept: Mary Richards would work in a TV newsroom. Unlike virtually every other actress on TV, she would make her own way in the world: Mary's character would be *divorced*.

The era of no-fault divorce had just begun, first signed into law by Governor Ronald Reagan of California in 1970. For television, divorce was the very definition of *new*.

Nervous, they pitched the idea to Moore and Tinker, who both loved it. Mary had gotten divorced herself, eight years ago. And in 1970, a divorced woman on television was revolutionary, as was a workplace comedy about a thirty-year-old woman.

The next hurdle was pitching the show to CBS in New York. Tinker wouldn't be going with them. It was up to Brooks and Burns to close the deal.

Divorces, Moustaches, and Jews

In 1970, two forces vied for the hearts of the networks. One was their eternal desire to play it safe, to avoid controversy, to stick to selling soap. The other was a rapacious desire to capture new audiences—in this case, the '60s generation that wanted to see characters like themselves, and probably not another version of *Green Acres*.

It was inevitable that these forces would go to war. The battleground turned out to be *The Mary Tyler Moore Show*.

As Brooks and Burns flew to New York, looking young and inexperienced, they knew that the fate of *The Mary Tyler Moore Show* was now squarely on their shoulders. CBS's iconic Black Rock HQ had just opened, increasing their sense of foreboding; they were on alien terrain. It was downhill from there.

At CBS, Michael Dann was vice president of programs, and he was having a very bad year. After years of trouncing NBC, CBS was now *losing*—and it was on his watch. Dann knew the clock was ticking. He could turn things around, or get ready for the ax. A new show with Mary Tyler Moore sounded promising. She could be his new Lucy, a younger Doris Day. Maybe it would be CBS's version of ABC's *That Girl* (1966–71), the popular story of an actress living on her own, starring Danny Thomas's daughter Marlo.

But Brooks and Burns had a different idea.

When they got to the divorce, Dann had had more than enough. Why go there? What was the point? Maybe viewers would think Mary had divorced Dick Van Dyke.

The country was ready, Brooks and Burns argued; it would make Mary sympathetic and real.

CBS countered: why did she have to say she was *thirty*? Women on TV *never* discussed their age.

Because, said Brooks and Burns, there are real women in America who are divorced and over thirty. And they are in the audience.

Dann, losing patience, did what TV execs did: he called for the research department man, who, reassuringly, explained why Mike Dann was right, "Our research says American audiences won't tolerate divorce in a lead of a series any more than they will tolerate Jews, people with moustaches, and people who live in New York."[3]

Thus did CBS research summarize the wisdom of '70s television management.

This was not a statement that invited a response, so the meeting concluded. Brooks and Burns flew home. Mike Dann called Tinker to say his writers were terrible and that he should fire them immediately. Tinker disagreed.

On the flight home, Brooks and Burns considered whether to quit. They still had *Room 222* to go back to, and working with Mike Dann would be tortuous. But if Tinker still had their back, they would give it another shot.

So Brooks and Burns made some adjustments, eliminating the divorce, and fleshing out a series of characters with whom Mary would work. Their idea was to create an *ensemble* show, one that featured an array of sympathetic characters, rather than one star with a retinue.

As they struggled to finish the script, Moore's manager Arthur Price called. Did they have a theme song for the show yet? It was a bizarre question, considering they hadn't finished the script. But Mary's manager had a Texan singer named Sonny Curtis who wanted to take a crack at writing the theme.

Price called back a few hours later. Curtis had written a theme song. Could he come by? Brooks and Burns agreed, and prepared to waste an hour of their time.

The song was perfect. In a few hours, with almost nothing to go on, Curtis's song had captured the fragility and hope that they were trying to write into the pilot. Reza Badiyi's opening sequence did the same, from Mary's opening tentative look to the exuberant toss of her beret. Slowly, *The Mary Tyler Moore Show* began to come together.

CBS casting pro Ethel Winant was one of the first female executives in television. Unlike her colleagues, she loved the pilot script. For one thing, she had good taste; for another, she was the lone woman in the office, before women even had a bathroom at CBS.

She set about populating the newsroom with a series of actors no one else would have chosen, three older, unknown actors who were perennially cast as heavies: Ed Asner as Lou, Gavin McLeod as Murray, and Ted Knight as Ted Baxter. She rounded out Mary's "home" cast with flighty movie actress Cloris Leachman, and an unknown named Valerie Harper.

Rehearsals began in an old Desilu lot, the same lot where *I Love Lucy* had been shot. Director Jay Sandrich brought another innovation: he encouraged his actors to speak softly. They were being miked and didn't need to project as if they were in a theater, creating another way in which the show felt more authentic.

Costume designer Leslie Hall worked with Moore and Harper to dress them in cutting-edge fashion. Most importantly, Brooks and Burns sought out women writers, making *The Mary Tyler Moore Show* the first TV production that was guided by women.

The first audience taping of *The Mary Tyler Moore Show* was a disaster. Audiences hated Mary's friend Rhoda. Phyllis struck the audience as grating. Lou Grant was a bully.

On the way home with Tinker, Moore burst into tears. Tinker called Brooks and Burns with one comment: "Fix it."

With one chance left, the writers made some minor changes, and in the second taping almost everything had been improved.

But Mike Dann still hated the show.

He offered to buy MTM out: take the money and walk away, he advised Tinker. Don't throw good money after bad. Tinker and Moore refused. They had a thirteen-episode commitment from him and were going to hold him to it.

So Mike Dann did what Paley would soon do with *All in the Family*. He put *The Mary Tyler Moore Show* somewhere no one would ever see it: on Tuesday nights between *The Beverly Hillbillies* and *Hee Haw*. It was precisely the timeslot to be seen by an audience that would hate it.

Then he waited for it to die.

The Rural Purge

I'm an experienced woman. I've been around . . .
Well, all right, I might not have been around, but I've been . . . nearby.
—MARY RICHARDS

The "Country Broadcasting System" of Jim Aubrey had continued into 1970, with one mind-numbing premise after another. That was good as long as it worked, as long as it generated profit.

But there was a problem: advertisers wanted the young and educated, and the young and educated didn't watch *Hee Haw*.

And the man who had left *Hee Haw* on in Aubrey's wake was Mike Dann. Dann's time was running out.

Dann resigned, heading to the Children's Television Workshop (CTW), and a new show called *Sesame Street*. Robert Wood became network president, and promoted Fred Silverman to vice president of program planning.

Wood gave Silverman immediate direction: get rid of the rural comedies. They were going to drag CBS into the present.

So that's what they did, canceling *Green Acres*, *The Beverly Hillbillies*, *Hee Haw*, *Mayberry RFD*, and *Lassie*, as well as *The Ed Sullivan Show* and *The Jackie Gleason Show*. It was the biggest schedule shift in television history. And it meant CBS needed new shows, pronto.

So Silverman flew to Los Angeles to see what Dann had in the can. And he found a pilot no one liked called *The Mary Tyler Moore Show*.

That was all it took. Silverman yanked *Green Acres* from Saturday at 9:30 and saved both *Mary Tyler Moore* and MTM.

Mary got another round of luck from a soon-to-be neighbor, another rescue case named Archie Bunker.

Mary and Archie

Even with a better time slot on Saturday nights, *Mary Tyler Moore*'s initial ratings were weak. Rumors spread that CBS was prepping a show to replace it. Execs peppered Brooks and Burns with helpful notes: "Mary should be presented with a problem. Toward the end she should solve that problem in a surprising and comical manner."[4] The producers resisted, and continued to hone their concept of a natural comedy, in which characters and real situations trumped punch lines.

Relief began with a midseason replacement, a beleaguered show that premiered four months after *Mary*. Paley had hated *All in the Family*, and stuck it in the Tuesday night graveyard where *Mary Tyler Moore* had been.

Though audiences may have missed the change, the Television Academy had been paying attention. At the 1971 Emmy Awards, *The Mary Tyler Moore Show* garnered four wins and eight nominations. *All in the Family* was right alongside, winning Best Comedic Series and Best New Series.

After the Emmys, both shows took off like a rocket. Soon more than 20 million people were watching *Mary*; by 1974, that number had grown to a 43 million. The *Wall Street Journal*'s Benjamin Stein called *Mary* "the best show on television, week in and week out. . . . [Viewers] are watching people much like themselves—doomed to live imperfect lives, often comically mixed-up lives, still stretching for a measure of dignity."[5]

MTM's next show, *The Bob Newhart Show*, joined CBS's Saturday night, as did *M*A*S*H* and *The Carol Burnett Show*. Bob Wood and Fred Silverman created the most successful one-night lineup that television has ever seen. In the years that this lineup aired, Americans stayed home by the tens of millions, and watched the same five shows at the same time.

It was the TV equivalent of the '27 Yankees, played out for as long as MTM and Norman Lear were there.

MTM grew into a major industry force. By 1974, it grossed more than $20 million, with eight comedies in production. And CBS returned to beating NBC handily.

Women, Television, and History

As *Mary* continued and MTM grew, Brooks and Burns continued to seek out women writers wherever they could find them. Many wanted nothing more than to write for the show. Though some thought the character didn't go far enough, millions of women saw Mary Richards as the only authentic woman on TV. Brooks and Burns deferred to their female-led writers' room on stories, best characterized by Burns's famous quote: "I know there is a wealth of comedy in my wife's purse, but I can't access that."[6]

By 1973, twenty-five of the seventy-five writers on *Mary* were women, far ahead of any other TV production. Female writers Treva Silverman, Pat Nardo, Gloria Banta, Susan Silver, and Gail Parent helped create a realistic portrayal of life in the '70s, most famously an arc in which Lou Grant's wife left him and they got divorced.

Mary addressed issues including equal pay, divorce, infidelity, and prostitution, but rarely pedantically and always from the perspective of the characters themselves.

TV Guide went from describing Mary Richards as "unmarried and getting a little desperate about it" to "thirty-three, unmarried, and unworried—Mary is the liberated woman's ideal."[7] In 1974 Mary Tyler Moore and Valerie Harper made the cover of *Time* as "TV's Funny Girls," confirming their influence on the women's liberation movement of the '70s.

Chuckles Bites the Dust

Mary's most famous episode came in its sixth season in 1975. Newsman Ted Baxter was asked to be grand marshal of a local parade and was crushed when he had to step down, only to be replaced by Chuckles the Clown, host of a children's show.

The next day, the news crew learned that Chuckles was killed in the parade. He had dressed as one of his characters, Peter Peanut, and an elephant mistook him for food and "shelled" him. The shock at his death and the absurdity of the circumstances drove the newsroom to make escalating jokes about Chuckles' manner of death. Mary was horrified.

The eulogy at Chuckles' funeral included a list of the characters he'd played, including Peter Peanut, Mr. Fee-Fi-Fo, Billy Banana, and Aunt Yoo-Hoo. Mary, who had been berating the others for their insensitivity, convulsed with laughter for the rest of the eulogy, and then burst into tears.

Reviewers noted that the episode broke perhaps the last taboo on television: it had looked at death with humor and humanity. Two writers from *M*A*S*H* attended the taping and shook their heads, wondering if they would ever write anything that good. The episode was ranked number one on *TV Guide*'s "100 Greatest Episodes of All Time" in 1997.

Mary cemented its status as the most sophisticated show on television. First Lady Betty Ford appeared on the show. Appropriately, Walter Cronkite, who had an audience of 20 million viewers every night, did a guest spot in the newsroom, playing himself. So did Johnny Carson, the most powerful man in television, who never appeared on any show but his own.

Mary could not get any bigger, but the world around it was changing.

Life after Mary

In 1974, Norman Lear's spinoff model spread to *Mary*, and Valerie Harper's Rhoda left to begin her own show. In 1975, so did Cloris Leachman with *Phyllis*. Key writers from *Mary* moved to other MTM productions. Then the FCC's "family hour" legislation pushed *All in the Family* to 9 PM, destroying the incredible CBS Saturday night lineup and scattering its components to different nights.

Fred Silverman left CBS for ABC, and began competing with his former team with more juvenile shows. It was becoming time to say goodbye, and the remaining major writers huddled to look for a suitable ending for *The Mary Tyler Moore Show*. They knew they'd be under the microscope for the final episode. Their premise: WJM-TV had been sold, and the new owner had fired everyone but Ted.

The writers' room was feeling the pressure. For rehearsal they had only about three-fourths of the script done.

They decided that Ted Baxter would sing the World War I–era song "It's a Long Way to Tipperary" on the air. The rest of the newsroom cast, recognizing the absurdity, would join him as a funny way of saying goodbye.

In the final shot, cast and crew were close to tears. Ed Asner's legendary line put them over the edge: "I treasure you people."

Moore also gave her famous final speech:

I just wanted you to know that sometimes I get concerned about being a career woman. I get to thinking my job is too important to me, and I tell myself that the people I work with are just the people I work with, and not my family. And last night, I thought, "What is a family, anyway?" They're just people who make you feel less alone and really loved. And that's what you've done for me. Thank you for being my family.

MTM's Legacy

Fueled by Tinker's willingness to let his writers run their shows, MTM became the place everyone wanted to work. Gary David Goldberg called MTM "Camelot for writers."[8] Of the Emmy awards for best comedy and best drama from 1971 to 1994, 50 percent went to shows produced by MTM or its former employees.

MTM alumni went on to dominate the next twenty years of television on shows including *Saturday Night Live, The Golden Girls, Cagney and Lacey, China Beach, Cheers, Chicago Hope, Cosby, ER, Family Ties, Frazier, Friends, Miami Vice, NYPD Blue, The Simpsons, Two and a Half Men,* and *Taxi.*

MTM's creators, James L. Brooks and Allan Burns, went their separate ways in 1978. Brooks created the cult comedy classic *Taxi,* which was extended for a season by Grant Tinker, who had returned to NBC. When *Taxi* was canceled, Brooks transitioned to film, where he produced, directed, and wrote *Terms of Endearment*—winning Academy Awards for Best Picture, Best Director, and Best Adapted Screenplay.

Brooks got two more nominations for *Broadcast News;* then *As Good as It Gets* won for both Best Actor and Best Actress.

In 1987, Brooks returned to TV for a project on a new fourth network, FOX. As producer of *The Tracey Ullman Show,* he ordered some interstitial cartoons from illustrator Matt Groening. FOX spun them off into their own show, which Brooks co-produced. *The Simpsons* became the longest-running comedy in TV history. To date Brooks has twenty Emmys and nearly fifty nominations.

———

In 1980, Mary Tyler Moore did what she'd done after *Dick Van Dyke*: she took a role 180 degrees against type, as a cold, sadistic mother in *Ordinary People*. This time she won a Golden Globe for Best Actress in a Drama. Powered by her performance, the film won the Academy Award for Best Picture.

The Mary Tyler Moore Show was cited as the original inspiration by a generation of performers and writers. In 2002, the cast was reunited by one of them. Oprah Winfrey said the show was "a light in my life, and Mary was a trailblazer for my generation. She's the reason I wanted my own production company." Winfrey's crew created an exact replica of the WJM newsroom and assembled the cast for a reunion. Moore gave Winfrey a version of Mary's iconic wooden "M"—a golden "O." Winfrey became speechless, then burst into tears.

In 1998, *Entertainment Weekly* named *The Mary Tyler Moore Show* the best TV show of all time.

CHAPTER 36

M*A*S*H

Television brought the brutality of war into the comfort
of the living room. Vietnam was lost in the living rooms
of America—not on the battlefields of Vietnam.
—Marshall McLuhan

I t was 1970. The Sixties were over. Only the Vietnam War remained. The body bags continued to pour in plane by plane, and were shown on the news in those uncensored days. Nixon promised to end the war, then expanded it quietly. Four protesting students were shot dead at Kent State. Public outrage grew.

A 1970 movie captured the dark mood of the times. Directed by Robert Altman, it was based on a 1968 novel about a mobile Army hospital during the Korean War. The doctors and nurses of the 4077th performed surgery on soldiers and civilians, under nightmarish conditions—while they drank, had sex, and tried to stay alive. *MASH* was biting and sardonic, one of a new crop of films for a new time. It received five Academy Award nominations, winning one for Best Adapted Screenplay.

In the '60s, the idea of turning *MASH* into a TV series would have been absurd. But the times were changing.

By 1971, Bob Wood's rebuilding of CBS was underway. *All in the Family* and *Mary Tyler Moore* were both on the schedule. 20th Century Fox had the rights to produce a series around *MASH*. So William Self, Fox's head of TV, approached CBS about creating a TV pilot.

Ideally, it could be a return of the "service comedy"—the format of military comedies such as *McHale's Navy* and *Gomer Pyle: USMC.*

CBS agreed to pay for pilot script development. If they liked it, they would shoot it as a possible series for 1972.

Fox tapped producer-director Gene Reynolds to develop the pilot. Reynolds saw the challenge: it would need jokes, at the least—but jokes that didn't undermine the tragedy of the circumstances.

He knew just who to call.

Larry Gelbart and Gene Reynolds

Larry Gelbart had been one of TV's most respected writers from the beginning, part of the legendary *Your Shows of Shows* team—with Carl Reiner, Mel Brooks, and Sid Caesar. After *Your Shows of Shows*, Gelbart had written the Broadway hit *A Funny Thing Happened on the Way to the Forum.* Then he moved to England, in 1963.

Gelbart liked English television; it was made for adults, focused on real themes, and was an order of magnitude beyond what was on in 1963 America. He enjoyed series like *Till Death Us Do Part*, the British show that had inspired *All in the Family.* He particularly liked that British shows often had only six episodes a season—as opposed to the twenty-two or more required in America. Soon, he'd have good reason to be jealous.

In 1971, Gelbart was running *The Marty Feldman Comedy Machine*, in London. His old friend Gene Reynolds visited him; Reynolds now worked at 20th Century Fox. The two discussed finding a project to do together, someday.

Soon afterward, Reynolds called Gelbart from Los Angeles. Did he want to write a pilot for *MASH?* Gelbart told Reynolds he would do it, then returned to working on the *Feldman* show.

———

What first inspired Gelbart was not *MASH*'s story—it was the song. The movie's haunting theme, "Suicide Is Painless" ran through his head, again and again. It inspired him to look for something funny but poignant, what he called "comedy written in a minor key."[1]

Reynolds called Gelbart two months later. How was the script going? Gelbart said he had just mailed it.

Reynolds hung up, elated.

Then Gelbart sat down to start writing the script.

Comedy in a Minor Key

Adapting *MASH* for television presented a series of major challenges. Though set during the Korean conflict, it was actually a commentary on Vietnam. Its antiwar spirit was typical for a '60s *film*—but almost impossible on network TV.

The show would have to walk a tightrope. It would have to question the Vietnam War, through the story of Korea. It would need to honor both the soldiers in the field and the families at home.

It should ultimately, Gelbart thought, respect everyone's point of view—not an easy thing to do in less than thirty minutes a week. It was the most daunting balancing act a comedy had ever attempted.

And there were production challenges as well. For one thing, *MASH* had a large ensemble cast. Large casts were kryptonite for a sitcom: they increased the cost of production, and diffused the focus on a show's lead actors. One of Gelbart's first jobs was solving that problem with a process he called "condensation and miniaturization."[2]

Gelbart decided that *M*A*S*H* would center on surgeon Hawkeye Pierce.

Around Hawkeye, Gelbart and Reynolds constructed a series of other characters, including Trapper John (best friend), Colonel Henry Blake (commanding officer), Margaret Houlihan (pro-war nurse), Frank Burns (pro-war zealot and Margaret's other half), Radar O'Reilly (an innocent boy from Iowa caught up in the war), and Max Klinger (a corporal who dressed like a woman, in a bid to be discharged from the Army).

Single-Camera Comedy

M*A*S*H got lucky in one respect: Fox had preserved the sets from the movie, which the series was able to inherit. Additional shooting occurred at a remote location in Malibu, a site preserved to this day.

That was more or less the only break that Gelbart and Reynolds got.

The logistical challenge for *M*A*S*H* would be creating a weekly movie-quality sitcom, one that would not cheapen the life-and-death stakes of its protagonists. The creative challenge for *M*A*S*H* would be living up to *MASH*.

And both required that *M*A*S*H* be as high-quality as a film.

All in the Family and *Mary Tyler Moore* each shot in front of a live audience. They did so using updates of the multicamera methods that Desi and Lucy had pioneered fifteen years earlier. This made production quick: three cameras (left, center, and right) shooting simultaneously, on every scene. As Lucy and Desi had foreseen, this generated a multitude of benefits.

Three-camera shows produce a variety of possible shots from each take. For every usable take, editors get three shots to choose from. So an entire show could be shot in *one evening*—with a live audience—in an experience that is similar to attending a play. This also means that comedies are shot with live audience laughter, cuing the audience at home to laugh along in the right places.

In contrast, movies were generally shot on *one* camera—meaning every shot is done separately, in a series of takes. One camera was the method for dramas: it allowed for a more nuanced, more cinematic final product.

On the downside, one-camera shows don't have a live audience, as there's nothing funny about watching actors perform the same lines over and over again. In one-camera production, each shot is painstaking, with close-ups, midshots, and wide shots all handled separately.

The decision was clear for Gelbart and Reynolds: to live up to its subject matter, *M*A*S*H* had to be shot on one camera, like a movie. But to generate enough episodes, it would have to get done on the compressed schedule of a three-camera sitcom. It was an insane proposition on its face, a brutal amount of ongoing pressure that would eventually yield a diamond.

Laugh Track

In a testament to how much edgier CBS was willing to be, it approved Gelbart's pilot script, and agreed to finance the pilot. The show would follow the lives of Hawkeye Pierce (Alan Alda) and the rest of the 4077th Mobile Army Surgical Hospital as they grappled with the reality—and absurdity—of modern war.

The pilot was sitcom-like, focusing on sexy "cot-hopping" between doctors and nurses. It wasn't the minor key comedy that Gelbart wanted to do yet. To get where they wanted to go, the producers would have to battle both CBS and FOX. The biggest battle was over the "laugh track."

Since M*A*S*H was not shot before a studio audience, CBS insisted on adding prerecorded laughter. This was a common, though terrible, tactic for decades of television, designed to let audiences know that the show they were watching was funny.

Gelbart and Reynolds were violently opposed. They wanted M*A*S*H to be shot *without* a laugh track—as the real Korean conflict had done, Gelbart noted later. He later said of laugh tracks:

> They're a lie. You're telling an engineer when to push a button to produce a laugh from people who don't exist. It's just so dishonest. The biggest shows when we were on the air were All in the Family and The Mary Tyler Moore Show, both of which were taped before a live studio audience, where laughter made sense. But our show was a film show—supposedly shot in the middle of Korea. So the question I always asked the network was, "Who are these laughing people? Where did they come from?"[3]

International audiences agreed with Gelbart; all DVDs would later let viewers remove the laugh track, which one British reviewer called "downright unbearable."[4]

It was the first of an ongoing series of battles.

Producing M*A*S*H

M*A*S*H went into production with a brutal weekly schedule: after a table read and rehearsal on day one, only three shoot days remained to shoot a thirty-five-page script. Gelbart and others would often write a scene until immediately before it was due. On some episodes, the show's cast would improvise major segments.

Gelbart and Reynolds would look for any new story premise they could find. They acted out scenes, talked through outcomes, and asked the actors for fresh ideas. Gelbart, as a former writer on *Your Show of Shows* and for Bob Hope, turned out punch lines like a machine. But over time, the jokes diminished and the show became more serious. And though many of the characters were brought over from the film, they were more nuanced in the series—more sympathetic and more human, especially over time. Gelbart would say, "*M*A*S*H* is the only successful one-camera show that television has ever produced."[5] Over time, it was also clear that *M*A*S*H* was finer than the movie that inspired it.

———

*M*A*S*H* premiered on September 17, 1972, and ran on Sundays at 7:30 PM, against *The FBI* and *The Wonderful World of Disney*. It struggled through its first season, coming in at forty-sixth with a 17.4 rating. In its second season, it got a miraculous gift: Silverman put it between the new breakout hits *All in the Family* and *Mary Tyler Moore*, which helped *M*A*S*H* become a sensation. The show finished its second season in TV's top ten.

Early on, the time pressures left some episodes feeling one-dimensional, so Gelbart hit on a new structure. An episode called "Dear Dad" featured members of the camp writing letters to loved ones back home. It created multiple stories within the same episode, to expand the format of the sitcom into something more complex. It was the first of a series of experiments.

As Gelbart and Reynolds had hoped, the characters grew to represent each point of view on the war, so that what people thought the show was saying was often a matter of interpretation. New characters were introduced and explored. CBS was concerned that the audience might be confused. But the audience stayed with the show. *M*A*S*H* became the first sitcom to employ multiple storylines, weaving a series of threads in thirty-minute scripts. The writers fought the network to take on serious themes rather than to play out a string of gags.

Gelbart and Reynolds would often begin an idea for an episode themselves, looking for a new premise and then working through the story beats. They would then assign the outline to a writer, or to Gelbart himself. If the writer had not grasped the tone of the series, Gelbart would rewrite the episode.

CBS censors focused on the amount of sex on the show, telling Gelbart to delete various uses of "hell" and "damn." He could use the word "God" and he could use the word "damn," but he could not use the word "Goddamn." CBS was also worried about scenes in the operating room.

There was a constant state of tension between the writers and the network. CBS required a one-paragraph description for each proposed story before M*A*S*H could start shooting. Eventually Gelbart stopped submitting them. By that point, the show was a hit.

Over time, M*A*S*H's cast became a major component of the writing process, as writers drew on character traits of the cast to deepen the characters. They also strove to break out of formula, however they could. They did this to shocking effect in the finale of Season Three.

"Abyssinia, Henry" (Season Three)

Actor McLean Stevenson played Colonel Henry Blake, and he was no longer happy. As several others on M*A*S*H would do later, he wanted to the leave the show. The writers resolved to turn this misfortune into something historic.

In the famous episode "Abyssinia, Henry," Blake receives word that he's being sent home. The camp has a party for him, and says their good-byes. Blake's plane leaves Korea. That's all the cast knew—until the final scene was shot.

In it, Radar O'Reilly enters the operating room. He tells a full crew of doctors and nurses that Blake's plane has been shot down: "There were no survivors." It was the first time a major TV character was killed instead of simply written out of the show. The death of Henry Blake spoke directly to the horror of war. The show received hundreds of angry letters, asking why he had to die. Gelbart and Reynolds answered each one by hand. They later donated the incoming letters to the Smithsonian.

M*A*S*H survived the exits of Wayne Rogers, McLean Stevenson, Larry Linville, and Gary Burghoff without weakening. None of them had a major success on television afterward.

"The Interview" (Season Four)

From the beginning, *M*A*S*H*'s writers conducted extensive research, meeting with doctors, nurses, pilots, patients, and others who had been in Korea or Vietnam. Reynolds and Gelbart visited South Korea's 8055th, the real-life model for the 4077th. Witnessing the damage the war had caused led to *M*A*S*H*'s finest hour: an episode called "The Interview."

It was inspired by Edward R. Murrow's seminal 1952 Christmas episode of *See It Now*, in which he had visited soldiers during the Korean War. Like Murrow's show, "The Interview" was shot in black and white.

Gelbart created a series of faux interviews that were ad-libbed by *M*A*S*H*'s actors. The actors were given a list of twenty questions, such as "What do you think about the war?" and "What do you miss about home?" Using their answers, Gelbart wrote a script, in which a Murrow-like war correspondent interviewed the unit.

"The Interview" was *M*A*S*H*'s most specific antiwar statement. Each character reflected the horror of war from his or her own vantage point. Alan Alda's Hawkeye mocked the Army, and proposed to First Lady Bess Truman. Jamie Farr's Klinger talked about missing home; his wife, Laverne; and Hungarian hotdogs. Mike Farrell's B. J. Hunnicutt (whom psychiatrist Sidney Freeman calls "an enigma in size 13 shoes") talked about his family.

Harry Morgan, as career military man Colonel Potter, talked about the loneliness of command. When asked what good would come from the war, he answered: "Not a damn thing."

William Christopher's Father Mulcahy delivered the most powerful lines of the series. When asked if the war had changed him, he responded:

> When the doctors cut into a patient, and it's cold, the way it is today . . . steam rises from the body . . . and the doctor will warm his hands over the open wound.

> How could anybody look upon that and not feel changed?

Soon after "The Interview," Gelbart and Reynolds left the series, exhausted by the schedule and their battles with the network. By this point, M*A*S*H's bench was so deep that it didn't seem to matter. By 1978, it was almost universally regarded as the best thing on television.

M*A*S*H created a national dialogue about the nature of the war. It brought a level of gravity to television comedy that had seemed impossible beforehand. As *The Sopranos* would twenty-seven years later, M*A*S*H became an American touchstone in an era in which Americans didn't know whom to trust.

When detractors pointed out that M*A*S*H had gone on longer than the war itself, Gelbart told them they were wrong. TV shows last thirty minutes a week. Wars never stop.

"Goodbye, Farewell, and Amen"

By 1982, the Vietnam War was long over. *The Mary Tyler Moore Show* and *All in the Family* were gone. A former actor was in the White House. A puny upstart called CNN was broadcasting twenty-four hours a day.

The notion of quality television was no longer ridiculed, because one show had made that impossible.

As M*A*S*H entered its eleventh and final season, everything around it had changed.

"Goodbye, Farewell, and Amen" was broadcast on February 28, 1983. The 2.5-hour finale allowed audiences to say goodbye to a group of characters who had grown to be part of many people's families. As it began, Hawkeye could no longer perform surgery. In repeated therapy sessions with psychiatrist Sidney Freeman, Hawkeye recovered a blocked memory of a woman murdering her own baby.

An announcement arrived: a ceasefire had been declared. The war is over.

Klinger, who had fought so hard to escape Korea, decided to stay and marry a Korean woman named Soon-Lee. Father Mulcahy performed the ceremony the next day. B.J. received a discharge—and was overjoyed to be going home—just in time for the second birthday of the daughter he had never met.

The 4077th camp was dismantled, and its characters disappeared one by one. Eventually, only B.J. and Hawkeye were left. Hawkeye was angry at B.J. for his refusal to say the word "goodbye," after all that they had been through together, but forgave him as they shared their last moments together.

Soon the chopper arrived to take Hawkeye home. As it carried him upward, B.J. waved.

As "Suicide Is Painless" began for the last time, Hawkeye noticed a huge array of stones laid out on the abandoned campsite. They spelled out a word: GOODBYE.

———

An audience of 121.6 million watched and said goodbye, too—over half of the population of America.

It is the most-watched television episode of all time, and probably always will be.

CHAPTER 37

PBS

The origins of public television came during the radio craze, when in 1925, the Department of Commerce met to consider the place of educational radio. The result was the creation of the National Association of Educational Broadcasters (NAEB). In 1938, the NAEB convinced the FCC to reserve five radio stations for educational broadcasting.

At around the same time, Edsel and Henry Ford established the Ford Foundation as the philanthropic arm of the Ford Motor Company. It became the largest funder of public radio and television, gifting $268 million from 1951 to 1974, the equivalent of $1 billion today.

One of the results of the Ford Foundation's largesse was the National Educational Television and Radio Center (NETRC). In the late '50s, the NETRC began pursuing an audacious goal: to become TV's fourth network.

With Ford Foundation funding, now called National Educational Television (NET), it began a series of groundbreaking programming. *NET Playhouse* included plays by Ibsen, Wilde, Shaw, and Tennessee Williams, performed by actors including Dustin Hoffman, Martin Sheen, and James Earl Jones. As quality at the Big Three networks declined, NET established a new standard for quality television. It was the "alternative network" with controversial, hard-hitting documentaries, a quantum leap beyond those on commercial TV.

The *NET Journal* created outstanding documentaries like *The Poor Pay More*, *Black Like Me*, *Appalachia: Rich Land, Poor People*, and *Inside North Vietnam*.

NET also launched children's programming—most notably, *Mister Rogers' Neighborhood,* which ran for over thirty years. It produced 895 episodes and generations of fans, becoming an essential part of American childhood.

Though critics loved NET's documentaries, many NET affiliates objected to what they saw as a liberal bias. Some loved NET; others hated it. And no one hated it more than Richard Nixon, the next president of the United States.

The CPB and PBS

> *Television is still a young invention. But we have learned already that it has immense—even revolutionary—power to change our lives. I hope that [the CPB] will direct that power toward the great and not the trivial purposes.*
> —PRESIDENT LYNDON JOHNSON

New York's Channel 13 was the giant of educational television. Its first broadcaster had been Edward R. Murrow, and it led the way in controversial programming.

NET attempted to merge with Channel 13 throughout the '60s, but the Ford Foundation blocked the merger. Then, in 1966, the foundation began to withdraw its funding.

To keep NET afloat, the government intervened, with the Public Broadcasting Act of 1967. The act established the Corporation for Public Broadcasting (CPB), a privately owned nonprofit; and, later, both the Public Broadcasting System (PBS) and National Public Radio (NPR).

The mission of the CPB was to ensure noncommercial, high-quality content.

There was a catch for NET: the act stipulated that 70 percent of CPB funding would be distributed to more than 1,400 locally owned public radio and television stations. In so doing, CPB would be able to check and balance NET's power. The installation of the CPB, in fact, acted as a gate on NET's programming, especially coverage of the war in Vietnam.

On October 7, 1970, the CPB replaced NET with PBS.

Sesame Street

In 1969, buoyed by the success of *Mister Rogers' Neighborhood*, the Ford Foundation gave $1 million to the Children's Television Workshop. The gift helped Joan Ganz Cooney and Lloyd Morrisett launch a new show, called *Sesame Street.*

Sesame Street's major innovation was to structure a show around the way children actually learned. Malcolm Gladwell wrote, "Sesame Street was built around a single, breakthrough insight: that if you can hold the attention of children, you can educate them."[1] *Sesame Street* revolutionized children's programming. It would win 150 Emmy Awards, more than any other children's show.

But after *Sesame Street*'s initial success, CTW hit a snag. The Nixon administration opposed funding PBS.

Public love for Sesame Street became CTW's weapon, and for a time, it won its own line item in the federal budget. Then in 1981, government funding for *Sesame Street* was terminated. Its new hero was the man who had jumped over from CBS before the rural purge. Mike Dann licensed *Sesame Street* to the rest of the world, putting it in front of 120 million international viewers in 140 countries. Next, he pitched a licensing strategy to Muppet creator Jim Henson, who owned the trademarks to *Sesame Street*'s Muppet characters.

Henson agreed, as long as the profits were used to fund CTW. The *Sesame Street* Muppets eventually brought in over $15 million a year in licensing revenue.

Over forty-six years and 4,000 episodes later, *Sesame Street* is still on the air. Over 95 percent of American preschoolers have seen it by the time they turn three.

Masterpiece Theatre

In 1971, PBS began extending its pedigree with the drama anthology *Masterpiece Theatre*. Overall, *Masterpiece* was a critical precursor of the finest dramas of the cable age.

Masterpiece was best known for its British-produced adaptations of novels and biographies. These include 1976's *I, Claudius*, which followed the story of Rome over twelve episodes. *The Six Wives of Henry VIII* aired in six episodes in 1970. *Jeeves and Wooster* was an adaptation of P. G. Wodehouse's "Jeeves" stories, and aired in the early '90s. *Sherlock* is one of the most recent adaptations, starring Benedict Cumberbatch.

Masterpiece also produced original dramas, which include its most famous, *Upstairs, Downstairs*. The show was set in a townhouse in London's tony Belgravia neighborhood during the first three decades of the century. From 1971 to 1975, it chronicled the lives of the wealthy Bellamy family "upstairs" and their servants living "downstairs."

More recent examples of original dramas on *Masterpiece* include *Downton Abbey* (2010–2015), a story set in a Yorkshire country house between 1912 and 1925; and *House of Cards*, a four-episode serial from 1990, which spawned the Netflix version starring Kevin Spacey and Robin Wright.

While CBS owned comedy in the '70s, PBS became the home of quality drama. *Masterpiece Theatre* proved out the miniseries as a format, as weekly cliffhangers brought viewers back week to week. *Masterpiece* inspired a generation brought up by television, who would grow up to reinvent it.

But in 1972, it all threatened to come apart. The man whom the press loved to kick around was back, and he would not let television beat him again. On June 30, President Richard Nixon vetoed major funding for the CPB, defeating a bill worth $863 million today. One newspaper called it "the veto to please Archie Bunker."[2] But that was wrong: the veto was personal, designed to make PBS crawl. Nixon was starving out an enemy, reducing PBS' ability to pay for quality programming.

Then Nixon inadvertently gave PBS the most riveting free drama anyone had ever seen.

CHAPTER 38

WATERGATE

If the president does it, then it is not illegal.
—RICHARD NIXON, 1977

Richard Nixon barely won the 1968 presidential election (43.4 percent to Humphrey's 42.7 percent), and knew the honeymoon would be brief. The media's antipathy toward him was too deep to ever go away. He was a realist above all, telling an aide, "The greatest mistake we can make is to try to do what Johnson did: to slobber over [the media] with the hope that you can 'win' them. It can't be done."[1]

Instead of trying to win reporters over, he'd fight them with every tool at his disposal. The White House, he knew, came with a lot of tools.

Once in the White House, Nixon instructed his chief of staff, H. R. Haldeman, to create a task force to monitor all three networks, and to respond aggressively to anything negative they had to say.[2] He ordered his staff to leverage the IRS, the FBI, and the CIA to prosecute his enemies.

The Silent Majority

To hell with history. Just knock the shit out of them.
—RICHARD NIXON, ON THE VIETNAM WAR

The antiwar movement grew stronger from 1969 to 1971, moving from campuses to suburbs, from students to parents. A unified demand for Nixon to end the war spurred a national day of protest, set for October 15, 1969.

In response, Nixon delivered a speech that would redefine the Republican Party.

In the televised address, Nixon argued that America could not walk away and leave South Vietnam to utter devastation. Most Americans felt the same, he said; and they were the ones he wanted to speak with, the "Silent Majority" of Americans who stood with him, rather than with the Vietnam protesters.

Once again, Washington insiders and the press were outraged: thousands were dying, and Nixon was blaming those who were trying to end the war. He had gone too far, they thought; now the public would see Nixon for the dissembler that he was.

They were wrong. Nixon's positive poll numbers increased. When asked whom they blamed for the problems in America, more Americans blamed the protesters than Nixon.

Nixon was euphoric. He had successfully used television to strike back at the media, and now he would do it again.

In the move that some called "the veto to please Archie Bunker," Nixon vetoed the funding for public television. They could get the funds to criticize the government from somebody else, but not from *his* administration.

Then he moved on to harness television for the greatest triumph of his life.

Nixon, China, and the U.S.S.R.

In the 1960s and 1970s, China was as distant as another planet. The regime of Mao was a mystery, as were Chiang Kai-shek and the great nation's history. Vietnam had brought concern about China to the fore, since North Vietnam had the sympathies of both China and the U.S.S.R.

Then the news broke: Richard Nixon, archetypal anti-Communist, would be the first American president to travel to China.

It was the biggest story in the world. The trip was scheduled for February 1972, immediately before Nixon's 1972 re-election campaign.

The administration announced there would be "some live television transmission" from Beijing, but in fact, the trip's logistical centerpiece was a TV coverage plan, which originally included bringing three remote TV trucks, each the size of school bus, from the United States to Beijing.

For eight days and nights, America watched its president in the first live images from China in over twenty years.

It was the biggest live television spectacle since the moon landing, and set the stage for Nixon's next trip, to the home court of America's nemesis.

———

A new term entered the American vocabulary during Nixon's reign: "détente."

A French word meaning "relaxation," "détente" was the term of art for improved relations between the United States and the Soviet Union that began in 1971.

Shortly after the trip to Beijing, Nixon arrived at Vnukovo airport. He was greeted by a welcoming party of leading Soviet officials; the ceremony was broadcast live by Moscow television. The historic trip included negotiations around the SALT Treaty, the Anti-Ballistic Missile Treaty, the Apollo-Soyuz Test Project, and the Agreement on Cooperation in the Field of Environmental Protection.

Nixon's trip to the U.S.S.R. may have been his finest hour. As he had intended, his prior meetings in China had rattled the Soviets. They had television, too.

Though neither trip helped end the Vietnam War, they accomplished their primary aim: Nixon's 1972 win against George McGovern was the biggest presidential win in American history.

As Nixon won re-election, one of his teams made another kind of history.

1972: The Plumbers

We've got some dirty tricks underway that may pay off.
—JOHN EHRLICHMAN, CHIEF OF STAFF, TO
PRESIDENT RICHARD NIXON

A top secret White House Special Investigations Unit had been formed by top Nixon aide John Ehrlichman, to prevent leaks from the White House. In a play on words, the "anti-leak" task force came to be known as "the Plumbers."

In the early hours of June 17, 1972, a team of Plumbers broke into Democratic National Committee headquarters at the Watergate building. The five men carried lock-picks, surveillance equipment, forty rolls of unexposed film, tear gas guns, and $2,300 in cash. They applied tape to the door lock to keep the door open, then foolishly left it ajar.

It was seen by a security guard, and the men were arrested at gunpoint.

Watergate and Television

*Good evening from Washington. In a few moments, we're going
to bring you the entire proceedings in the first day of the Senate
Watergate hearings—hearings to bear the truth about the wide range
of illegal, unethical or improper activities established or still merely
alleged, surrounding the reelection of President Nixon last year.*
—ROBERT MCNEIL, PBS, MAY 1973

The Watergate break-in at the DNC was a small story at first, confined to *the Washington Post and the New York Times.*

Then in October 1972, *Walter Cronkite* devoted an unprecedented 50 percent of the *CBS Evening News* to the break-in. After Cronkite, Watergate became a national topic, and all of the networks piled on.

On February 7, 1973, the Senate voted 77–0 to begin hearings on Watergate. In a landmark decision, the select committee decided to allow TV cameras into the proceedings.

The three major networks agreed to alternate coverage, with each network airing the hearings every third day. PBS announced that it would run the hearings every night, in their entirety:

> We think these hearings are important and because we think it is important that you get a chance to see the whole thing and make your own judgments . . . we are doing this as an experiment.[3]

Many PBS affiliates had not wanted PBS to produce news. Its controversial documentaries in the '60s had been disliked by many in Washington. But Watergate was simply too big an opportunity to pass up. It was important, it was cheap, and it was good for the brand.

Watergate gave PBS what it needed after Nixon cut its budget: over 250 hours of free programming, perfectly targeted at the "smart" demographic. PBS marketed the proceedings that way: "What you're going to be able to watch this evening is a rare glimpse given by real adventurers into the world of mystery and intrigue we normally hear about in spy novels," said reporter Robert MacNeil.[4]

Watergate criminal James McCord soon obliged, showing the audience how to tap a phone. The hearings became national theater, leading to one central question, from Vice Chairman Howard Baker: "What did the president know, and when did he know it?"

On June 25, 1973, White House lawyer John Dean appeared before the cameras to give America an answer.

Dean's reading of his 245-page statement was damning: "I began by telling the president that there was a cancer growing on the presidency—and if the cancer was not removed, the president himself would be killed by it. I also told him that it was important that this cancer be removed immediately because it was growing more deadly every day."

It was clear that John Dean appeared to save himself from prison. What wasn't clear was who to believe. It was John Dean's word against Nixon's, until July 16, 1973.

Impeachment

Fred Thompson would later be a world-famous actor, on TV hit *Law and Order*, and in movies including *Die Hard 2* and *The Hunt for Red October*. He would eventually be a senator, a lobbyist, and a presidential candidate.

But in 1973, he was the thirty-one-year-old Republican minority counsel. And on July 16, he questioned White House lawyer Alexander Butterfield.

> Thompson. Mr. Butterfield . . . are you aware of any listening devices in the office of the president . . . [and] were you aware of any devices installed in the executive office building office of the president?
>
> Butterfield. Yes sir.

Butterfield had hoped this question would not be asked. Like Dean, he was terrified that he would be sent to prison, for obstruction of justice or worse.

So Butterfield, one of the perhaps three people (other than the Secret Service) who knew, revealed that Nixon's conversations had been tape-recorded for the past two years.

The committee (and the country) now knew that Nixon's people had tapped phones, broken into offices, and committed potentially dozens of crimes. But they still did not know what Nixon himself knew about all of this. This is what recordings of his meetings could show.

The committee demanded that Nixon turn over the tapes. He refused, citing executive privilege: the tapes of the president contained matters of national security.

On July 31, top Nixon aide H. R. Haldeman testified:

President Nixon had no knowledge of, or involvement in either the Watergate affair itself or the subsequent efforts of a cover-up of the Watergate. It will be equally clear despite all the unfounded allegations to the contrary, that I had no such knowledge or involvement.

After Haldeman's testimony, PBS's Jim Lehrer opined:

Unless the tapes are made public or some other revelation should come, the senators as well as the rest of us who are following are going to have to eventually make a choice of believing John Dean or Bob Haldeman. That's the way it looks to me, at least at 3 or so in the morning. Feel free to disagree.

PBS eventually received over 70,000 letters commending the coverage. The network Nixon had tried to strangle was effectively helped to strangle him.

The Tapes

I think we may just be doing it to damn legalistically. . . . Now here's the point, Bob: please get me the names of the Jews, you know? The big Jewish contributors to the Democrats. . . . Could we please investigate some of the cocksuckers?
—NIXON TO AIDE BOB HALDEMAN

Nixon could have erased the tapes, but chose not to, and withheld them—causing what was widely viewed as a constitutional crisis. Eventually, Special Prosecutor Archibald Cox demanded the tapes. On October 20, 1973, Nixon fired him, infuriating Congress and the public at large.

In a press conference on November 17, 1973, with 400 Associated Press reporters, Nixon defended himself from accusations that he'd known about the break-in: "In all of my years of public life I have never obstructed justice," he said. "People have got to know whether or not their President is a crook. Well, I'm not a crook."

———

On February 6, 1974, the House gave its Judiciary Committee authority to pursue impeachment charges against Nixon. Both the House and Senate voted to allow television coverage of impeachment proceedings.

On July 24, 1974, in *United States v. Nixon*, the U.S. Supreme Court ordered Nixon to turn over sixty-four Watergate-related tapes and documents.

On July 27, 1974, the House Judiciary Committee recommended the first article of impeachment, *obstruction of justice*, followed shortly by *abuse of power* and *contempt of Congress*.

When Nixon finally released transcripts of the Watergate tapes, it was clear that he would not survive.

1974: Resignation

> *I gave them a sword. And they stuck it in. . . . I guess if I had*
> *been in their position, I'd have done the same thing.*
> —RICHARD NIXON

On August 8, 1974, in a televised speech, Richard Nixon resigned as president.

When he told his wife and daughters he was finished, they knew whom to blame: television. "It was too much, they said, after all the agony television had caused us."[5]

But Nixon knew otherwise. Television had saved him with the Checkers speech. It had allowed him to reach past his enemies in the press, to the silent majority that loved him. It had made him the foreign policy president par excellence, with his appearances in Moscow and Bejing.

Nixon stayed out of sight until 1977. Then he signed with British interviewer David Frost, for an exclusive series of interviews.

Once again, Nixon banked on television to resuscitate his reputation.

Later that year, President Gerald Ford granted Nixon a full and unconditional pardon.

CHAPTER 39

STANTON'S LAST STAND

For decades, Bill Paley had been the voice of CBS, while Frank Stanton had been the architect who ran it day to day. Stanton was involved in everything from the iconic CBS logo to the sign on the men's room. Paley spoke for CBS; Stanton protected Paley.

Stanton, one colleague would say, "was the total extension of Bill Paley's will."[1]

Murrow and Stanton had once competed for Paley's affection. The two grew to hate each other, which may have pleased Paley. Stanton had been deeply hurt when Murrow was invited to Paley's wedding and he was not. But when the chips were down, Stanton supported Murrow as best he could.

Then Murrow was gone, and Stanton's place was uncontested.

As his stature grew, Stanton received countless offers, and could have had the top job almost anywhere he chose. But the only job he wanted was to be CEO of CBS. So he stayed.

"What the hell does Frank want?" Paley asked. "He wants to be named CEO," he was told. "Why, for God's sake? He's the president. Everybody thinks he runs the place anyhow."[2]

By the early '70s, Stanton had worked for Paley for over thirty years, taking on progressively larger roles at CBS.

But Bill Paley could not let go. He would leave for months, but always returned, seizing the reins before heading off again. And Stanton became an old man playing a young man's waiting game.

The relationship degenerated until 1973, when Stanton reached CBS's mandatory retirement age of sixty-five. It had applied to everyone but Paley, who was now seventy-two.

Paley let Stanton know that he would be no exception. It was time for Stanton to go.

A consultant agreement was discussed; the process turned into a war. Stanton could have an office, but not on CBS property. Paley and Stanton argued about Stanton's support staff, his car, and the amount of space he could have. Once Stanton moved into his new office, he felt lost at sea. In David Halberstam's words,

> Stanton felt totally cut off from the company, which was precisely what Paley intended. When Stanton talked with old friends he could no longer control his anger about the Chairman. He felt used, badly used. It was beyond him to say a kind word about Paley.[3]

In 1977, an opportunity emerged: PBS had an opening for a new chairman. Stanton wanted the job, but told PBS he would have to check with Paley.

Paley sent word back through an attorney: if Stanton took it, he'd lose his CBS board seat, his consultancy, and all the perks. Stanton declined the PBS job.

Paley rescinded Stanton's board seat anyway.

If Stanton had stayed, perhaps what came next might have been averted.

———

What had started as a cigar factory had been grown beyond imagining. Paley's desire for the country club had taken him beyond the club, beyond the elite, to something beyond what even Sarnoff had predicted.

CBS was an architect of societal consensus. It shaped public opinion; it had helped end a war; it was helping to bring down a president.

CBS executives reflected their supremacy: they wore the right suits, knew the right people, went to the right restaurants, and stayed a cut above.

But programmer Fred Silverman did not. He was messy. He ate too much. He spoke too loudly. He dressed poorly. Over time, it became clear that Fred Silverman had gone as far as he could go at CBS.

So Fred Silverman took everything he'd learned to the network that needed him, the one that had always been number three. He went to ABC.

It would take CBS twenty-five years to recover.

CHAPTER 40

ABC AND SILVERMAN

F red Silverman was the son of a television repairman, the first TV exec who'd grown up on TV. He'd fallen in love with television early, and went to Syracuse University to study the medium. His 400-page master's thesis was a prescient analysis of ABC's 1950s programming.

In the document, Silverman proposed several theories. He said that weekly series built *audiences*, while TV specials yielded *ratings*. He also believed in the power of audience research, and in targeting a younger, urban audience. And he emphasized the importance of a network promoting its own programming.

Way ahead of its time, Silverman's thesis was a critical piece of work that would guide the rest of his career.

———

In 1958, Silverman got a job in the ABC mailroom. There he met Fred Pierce, then manager of ABC's television research. The two became friends, and Pierce recommended Silverman for a job at ABC.

Though Silverman didn't get that job, he got one at CBS, where he and Bob Wood reinvented the network. They dominated the '70s by scheduling *All in the Family, The Mary Tyler Moore Show, M*A*S*H, Sanford and Son, Maude, The Jeffersons, Rhoda,* and *The Bob Newhart Show*. Silverman and Wood made CBS the envy of the business.

But as many executives have learned before and since, Silverman's success didn't mean that CBS liked him.

They did not. Irwin Segelstein, CBS programming vice president, was unofficially Silverman's handler, keeping him way from the executive team. Paley and Stanton viewed Silverman as a technician—ironically, just what his father had been. Silverman was a guy who moved stuff around the schedule, not someone to be trusted with leading a network.

Silverman seethed. No matter how well he performed, he could not move up. Stanton and Paley kept him at a distance.

Then Silverman's ship came in. In 1974, Frederick Pierce was named president of ABC, and he remembered his old friend from the mailroom. He made Silverman an offer: president of ABC's entertainment division.

It was the job had always wanted, at the very network he had studied in college. It offered more of everything—money, power, and status—all things he would never get at CBS.

Silverman's first day at ABC was June 16, 1975. He was thirty-eight years old. When Wall Street got word of Silverman's jump, ABC's stock rose two points.

The market was right.

Silverman's ABC

ABC had been in the doghouse since the decline of the Westerns. In the fifteen years from 1960 to 1975, ABC had only eleven shows make it to the top ten. ABC, according to one joke, was the "Almost Broadcasting Company." Silverman had his work cut out for him.

From what he'd experienced at his time at CBS, Silverman suspected that the times were changing again. The '60s were over. Vietnam and Watergate were done. A big part of the audience just wanted to forget.

Silverman knew that much of CBS's success was based on its star power. So as Paley had three decades earlier, Silverman went on a talent raid of his own. He went after Jimmie Walker, the star of Norman Lear's *Good Times* on CBS, offering him a deal so rich that Walker no longer cared about *Good Times*. Then he did the same for Redd Foxx from NBC's *Sanford and Son*.

To complete the carnage, Silverman signed LaWanda Page, Harvey Korman, Rob Reiner, Rue McClanahan, Nancy Walker, Peter Strauss,

Cloris Leachman, and Cher. He also hired *Mary Tyler Moore*'s top writers, James L. Brooks, Dave Davis, Stan Daniels, and Ed Weinberger.

Silverman's predecessor, Martin Starger, liked highbrow series like *The Life and Times of William Shakespeare* and *Eleanor and Franklin*, a two-parter on the Roosevelts. Silverman would take things as far as possible in the opposite direction, as quickly he could.

But as Silverman began at ABC, it had not one top ten series. Silverman began by focusing on what he knew: comedy. "ABC had a few elements—*Happy Days, Welcome Back, Kotter, Barney Miller,* but it needed a comedy *structure*," he'd later say.[1] Silverman had the *Welcome Back, Kotter* producers add more comedic elements—but it was *Happy Days* that turned the tide.

Happy Days

Silverman inherited *Happy Days* from Michael Eisner. He went along with Eisner's request to make Fonzie a central part of *Happy Days*. Even though Silverman had persuaded him to stay on, Eisner decided his days at ABC were numbered. He lasted about a year at ABC under Silverman, but would have the last word when he bought ABC in 1996.

Garry Marshall suggested that the Fonz broke a new world record by jumping over fourteen garbage cans. Silverman did him one better: they would broadcast the stunt live. Marshall called it the turning point of the show: "Fred's promotion took a show that I thought was solid and turned it into a #1 show."[2]

The promotion worked, and *Happy Days* began to rise in the ratings. It became a top thirty show in 1975 and was number one in 1976.

As he had done at CBS, Silverman ordered creator Garry Marshall to create a *Happy Days* spinoff. Silverman suggested giving the Fonz his own show, but Marshall demurred, arguing it would take down the show.

Instead, Marshall suggested a show about two of Fonzie's female friends from an earlier episode. With no time for a pilot, Marshall filmed a ten-minute scene featuring Laverne DeFazio and Shirley Feeney. ABC immediately green lit the show.

In January 1976, Silverman used his old crossover technique: the Fonz himself introduced *Laverne and Shirley*. The show quickly rocketed to number one in its time period, and finished the season at number three in the ratings.

Silverman used the trick again: *The Six Million Dollar Man* spawned *The Bionic Woman.* It too went into the top ten.

By the end of the 1975–76 season, ABC was number one in the ratings. *Starsky and Hutch, Welcome Back, Kotter, Laverne and Shirley,* and *The Bionic Woman* joined *Happy Days* and *The Six Million Dollar Man* in the top ten.

In the wake of the success of PBS's *Masterpiece Theatre,* ABC jumped on the miniseries bandwagon. *Rich Man, Poor Man* aired in 1976 and was a hit, averaging 41 million viewers an episode. This gave Silverman the courage to spend $6 million on the biggest triumph of his ABC career.

Roots

In 1974, producer David Wolper approached ABC about doing a miniseries based on Alex Haley's book *Roots.* ABC gave Wolper $50,000 to write a few sample scripts.

When ABC executives Barry Diller and Martin Starger left ABC in 1975, VP Brandon Stoddard took control of the project. He asked Silverman for $6 million for the twelve-hour miniseries. Silverman wisely said yes.

ABC added TV stars including Ed Asner and Lorne Greene to play the villains. ABC promoted the series as a soap opera, afraid that a historical drama would keep viewers away.

Silverman had planned to air *Roots* weekly, similar to *Rich Man, Poor Man*; but as time went on he began to lose some faith. Instead of having *Roots* do poorly for two months, he would air it eight nights in a row, and risk only one week's ratings.

At ABC headquarters, execs were predicting a 30 share (30 percent of TVs that were turned on) for the series. Then they held their breath.

Roots blew through every conceivable record. It was watched by an estimated 130 million total viewers, more than any other program in history. Ninety million viewers watched the finale alone.

Roots won nine Emmys and earned a 66 share. Seven of its eight episodes landed in the top ten most watched programs of all time.

ABC won the 1976 season by almost three full ratings points.

In 1977, ABC placed seven shows in the top ten. It beat CBS decisively, 21.6 to 18.7. In a year when an average show garnered $60,000 per commercial, ABC now charged advertisers $200,000 for its top shows.

In 1977, *Time* magazine put Fred Silverman on its cover, calling him "the man with the golden gut." *Time* would summarize his run at ABC by writing,

> There is no parallel in the history of broadcasting—and few in any well-established industries—to ABC's sudden rise. It is as if, in the space of two years, Chrysler had surged past General Motors and sent Ford reeling back to Dearborn.[3]

At Black Rock, William Paley exploded with rage. Though he may not have known it, his era was ending.

Silverman became a television emperor. He touched every aspect of ABC's broadcast business: producers to talent, advertisers to sales, research to writing. His 1958 master's thesis had been a divining rod, and it seemed to be working across the board: "I still get a kick out of reading the recommendations. It really is the key to a whole scheduling philosophy. I don't care whether it is ABC, CBS, or NBC, those recommendations are as valid today as they were in 1959."[4]

Master of Promotion

One of Silverman's central theses had been the value of network promotion—networks using ad time to promote their own shows. If people didn't know the show was on, how would they know to watch it?

At CBS, Silverman's arguments had been ignored. At ABC, he made up for lost time, pioneering the concept of "block promotion." In this, ABC would run condensed ads for an entire night of programming. The ads ran for twenty to thirty seconds and often aired three times per thirty-minute show. Garry Marshall summarized Silverman's promotional philosophy, "When you've got something to promote, promote the hell out of it."[5] The quality of Roots gave Silverman the ability to increase production of "fast food TV." The leader of that trend was producer Aaron Spelling.

Aaron Spelling

Aaron Spelling grew up poor and Jewish in Dallas, the son of Russian and Polish immigrants. He began as an actor, with over twenty-five small film and television appearances. Scrawny and bug-eyed, Spelling experienced plenty of rejection. He appeared in episodes of *I Love Lucy* and *Dragnet*, but gave up on acting and resolved to become a writer instead.

His first producing mentor was Dick Powell, who hired Spelling as a writer on the anthology *Zane Grey Theatre*.

When ABC began looking for modern shows in the '60s, Spelling delivered a hit featuring three hip undercover detectives. *The Mod Squad* became a sensation and one of the primary drivers in convincing CBS to modernize its lineup as well.

Soon ABC was running a host of Spelling shows: *The Rookies*, *S.W.A.T.*, and *Starsky and Hutch*, as well as made-for-TV movies including *The Boy in the Plastic Bubble* with John Travolta.

Spelling began partnering with former ABC executive Leonard Goldberg in 1972. Two years later they came up with their biggest hit. They liked the idea of beautiful women on television: why not combine this with *The Mod Squad?* They put the two formats together, in a show called *The Alley Cats*, which they pitched to Diller and Eisner at ABC.

Michael Eisner said it was the worst idea that he had ever heard. Diller thought they were crazy. But Spelling and Goldberg already had a $25,000 pilot agreement in place, so Eisner agreed to pay for the pilot.

The Alley Cats was retitled *Charlie's Angels*. It debuted in the spring of 1976 and became a top ten hit with a 54 share. Farrah Fawcett became the biggest TV star in America, with posters in bedrooms across America. Critics derided the show as "T&A TV." Spelling never denied his brand, proudly calling it "fast-food entertainment."

By 1976, ABC and Spelling were leading in the ratings. Spelling hits *Love Boat*, *Fantasy Island*, *and Dynasty* dominated the second half of the '70s. After being inundated with television about Vietnam and Watergate, the country wanted escape—and Aaron Spelling was there to give it to them.

Love him or hate him, Aaron Spelling became the biggest producer in television, with seven hours of ABC programming a week—more than a third of its prime-time schedule. The industry began referring to ABC as "Aaron's Broadcasting Company."

Critics and watchdogs blamed Fred Silverman for dumbing down television, and called him the architect of "jiggle TV." The man who had scheduled *The Mary Tyler Moore Show* and *All in the Family*, they said, was now pandering to America's worst instincts.

Silverman and NBC

Silverman tried several times to increase his role at ABC. He had been disappointed by Pierce and Goldenson's decision not to promote him to head of ABC News.

Silverman's contract was up in June of 1978. He had some decisions to make.

During his last year at ABC, Silverman found backers for a new family entertainment network. This would allow Silverman to create and rule his own kingdom, something he had been fighting for since CBS.

But then Edgar Griffiths, the chairman of RCA, called. Did Silverman want to be president of NBC? The offer eventually reached over $1 million dollars per year.

If Silverman took the job, he would be the only executive in history to have had senior roles at all three networks. He would be the king. He took it.

ABC was stunned.

On the day the deal was announced, RCA's stock jumped $1.25 a share, and ABC's dropped $1.75. The market was pricing in the value of the man with the golden gut.

This time, the market was wrong. Silverman's tenure at NBC would be a disaster.

CHAPTER 41

JOHNNY CARSON AND *THE TONIGHT SHOW*

*Talent alone won't make you a success. Neither will being in the right place
at the right time, unless you are ready. The question is, "Are you ready?"*

—JOHNNY CARSON

I n the *Foundation* trilogy, science fiction author Isaac Asimov offered
a world in which the future is predictable. The science that makes it
predictable is called psychohistory, in which math and social science
are combined to successfully predict the future of large populations.

What psychohistory could not predict was the effect of one massive
outlier, one individual with abilities so unique that they could change
the course of history. A civilization guided by psychohistory was always
vulnerable to the outlier, the individual so rare that his occurrence is
beyond prediction.

Psychohistory would have been crushed by Johnny Carson.

Steve Allen and Jack Paar

In its earliest days, television was all about prime time; mornings and
late night were harder to make money from. The first non-prime-time
hit was a series of late-night movies called *The Knickerbocker Beer Show.*
Then Knickerbocker Beer decided to sponsor a variety show, with a host

named Steve Allen. The *Steve Allen Show* began on NBC New York in 1953, and was the coolest thing on TV.

The show began with Allen riffing at a piano, then segued to a mélange of sketch formats and guests. It became a phenomenon—the hippest room in New York, the place in which everyone wanted to be—at precisely the right time.

NBC president Pat Weaver had been working on new shows for new time slots. He created one for the morning, called *Today*. No one expected much from it.

Weaver also saw the potential of late night. It could bring in new advertising revenue and elevate the schedule, especially via the high-culture moments that Allen brought to the screen. Weaver took the program national, and renamed it to match his strategy, and the *Steve Allen Show* became *Tonight*.

Steve Allen opened *Tonight*'s first national broadcast with a joke that targeted the show's length, a grueling 1 hour and 45 minutes: "This show is gonna go on . . . forever." Over sixty years later, it appears that he was right.

Allen, however, did not last. He left *Tonight* after two years, to move to a variety show. *Tonight* was eventually resurrected as *The Tonight Show*, with the volatile Jack Parr.

Allen may have defined the late-night format, but Parr turned it into a high-wire act. On some nights, he would insult guests; on others, he would burst into tears. More than anything else on TV, people *had* to watch *The Tonight Show*—so they didn't miss the bizarre thing that Parr might do next. Within a few years, his *Tonight Show* had 8 million nightly viewers, beloved by audiences, advertisers, and affiliates alike.

Parr was electric, eccentric, and unique; a few times, he even walked off his own show. After a joke was censored, he left for three weeks, demanded an apology from NBC, and refused to return till they gave him one.

Eventually, 105 minutes a night wore Parr down. In 1962, amid tumult and fanfare, he announced he was leaving the show.

NBC scrambled to find a replacement. Jackie Gleason, Groucho Marx, Bob Newhart, and Joey Bishop all turned the network down. NBC even asked the star of an ABC game show. He refused as well.

But NBC came back to him with a second offer. And this time, Johnny Carson agreed.

On October 1, 1962, Groucho Marx introduced Johnny Carson to America, as the new host of *The Tonight Show*. Critical opinion was that Carson could never fill Jack Paar's shoes.

What they didn't know was that Carson's entire life had been pointing in this direction.

Johnny

> *I was so naive as a kid I used to sneak behind the barn and do nothing.*
>
> —JOHNNY CARSON

John William Carson was born in 1925 and grew up in Norfolk, Nebraska. A shy boy, he was captivated by Jack Benny's radio show, and he would memorize and recite it to the other kids at school. His mother, Ruth, was the seminal figure in his life—but not for the good. She was raucously funny, but cold and withholding, at least to her son. For the rest of his life, Carson hungered for Ruth's approval, which he never received.

At age twelve, Johnny became fascinated by magic, and ordered a magic kit that he practiced with for hours at a stretch. Soon he was performing at the local Rotary Club, where he received the approbation that he never got at home. Immediately after high school, he hitchhiked to Hollywood, then joined the Navy in 1943.

It was on the USS *Pennsylvania* that Carson would see his future, when he was sent to deliver a message to U.S. Secretary of the Navy James V. Forrestal. When Forrestal asked Carson what he wanted to do after the service, Johnny said he wanted to be a magician. Forrestal gave him a deck of cards and told him to do his stuff. Carson found himself making the head of the Navy laugh until dawn.

Inspired, Johnny learned ventriloquism and purchased a dummy, which he used to perform shows in front of the troops. He studied his audiences, practiced nonstop, and grew into a confident performer. Offstage, he was edgy and depressive; onstage, he was likeable, witty, and poised.

Johnny returned home and enrolled at the University of Nebraska in Lincoln. He continued to hone his act, as an emcee at large college events. He was getting better, pushing the limits, learning how to seduce the audience. When an orchestra leader name Johnny Cox was late to the show, Carson pointed to the waiting orchestra: "I'm afraid we have a problem—it looks like we've got ten men, and no Cox."[1]

It was Carson's college thesis that cemented his future: on radio comedy, it was titled "How to Write Comedy Jokes." Carson spent months preparing a tape of moments from leading performers, including Jack Benny, Bob Hope, and Milton Berle. He dissected and analyzed each segment in voiceover. Unlike casual observers, who assumed that stars performed off the cuff, Carson understood that the *writing* was central to success on radio.

Carson unpacked them all, learned their tricks, and made them his own. And he began working in radio.

Half of Johnny's success was due to timing. He had been young enough to miss combat in World War II, old enough to return home in time for a revolution.

But the other half was due to was a hard work and intuition. Johnny had used magic to learn to master audiences. He'd learned ventriloquism to play two parts at one time. He'd studied radio to reverse engineer the best comedians in the world. In short, he'd developed a unique set of skills at the perfect time. Now, he was in Omaha looking for work in the summer of 1949.

And that summer, WOW-TV of Omaha launched one of the first television stations in America.

Inventing Johnny Carson

As word of television began to spread, WOW-TV started airing test patterns. These were watched by the fifteen hundred residents with TVs, and by others who gathered to view them at the Greyhound bus station.

WOW-TV went on the air on August 29, 1949. Johnny Carson was there. He dived into TV at its literal beginning, and did not stop for forty-three years.

All of this might have meant nothing had Carson not been extraordinarily prescient. While every broadcaster on television was aping what worked on radio, he saw something else: "My experiences on radio didn't help me in TV at all," he said later. "I learned a lot though, from doing my magic and ventriloquism acts."[2]

Carson, more fully than anyone in the twentieth century, saw immediately what TV performance was: it was about creating an *illusion*. And the illusion was layered.

It was the illusion of pretending that the studio was a living room. It was the illusion that hosting a show was *easy*, rather than the massive stress that it was. Most importantly, it was the illusion of being someone else: someone likeable, someone good.

Like a machine built for one specific task, Carson tuned in on the qualities that worked best: being affable, witty, and smooth. In a tiny studio in Omaha, he became the person whom everyone wanted to watch. He became Johnny Carson. And he *worked*.

Carson's first TV show was *Squirrel's Nest*, a fifteen-minute talk show in which he tried everything he could think of. According to a colleague,

> Carson was there an hour or more ahead of time. He would check the news wires and look over everything, looking for something that he could use on his show. He did his show, then he had his regular shift. I'd often do the news at ten p.m., and John would be there still recording things and working out skits and stuff. I've seen him put in an hour or so working on a thirty-second gag.[3]

Carson brought friends onto the show. He had turtle races. He created satire around national and local news. In short, *Squirrel's Nest* was a testing ground for the future of late-night television, the place much of it was invented. Soon Carson became a star in the five states that could see him.

But to get where he wanted to be, Carson needed to get to New York or Los Angeles. His next break came from a childhood friend, with a job offer as an announcer. If he wanted it, he'd have to be in Los Angeles in a week. So Johnny Carson said goodbye to his wife, and drove to LA with a U-Haul.

In 1951, the coaxial cable that connected LA to New York had not been completed. Cut off from the source, Los Angeles had to come up with hours of its own TV programming, creating a need for local shows that came and went with the wind.

Once again, Carson was in the exactly right place. He took any job he could get, moving through a series of shows, in work, then out of work, then working again.

His breakthrough came in October of 1952, with a show called *Carson's Cellar*. It began,

> The program you are about to see is true; only the jokes have been changed to protect the station. . . . KNXT, in cooperation with the itinerant yam pickers of southern California, cautiously presents . . . Carson's Cellar!

The show capitalized on everything Carson had mastered: the satires of radio, television, and commercials ("a limited time only: a beautiful illustrated book titled *How to Perform Operations at Home!*"), impersonations, and topical humor. It was a tour de force, but not what advertisers wanted. So *Carson's Cellar* was canceled.

But Carson was becoming known. One person who saw him was young James Aubrey of CBS. Aubrey told sales to put Carson with a coffee sponsor, and gave him a five-minute joke segment at 9 am. The segment was canceled, too.

Next, Carson was given a sponsored program called *The Johnny Carson Show*. Unfortunately, it never found its voice, and went through eight writers and seven directors before being canceled. It was a bitter experience for Carson, who recalled, "I found myself and my material subject to the opinions of businessmen."[4] He vowed that would never happen again.

It was the low point of his life: Carson was a three-time loser, with no income, three kids, and a failing marriage.

Things picked up some when Carson guest hosted for comedian Red Skelton in 1954, got a new manager, and fired his agent. Then he moved to New York in 1954, to host a game show called *Who Do You Trust*, a talk show–like format in the wake of the quiz show scandals. With a strong writing bench, it gave Carson a chance to shine, to grow his reputation after the failures in Los Angeles. Most importantly, it gave him years of interview experience, perhaps the only major skill he lacked.

As Carson's reputation grew, he appeared around town, at institutions like the Friars Club.

In 1958, he guest hosted for an institution, filling in for Jack Paar on *The Tonight Show.*

In 1962, Jack Paar announced his retirement. His last show was a legendary send-off, featuring Robert Kennedy, Richard Nixon, Jack Benny, and Bob Hope.

No one dared to fill Paar's shoes. No one but Carson, who'd been in training for twenty-five years.

Carson's Tonight Show

Carson came onto *The Tonight Show* with the national spotlight bearing down on him. His monologues were stellar from the beginning. But he faced the same massive challenge that Paar had: 105 minutes of air time per night, a total of nine hours of time to fill per week—*live.*

One indispensable asset was his sidekick, Ed McMahon. McMahon had been with Carson since the beginning of *Who Do You Trust.* They had been (hard-) drinking buddies throughout the New York years, and would be through the collapse of Carson's first marriage, which would end in 1963. On *The Tonight Show,* the two became archetypal male pals of their generation—as Laurel and Hardy, and Hope and Crosby had been in film before them. Their banter would be the glue that tied the show together for the next thirty years.

In the first few months, Carson was tense, a fundamental loner forced to banter for nine hours a week. There were "unseen cords of inhibition in Johnny," said competing talk show host Dick Cavett.[5]

But in working long hours, as he always had, Carson made an intuitive leap that put him ahead. And that was to be *cool.* Like the jazz he loved, like the way he drummed, Johnny learned to be *cool,* not hot. He would not be drawn out, would never fully reveal himself, would always step back slightly from the camera. If the audience wanted him, it had to meet him halfway.

This both saved him from exhaustion and made his career. Because soon there would be an endless parade of challengers, all of whom would overheat and burn out. By refining the illusion of "Johnny Carson" to "cool," Carson distinguished himself from Paar, Allen, and the next dozen challengers.

It made him the perfect creature for television.

Over time, Carson developed another set of tricks, the characters he inhabited on and off for the next three decades, including Art Fern, Aunt Blabby, Carnac the Magnificent, El Mouldo, evil Mr. Rogers, and Floyd R. Turbo: American. These alter egos allowed Carson to do the "uncool" things: to be liberal, to be critical, to be mean.

Carson managed the grueling schedule by developing daily routines: he read a large group of newspapers and magazines early in the day, looking for the day's punch lines. He dispatched his ideas to his producer, who conveyed Johnny's requests to the writers' room. When the jokes came back in late afternoon and early evenings, Carson selected, edited, and rearranged—then locked down his monologue.

Carson avoided his guests and kept to himself; all that mattered was what happened before the camera. Guests expecting to get to know Johnny were always disappointed. People who appeared for decades never really got a handle on him.

Competitor and sometimes guest Dick Cavett opined, "I felt sorry for Johnny in that he was so socially uncomfortable."[6] Maybe so, but no one had as much pressure, either. Unlike Jack Paar, Carson rarely trotted out his personal life; no one saw behind the curtain.

The man who knew him best put it best: "Johnny packs a tight suitcase," said Ed McMahon.[7]

And it worked. By 1965, the *Daily News* called Carson "the most familiar face in America." He was the last thing people saw before they fell asleep, and the person they discussed over breakfast. He became the master curator of American culture, introducing two generations of new performers and themes. If it mattered in America, it showed up on *The Tonight Show*.

We'll never know as much as we should about those years, because NBC bulk-erased the first ten years of *The Tonight Show* in 1972, so that they could reuse the tape. Those years included appearances with Carson by John Lennon and Paul McCartney, Martin Luther King, Jr., Richard Nixon, Robert Kennedy, and many others. It was a tragic error by a confused network that had no idea what it had in *The Tonight Show.*

But Carson did—and he moved to grow it into a dynasty. In 1972, Johnny Carson said goodbye to New York forever, and moved *The Tonight Show* to Los Angeles.

Los Angeles

> *New York is an exciting town where something is*
> *happening all the time—most unsolved.*
> —JOHNNY CARSON

At the beginning of the 1970s, Carson was nearing the peak of his power. He knew it.

At age forty-five, no one could touch him, except on the streets of New York. "I'll never move to California," Johnny had said. "Those people are weak. They have no books to read. It's awful."[8]

But in 1972, Carson decided to move to Los Angeles.

There were several reasons for the move. The guest pool was the reason Johnny gave: in LA, he could draw on all of Hollywood, rather than scraping by on who was around in New York. Since he had taken over *The Tonight Show* and as live TV decreased, more shows migrated to Hollywood, to take advantage of the growth of production studios. Carson's move was the watershed moment: once he left New York, the rest of television followed suit.

But ultimately it was a lifestyle decision: in LA, Johnny could live on his own terms. And in 1970, Carson's second wife filed for divorce. One chapter was ending, another beginning.

Los Angeles brought Carson a much wider pool of guests, as the entire industry vied to get booked. Carson moved from an industry fixture to a godfather, the undisputed kingmaker of popular entertainment. His support of his guests was genuine: he wanted them to look *good.*

For comedians, making Johnny laugh became a career-making event. Jerry Seinfeld would say it best: before you were on Carson, you *wanted* to be a comedian. After you appeared with him, you *were* one.

Carson continued his strict routine: newspapers, show postmortem, joke topics in the morning; monologue review, prep, and rehearsal in afternoon. During a writers' strike in 1972, he wrote the entire show for weeks. He never took success for granted, never stopped worrying that he might lose the crowd. Because of this, he never did.

Carson's monologue became the tealeaves of the most powerful nation on Earth. When he skewered preacher Oral Roberts, Roberts became a laughingstock. When he began joking about Watergate, Nixon was doomed. When Carson joked about a national toilet paper shortage, Americans bought so much toilet paper that stores had to ration it for weeks. When major events would break, people would wonder what Carson would say that night. Critic Tom Shales called him the "electronic Mark Twain."

Critics began calling him the Walter Cronkite of entertainment. And this was true, for reasons beyond what they intended. Like Cronkite, Carson had the trust of tens of millions. Like Cronkite, he was a survivor, a king in a field where no one lasts. After Cronkite, broadcast news declined. After Carson, late night would do the same.

In an age of disposable celebrities, Carson was broadcast to American homes thousands of times, eventually spanning seven American presidents. He tipped the scales for and against politicians, influenced tens of millions on abortion and birth control, was the last voice people heard at night and the one that inhabited their dreams.

Carson faced challenger after challenger for three decades: Dick Cavett, David Frost, Geraldo Rivera, Alan Thicke, Jerry Lewis, Joan Rivers, David Brenner, and others. All were canceled. The standing ovation that began every show was now the nightly re-coronation of a king.

On Carson's tenth-anniversary show, his childhood hero appeared with a question. Jack Benny asked Carson, "Remember [when] you were the toastmaster at a testimonial dinner to me?" Carson nodded. "At this dinner I said that for many years I've been Johnny Carson's idol." Carson nodded again.

"And all of a sudden the whole thing switched," said Benny. "And you want to know something? It's not as much fun this way."

———

Everyone adored him, except the one person whose approval he craved. When Ruth Carson was interviewed by *Time* magazine, she and a reporter watched her son's monologue on TV. As always, she was unimpressed: "That's not funny," she said. Then she left the room.

When Ruth Carson died, she had left a box in her closet, packed with newspaper clippings of her son, from the very beginning. Johnny Carson took the box. It was in his bedroom for the rest of his life.

By now, her boy was the Great American Sphinx, one of the only sources of constancy in a decade of tumult.

———

In May 1976, Carson went home to give the commencement address at his high school. "You don't know how terribly proud I am to be here today," he said, then tellingly. "I've found that there is more unhappiness than happiness in life. . . . I always have doubts and concerns, with ups and downs. Then I have to sit down and examine myself. . . . If I had it to do over I'd stumble along as I did."

He was being modest. His personal life may have been difficult, but professionally, he had rarely stumbled.

By 1974, Carson had logged 3,500 hours on the air—five months of consecutive shows. He had been watched by viewers for 22 billion hours.

Carson vs. Silverman

Executive Fred Silverman had gone from CBS to ABC in 1975, then to NBC's top job in 1978.

NBC's profit had dropped $16 million (around 15 percent) in the previous year. Silverman's new fall schedule made the losses much worse; he put an unprecedented slate of forty new shows on the air, almost all of which were canceled.

Silverman pushed Carson to book more actors from his shows, the terrible flops he needed to promote. Carson refused.

Silverman suggested a new show after *The Tonight Show*, starring Steve Allen. It would be the first and current hosts of *The Tonight Show*, back to back.

Johnny thought it was ridiculous. There were better people to go on after Johnny—for example, said Johnny, a young comic named David Letterman.

Though Carson generated an incredible 17 percent of NBC's revenue, Silverman began haranguing him for sloth. He told the press Carson was taking too much time off. It was hurting the show. To *Newsweek* he said, "I don't think he must enjoy reading that [*The Tonight Show*] is slipping."

Silverman was playing with fire, and Carson took him on. In one monologue, he noted that "NBC now stands for 'nine bombs canceled.'"

Then Carson told his lawyer Henry Bushkin: "I've had enough. Their schedule is a wasteland, I have to maintain ratings without having a single worthwhile lead-in, and I have no confidence that the genius Fred Silverman will be able to yank his nuts out of the fire."[9]

When he got word, rather than placate his biggest star, Silverman threatened to sue Carson for $100 million.

So Carson told the world that he was done with NBC.

―――

The story was immediate front-page news. On *NBC News*, David Brinkley noted, "Johnny Carson wanting to get off the Tonight Show is roughly equal to George Washington wanting to get off of the one dollar bill." The battle between Carson and Silverman became a national story, but behind the animosity there was another force at work.

And that was the job itself. The work had gotten easier, but it was never easy. Carson made it look effortless, but appearing effortless was hard work. He had more money than he could spend. His third marriage was failing. Maybe it was enough.

When Silverman said Carson was under contract until 1981, Carson called his bluff. They would let the courts decide.

The decision hung on one principle of California law. Decades earlier, actors had sued studios to escape the rapacious deals that studios demanded that made them indentured servants. Eventually the State of California agreed, and—in a suit brought by actress Olivia de Havilland—had limited employment contracts to a maximum of seven years.

Carson had worked for NBC since 1962—seventeen years. He said he was free to go wherever he pleased.

No, countered Silverman. Johnny had re-signed three times since 1972—and each of those deals reset the clock. Johnny owed NBC another two years.

Both parties agreed to go to private litigation, to avoid a saga in newspapers around the world. Fred Silverman held his breath. Carson's team weighed its options.

The judge delivered his verdict: Carson had been under contract for seventeen years, ten years longer than the threshold.

Carson was free to go wherever he chose.

Carson received an offer from ABC—then offered NBC the ability to counter. If NBC wanted him to stay, he had demands:

- *The Tonight Show* would go from ninety to sixty minutes.
- Johnny would work three nights a week, thirty-seven weeks a year, with guest hosts on Monday and reruns on Tuesday.
- NBC would surrender full ownership of *The Tonight Show* to Carson Productions, including full rights to every existing recording.
- After *The Tonight Show*, NBC would air *Late Night with David Letterman*, to be produced and owned by Carson Productions.
- Johnny Carson would receive $25 million a year, making him the most highly compensated artist in history.

NBC agreed to every one of Carson's demands.

Fred Silverman left NBC in 1981. He never had a job in network television again.

Finale

In the 1980s, Johnny Carson hosted the Academy Awards five times. He is generally considered the best host in its history.

In 1983, he named Joan Rivers the permanent guest host of *The Tonight Show*. She had appeared on the show since 1963, and said she owed her career to his support. In 1986, the Fox Broadcasting Company was attempting to build a fourth network. Looking to make a dent in late night, it hired Rivers, who did not tell Carson until the day it was announced.

By the time she called him, he'd already heard. He hung up on Rivers and never spoke with her again.

In 1987, though he'd sworn he never would, Carson got married for the fourth time.

In the early 1990s, Johnny was awarded the Presidential Medal of Freedom, a Kennedy Center Honor, and a Peabody Award. The Peabodys noted that Carson was "an American institution, a household word, and the most widely quoted American."

In 1991, Carson's son Rick was killed in a car accident. In a sober and moving segment, Carson closed the show with his son's photographs. Near tears, Carson ran over the time limit—as from the wings his producer, Freddie De Cordova, signaled aggressively for Carson to "wrap it up."

Carson fired De Cordova and banished him from the set. They had been together for twenty years. They never spoke again.

———

On May 22, 1992, Johnny Carson gave his final *Tonight Show*. More than 50 million people tuned in. In tribute to Johnny, multiple networks went dark for the entire hour of this last show.

Carson closed,

> I am one of the lucky people in the world; I found something I always wanted to do and I have enjoyed every single minute of it. . . . And I hope when I find something that I want to do [again], that you'll be as gracious in inviting me into your home as you have been.

Then he disappeared.

When Freddie De Cordova died, his widow asked Carson to attend the memorial service. According to his friend Gore Vidal, Carson considered it, then told her he could not:

> I can't do it because everyone thinks I'm still Johnny Carson but I'm not anymore. I wouldn't even know how to fake it.[10]

Instead, he sent her a large check, as he had done for many people. She was grateful. Vidal went on to wonder, "How odd it must be not to be the self you have spent a lifetime perfecting."[11]

———

On May 13, 1994, David Letterman announced one of his trademark Top Ten lists. It was delivered by a surprise walk-on, Letterman's mentor and boss.

As Carson walked out and sat behind Letterman's desk, the audience exploded into a standing ovation that lasted for minutes—so long there was simply nothing left to say. Genuinely moved, Carson sat in the chair, gave Letterman the list, then left without saying a word. He never appeared in public again.

———

In 2005, Johnny Carson died.

Immediately, his legacy seemed even more immense than it had before his death, and in many ways, larger than that of anyone else in show business.

In thirty years, he had logged over 5,000 shows, 23,000 guests, and more billions of views than anyone in history. To say he'd changed TV, or America, was too obvious.

In comedy in particular, his contribution was hard to believe.

Most curators are happy to discover one star. Carson discovered— by their own report—Woody Allen, Louis Anderson, Roseanne Barr, David Brenner, George Carlin, Drew Carey, Jim Carrey, Bill Cosby, Ellen

DeGeneres, Andy Kaufman, Jay Leno, David Letterman, Bill Maher, Steve Martin, Richard Pryor, Joan Rivers, Ray Romano, Jerry Seinfeld, Garry Shandling, and Steven Wright.

———

After Carson's death, the Carson Foundation gave $156 million to a variety of charities, including the Children's Hospital of Los Angeles and Planned Parenthood. It became the largest charitable fund in the history of show business.

His heirs discovered that Carson had been writing checks to people in need that he read about in the papers, for years. He had just never talked about it.

———

The month of his death, his heir, David Letterman, performed a monologue, every joke of which had come from Carson. It turned out Johnny had been faxing them in since his retirement. Carson would watch Dave to see which jokes worked and which didn't. He wanted to see if he still had it. He did.

———

The reason we're all doing Johnny's "Tonight" is because you think, "Well, if I do Johnny's Tonight Show, maybe I'll be a little like Johnny, and people will like me more." But it sadly doesn't work that way.

It's just—if you're not Johnny, you're wasting your time.
—David Letterman

Since Carson's death, the number of late-night hosts has proliferated, each garnering perhaps 15 percent of Carson's ratings. With minor exceptions, they live in the illusion he created: desk, monologue, sidekick, and interviews, frozen in amber to this day. Once he was gone, late night splintered into a dozen fragments, well-intentioned knock-offs of a thing they could not touch.

The lonely boy from Nebraska was seen by more people on more occasions than anyone in human history.

The real trick, for all those years, had been simple misdirection, a set-up to distract the audience and the host from the truth.

The Tonight Show was simply a talk show. Johnny Carson had been magic.

CHAPTER 42

Monty Python, SNL, and SCTV

I n the 1970s, Carson was king, but the children of television were starting to grow restless. The Baby Boomers were coming of age, and the World War II generation would never speak for them.

And outside of America, *The Tonight Show* did not exist. In three different nations, three very different shows began the shift away from the era of broadcast TV.

In the Big Three's final dominant decade, TV got the best ensemble comedies it has seen to this day.

Monty Python's Flying Circus

> *After the Beatles,* Monty Python *was my favorite thing.*
> —George Harrison

According to legend, Eric Idle of *Monty Python* once asked former Beatle George Harrison why he had been so extraordinarily generous to Monty Python. He had, after all, financed almost all of their movies. "Because," Harrison allegedly said, "whatever magic we had, left us and went into you."

Terry Jones, Michael Palin, John Cleese, Graham Chapman, Eric Idle, and Terry Gilliam met in college at Cambridge and Oxford, and worked in almost a dozen British shows in various combinations in the late 1960s. They were offered individual shows from multiple networks, but decided to join forces and create a show they could control. They considered names for the show including "Owl Stretching Time" and "Vaseline Review" before settling on a name the BBC hated—and *Monty Python's Flying Circus* was born.

Monty Python's power came from its chemistry. Palin and Jones wrote as a pair, as did Cleese and Chapman. Palin and Jones's work tended to be the longer parodies, often based on one central, absurd premise—such as "The Spanish Inquisition" or the "Summarize Proust" game show. Palin was usually the straight man, while Jones was the most frequent Python in drag.

Jones was also the unofficial leader of the troupe, of whom biographer George Perry said that on "subjects as diverse as fossil fuels . . . mercenaries in the Middle Ages or Modern China . . . [if you talk to Jones] you will find yourself hopelessly out of your depth, floored by his knowledge."[1]

Cleese and Chapman worked differently, with largely different roles. Cleese would often create a first draft and then bounce it around with Chapman. One of these involved an incident Cleese had with a car salesman who had "an excuse for everything." Cleese took Chapman through a draft that featured rounds and rounds of denial from the car salesman, who took no responsibility for the lemon he had sold.

Chapman thought about it, then gave Cleese one note. "Make it a parrot."

The "Dead Parrot" sketch was born:

Mr. Praline. I wish to complain about this parrot, what I purchased not half an hour ago from this very boutique.

Owner. . . . What's wrong with it?

Mr. Praline. I'll tell you what's wrong with it, my lad. He's dead, that's what's wrong with it!

Owner. No, no, he's resting.

Gilliam, the sole American Python, was responsible for all of its signature animations. Idle contributed the musical segments, as well as Python's many smarmy characters, including the Nudge Nudge man, and Awards show host Dickie Attenborough:

> Ladies and gentlemen, seldom can it have been a greater pleasure and privilege than it is for me now to announce that the next award gave me the great pleasure and privilege of asking a man without whose ceaseless energy and tireless skill the British Film Industry would be today. I refer of course to my friend and colleague, Mr. David Niven. Sadly, David Niven cannot be with us tonight, but he has sent his fridge.

> This is the fridge in which David keeps most of his milk, butter and eggs. What a typically selfless gesture, that he should send this fridge, of all his fridges, to be with us tonight.[2]

Then the six would come together and review everything as a team.

———

The alchemy of the Python Six would be a constant source of breakthrough and reinvention, initially for the four-year run of the show, and eventually for decades. *Python* episodes were a new kind of comedy, combining surrealism, intellectual references, and risqué humor with inimitable style.

The Pythons smashed the conventions of television. They broke the fourth wall, with characters making comments directly to the audience. They ended sketches abruptly by dropping a sixteen-ton weight on the cast, or by crushing them with an enormous foot. Other segues were managed by violent, semi-blasphemous animations. One recurring walk-on summed up the proceedings: Cleese's serious announcer would randomly appear to say "And now: for something completely different."

But *everything* about *Python* was different. The show was a sensation on the BBC from 1969 to 1974, three seasons of fourteen episodes and a final season of six (without Cleese, of whom Idle would later say, "He's a difficult man, not easy to be friendly with. . . . He never wanted to be liked [which] gives him a certain fascinating, arrogant freedom").[3]

The U.S. rights to *Python* were owned by Time-Life Films, which decided the surreal show would never work in America. They felt the risk wasn't worth the cost of converting the show to the U.S. TV format (from the European TV standard PAL to American TV format NTSC).

Then in 1974, based on *Python*'s success in Europe, NBC decided to show *Python* clips in summer series *The Dean Martin Comedy World*. NBC's use of "Bicycle Repairman" and 'The Dull Life of a Stockbroker" paid for the series' conversion.

The manager of Dallas's PBS affiliate soon fell in love with *Monty Python's Flying Circus*. PBS affiliates in New York, Chicago, Miami, and D.C. followed suit—and *Python* spread into 113 PBS markets, beginning five years to the month from its BBC debut.

Python sketches became comedy anthems in America, including "Spam" (which led to the term "spam" for bad email), "Dead Parrot," "The Lumberjack Song," "The Parana Brothers," "Upper Class Twit of the Year" (an Olympic-style competition including "Kicking the Beggar" and "Shooting Yourself"), "Argument Clinic," "Nudge Nudge," "The Spanish Inquisition," "Cheese Shop," and "The Ministry of Silly Walks"—two years before *Saturday Night Live* began.

In 1975, ABC tried to get a piece of the action, and aired ninety-minute specials composed of three episodes each. But ABC censored the episodes heavily and cut them to shreds. Furious, and concerned that ABC would destroy the market for the real shows, Python sued ABC. In *Gilliam v. American Broadcasting Companies, Inc.*, Python won.

Eric Idle explained later, "We were always very insistent that we would not be on commercial networks. . . . We were always very keen that the show is shown in the way we wanted it to be shown. And that's the great thing about PBS."[4]

After the series, Python released a series of movies including *And Now for Something Completely Different, Monty Python and the Holy Grail, The Life of Brian,* and *The Meaning of Life*—all of which were met with massive acclaim.

———

> *It is absolutely impossible to get even a majority of*
> *us together in a room, and I'm not joking.*
> —JOHN CLEESE

Since then, the members of *Monty Python* have released and performed (in various combinations) in projects including the Secret Policeman's Balls, *A Fish Called Wanda, Time Bandits, Jabberwocky, Brazil, The Adventures of Baron Munchausen, Ripping Yarns, The Wind in the Willows, Fawlty Towers,* Beatles mockumentary *All You Need Is Cash* (financed and with a cameo by Harrison), and *Parrot Sketch Not Included—20 Years of Monty Python.*

The remaining cast members gathered in 2005 for the premiere of Idle's Broadway musical, *Spamalot.* It won three Tony Awards, and was nominated for fourteen. When asked about a reunion, Idle replied, "Just as soon as Graham Chapman comes back from the dead. . . . We're talking to his agent about terms."[5]

In 2002, four Pythons appeared together at George Harrison's memorial, where they performed "The Lumberjack Song" and "Sit on My Face." He would have been proud.

In 2012, every remaining Python but Idle appeared in a posthumous film based on Chapman's memoir, *A Liar's Autobiography.* In 2014, the five remaining Pythons performed for the first time in thirty-four years, in a lawsuit-driven London show called *Monty Python Live (mostly): One Down, Five to Go.* They continue to influence a new generation, including Sacha Baron Cohen, Seth MacFarlane, Matt Stone and Trey Parker of *South Park, The Simpsons'* writing staff, Elon Musk, the author of the programming language Python, and philosophers and shut-ins all over the world.

Saturday Night Live

> *We wanted to redefine comedy the way the Beatles*
> *redefined what being a pop star was.*
> —LORNE MICHAELS

"Okay, send the kids in," said the most powerful man in television. In came Dick Ebersol and Lorne Michaels, for the audience with Johnny Carson that would make or break their careers.

In 1974, Carson had given NBC orders: he didn't want *The Best of Carson* on the weekends anymore. He wanted to keep the reruns on weekdays, so he could take more time off. He gave NBC until the summer of 1975 to get his shows off of their weekend schedule.

The shepherds of the new show were light years from Carson. At age twenty-seven, Ebersol was NBC's director of Weekend Late Night Programming; producer Lorne Michaels was twenty-nine. That didn't bother Carson, but he wanted to get some things straight.

"So you guys are only going to be on one night a week, huh?" asked Carson.[6] Correct. Would there be talk-show segments? No. Would there be guests? Well, guest hosts—and some musical guests. Carson considered this, then laid out one rule: no guests within two to four weeks of their appearance on *The Tonight Show*. Ebersol and Michaels agreed. Carson gave NBC his OK.

Later on, seeing what he had wrought, Carson would tell critic Tom Shales that *Saturday Night Live* had "some very clever things . . . some very bright young people" but that the cast couldn't "ad-lib a fart at a bean-eating contest."[7]

The feeling was mutual. When Carson announced that he would do some episodes live, *SNL*'s "Weekend Update" reported on the welcome change, since Johnny had been "doing the show dead for the past fifteen years."[8]

———

I have great affection for old-time show business. But it had become corrupt. . . . [SNL] was trying to get away from that.
—LORNE MICHAELS

Ebersol had been hired away from ABC, and had resigned the same day that Nixon had. He had spoken with comedians including Richard Pryor, Lily Tomlin, and George Carlin, but nothing materialized, and the clock was ticking.

Then Ebersol met Lorne Michaels, a Canadian who had worked on *Rowan & Martin's Laugh-In* and was fully wired into the underground comedy scene. Michaels's effortless air and expertise in assessing talent made him a perfect choice. Michaels pitched a vision of what this new show could be, a combination of *Monty Python* and *60 Minutes*:

> The year 1975 was a hinge moment in America. The president of the United States had recently resigned in disgrace, and politics was deeply unsettled. The Vietnam War had ended with the last helicopter taking off from the roof of the American Embassy in Saigon. New York City was flat broke. It was a moment of chaos, doubt, and, of course, opportunity. The perfect time to start a new comedy show.

NBC president Herb Schlosser gave them two critical directives. First, everything had been moving to Los Angeles for years. NBC's headquarters, 30 Rockefeller Plaza, was becoming a production ghost town. Schlosser wanted Michaels and Ebersol to do the new show in New York, in ancient Studio 8H. And in another throwback, he wanted the show to be *live*.

Schlosser's selected location would turn out to be prophetic. *SNL* marked a return to the beginning of television, the beginning of NBC, and the genre that had started it all: the variety show. But this show would be a new version of the format, with a very different spirit.

Michaels saw the show as a pivotal event, one that would bring the language of a new generation to television.

It would feature a company of young comedians, with a staff of young, hip writers. As for Carson's concern about an overlap, that simply would not happen. Anything that felt like old-time show biz would be banished from the premises. Michaels and Ebersol fought off a phalanx of old-school host suggestions, including impressionist Rich Little, quarterback Joe Namath, and singer Connie Stevens, who they thought would be the kiss of death for the statement the show intended to make.

NBC soon learned whom they were dealing with. Michaels reviewed Studio 8H, and said it needed $300,000 in renovations. As the studio was updated, he recruited performers from untapped gold mines like Chicago's Second City comedy troupe and the National Lampoon. Until then, breakthrough comedy was limited to the coolest (and tiniest) audiences. By bringing their underground sensibility to television, Michaels would change it forever.

———

It was our turn. The 1970s, I realize now, were a time when things were both coming undone and being put back together in a different way.
—LORNE MICHAELS

As the premiere date approached, ABC launched its own variety show, starring the very old-school Howard Cosell. Cosell's young co-stars were billed as the Primetime Players—so *Saturday Night* made theirs the "Not Ready for Prime Time Players": Dan Aykroyd, John Belushi, Chevy Chase, Jane Curtin, Garrett Morris, Laraine Newman, and Gilda Radner. All were unknowns.

On October 11, 1975, *Saturday Night* began with the first of hundreds of "cold opens," a beginning of a show with no explanation, credits, or music. *SNL* writer Michael O'Donoghue played an English teacher; John Belushi played an immigrant who speaks no English. O'Donoghue maliciously taught him nonsense phrases, such as "I would like to feed your fingertips to the wolverines."

Belushi's immigrant copied him slavishly—including when O'Donoghue keels over, dead. Belushi fell to the floor, copying him, and Chevy Chase emerged, saying, "Live from New York: it's Saturday Night!"

The Not Ready for Primetime Players quickly became the rock stars of comedy. Frequent host Tom Hanks said that it was "the cultural phenomenon of the age." Soon NBC censors had to give the show more leeway because of its enormous popularity and the fact that it was aired live. Like nothing on television since the days of Jack Parr, *SNL* was dangerous.

As the first host of "Weekend Update," Chevy Chase looked for a version of newscaster Roger Grimsby's nightly opening, "I'm Roger Grimsby; here now, the news." He came up his own iconic turn: "I'm Chevy Chase, and you're not."

"Weekend Update" cemented *SNL*'s place in American culture. Chase rocketed to fame, quickly appearing on the cover of *New York* magazine. He became a national celebrity and the cast's most famous member.

At first, the show was a pastiche of whatever the team had cobbled together, with a monologue for a guest host in front, and a film by Albert Brooks. Frequent host Buck Henry saw a better way, however: he had liked a skit called "Samurai Hotel," featuring Belushi's absurd depiction of a hotel run by a Japanese warrior.

"Do you want to do the Samurai again?" Henry asked Lorne Michaels. It was a pivotal moment in *SNL*'s evolution, beginning the move from free-standing pieces to the most popular comedy properties in the world. "Samurai Hotel" would be followed by a string of Belushi classics including "Samurai Delicatessen," "Samurai Hitman," "Samurai Stockbroker," and "Samurai Optometrist." Michaels would give the credit to Buck Henry.

In addition to innovations "Weekend Update" and the format itself, the original cast created iconic bits including Baba Wawa, Bad Conceptual Theater, Bass-o-Matic, the Blues Brothers, Cheeseburger Cheeseburger, The Coneheads, Emily Litella, Ernest J. Mainway, The Festrunk Brothers, Fred Garvin Male Prostitute, Killer Bees, Land Shark, the Mr. Bill Show, News for the Hard of Hearing, Nick the Lounge Singer, Roseanne Roseannadanna, and Todd and Lisa.

SNL became the favorite show of a generation. It hit its first speed bump at the end of Season One, when Chevy Chase announced he was leaving. Though it was traumatic at the time, Michaels would later say it had helped the show, by forcing *SNL* to make its way as a true ensemble comedy.

Chase was replaced by one of Michaels's early picks, and Bill Murray became a star.

The first cast and writing staff of *SNL* were its most fearless, inventing the format and pushing the limits. Of the original and most famous cast, Bill Murray would later say,

> We'd learned working together as a group in a service way. Nowadays there's probably more stand-ups that end up on the show, sort of more individual guys. . . . They're individually good but they maybe don't have that particular skill.[9]

By its third season, *SNL* was a staple of popular culture, garnering a 12.6 rating and a 39 share, and beating *The Tonight Show*.

———

With *SNL*'s amazing success, newly installed NBC president Fred Silverman saw an opportunity, to use its stars as he had Norman Lear's on CBS: as a way to spin off new shows. Silverman offered Gilda Radner her own show, but eventually she declined, beginning a rift between Silverman and Michaels that got worse over time.

The relentless pressure and massive celebrity began to grind the original team down.

In 1979, Silverman fired Dick Ebersol. Lorne Michaels left *SNL* in 1980, along with those who remained from the original cast. Michaels's chosen successor was writer Al Franken—but Franken buried that by savaging Silverman on the air.

In a bit called "Limo for a Lame-O," Franken skewered the failing network head, urging viewers to write to NBC to tell them to transfer Silverman's limo to Franken. When they wrote in by the hundreds, Silverman was apoplectic. This ended Franken's chance to take over the show.

Franken recovered and later returned as a writer. Today, he is a U.S. senator.

Jean Doumanian, a producer and close friend of Woody Allen's, took over *SNL* once Lorne Michaels left. Her tenure was a legendary disaster. After ten months, when one of Doumanian's new cast said "fuck" on live TV, Silverman fired her. She was succeeded by a returning Dick Ebersol, who ran *SNL* for a time, until Lorne Michaels returned in 1985.

———

Michaels has presided over *SNL* for the past thirty years, introducing by far the largest contingent of stars ever associated on one show. Its casts have included Fred Armisen, Jim Belushi, Dana Carvey, Billy Crystal,

Joan Cusack, Robert Downey, Jr., Chris Elliott, Jimmy Fallon, Chris Farley, Will Ferrell, Tina Fey, Al Franken, Janeane Garofalo, Gilbert Gottfried, Christopher Guest, Phil Hartman, Julia Louis-Dreyfus, Jon Lovitz, Norm Macdonald, Michael McKean, Tim Meadows, Seth Meyers, Dennis Miller, Tracy Morgan, Eddie Murphy, Bill Murray, Mike Myers, Kevin Nealon, Joe Piscopo, Amy Poehler, Randy Quaid, Colin Quinn, Chris Rock, Maya Rudolph, Andy Samberg, Adam Sandler, Horatio Sanz, Rob Schneider, Paul Shaffer, Harry Shearer, Martin Short, Sarah Silverman, Robert Smigel, David Spade, Ben Stiller, Damon Wayans, and Kristen Wiig.

SNL has been on NBC for over forty seasons—an on-and-off, mutating voice of generations to come.

SCTV

> [SCTV *is*] *the most intricate, complex, and in a*
> *way beautiful comedy show ever made.*
> —CONAN O'BRIEN

When *Saturday Night Live* was being created and scouting for talent, Lorne Michaels had an ace in the hole. It was called Second City, the most successful comedy troupe in history. It began in Chicago (the name came from a classic ding on Chicago, the "second city" to New York) in 1959, and opened a second theater in Toronto in 1973.

From Second City, Michaels tapped John Belushi, Gilda Radner, and Dan Aykroyd—three of the six original Players. *SNL* would go back to Second City for years, bringing on Bill Murray, James Belushi, Julia Louis-Dreyfus, Mike Myers, Chris Farley, Tina Fey, Amy Poehler, and many others.

As *SNL* grew into a phenomenon, another group of Second City comics started working on a show of their own. *Second City Television* (*SCTV*) was born. Its cast eventually included John Candy, Eugene Levy, Catherine O'Hara, Dave Thomas, Joe Flaherty, Andrea Martin, and Martin Short.

SCTV satirized television itself, built on the premise of a tiny TV station. The station was populated by truly awful performers and shows, and run by a larcenous set of execs.

From this difficult premise and a minuscule budget, *SCTV* became one of the greatest comedies in history. Its success stemmed from blurring the lines between reality and parody.

While the most popular comedy shows of the time were built on individual sketches, the genius of *SCTV*'s concept was creating a complete living parody of a local TV station set in the fictional town of Melonville. The fictional station was run by criminal Guy Caballero, who rode around in a wheelchair that he didn't need.

SCTV followed the programming day of the fictional network. Their morning show was *Farm Film Report*, in which hayseeds Big Jim McBob and Billy Sol Hurok invited celebrities onto *SCTV*, and blew them up with explosives.

SCTV's movie feature was *Monster Chiller Horror Theater*, hosted by faux-vampire Count Floyd. His low-budget movies included *Tip O'Neill's 3-D House of Representatives* and *Dr. Tongue's 3-D House of Stewardesses*.

SCTV's game shows were *Half-Wits* and *High-Q*, populated by imbecilic contestants and perennially irritated host Alex Trebel. Advertisers during the *SCTV* programming day included Harry the Guy with the Snake on his Face and Tex and Edna Boyle's Organ Emporium.

SCTV News was anchored by alcoholic Floyd Robertson and his moronic sidekick, Earl Camembert.

Various segments included two Martin Short creations: albino singer Jackie Rogers, Jr., and the exuberantly mental Ed Grimley. Short took both of these with him for his one season on *SNL*. Others featured the Shmenge Brothers, variety show hosts and leaders of polka band The Happy Wanderers, famous for their hit "Cabbage Rolls and Coffee." In *The Last Polka*, an HBO special, they staged a false retirement, to defraud their fans by pretending that Michael Jackson would appear at their final concert.

SCTV's stellar late-night parody was *The Sammy Maudlin Show*, a third-rate *Tonight Show* starring talentless, two-faced hacks. Scams of the Maudlin team included an *Ocean's Eleven* knockoff called *Maudlin's Eleven* and various absurd fund-raisers.

SCTV's most famous recurring skit grew from the Canadian Broadcasting Company's request that *SCTV* feature a few minutes of "identifiably Canadian content" in each episode. To spite them, Flaherty and Rick Moranis developed Canadian stereotypes Bob and Doug McKenzie, two genial drunks in parkas and toques. Bob and Doug become stars with a hit comedy album, a movie, and a single with Geddy Lee, singer of Rush—bringing performers Dave Thomas and Moranis a windfall of cash.

SCTV's impressions were a direct result of its tiny budgets: "We couldn't afford guest stars, so we had to impersonate celebrities," said Dave Thomas.[10] This led to the best impersonations on television, including Brooke Shields, Meryl Streep, Woody Allen, Perry Como, Orson Welles, Julia Child, Tip O'Neill, Alex Trebek, Kirk Douglas, Milton Berle, Gene Shalit, Merv Griffin, Barbra Streisand, Dick Cavett, George Carlin, Jerry Lewis, G. Gordon Liddy, and Michael Caine. As *SCTV* became better known, a crop of celebrities came on to appear within its "shows"—including Tony Bennett, John Mellencamp, Bill Murray, and Robin Williams.

In 1981–83, after Lorne Michaels left *SNL*, *SCTV* aired on Friday nights on NBC. It won Emmys in both 1982 and 1983 for outstanding comedy writing. TV critic James Wolcott called *SCTV* "the only entertainment show on TV that matters."

For the 1983–84 season, NBC took the Friday night slot back and offered *SCTV*'s producers a Sunday night slot, opposite *60 Minutes*. But *SCTV*'s producers would have had to change the show's format, so they declined. It was America's loss.

CHAPTER 43

GOLDENSON, DILLER, AND EISNER

Business management can be viewed as a three-act play—the
dream, the execution, and the passing of the baton. Leonard
Goldenson will be remembered as a master of all.

—WARREN BUFFETT

When Goldenson had engineered the United Paramount merger with ABC in 1953, ABC had been a third-rate broadcaster. Goldenson retooled the network to take it to places Sarnoff and Paley had never gone, making ABC a lean and equal competitor. He moved ABC into new genres, away from radio and closer to motion pictures—and hired executives who did the same.

Goldenson brought movies to television, pioneered "event" television, and introduced made-for-TV movies and the miniseries. He green lit the shows that defined sports on television, *Wide World of Sports*, *Olympic* coverage, and *Monday Night Football*.

He did it by championing three of the most important executives of the era.

Barry Diller

As the '60s progressed, the space age began, and Westerns began a decade-long crawl to oblivion. In 1964, ABC's West Coast head, Elton Rule, hired a new assistant named Barry Diller.

Diller was a force to be reckoned with from the beginning. When Rule was promoted to president of ABC, Diller was put in charge of negotiating ABCs rights to feature films.

Movies had been good to ABC; the new goal was to expand them to become an even bigger part of the schedule.

With VP Leonard Goldberg, Diller commissioned a plan for twenty-six 90-minute movies, to be produced exclusively for ABC.

When each studio wanted the full slate of twenty-six movies, Goldberg split it across a range of producers. One of them was an ex-actor named Aaron Spelling.

ABC did the best it could with the budgets it had. Diller said later, "In the early period we did a lot of junk movies—but we also proved that you could do movies every week."[1]

With no time to build ratings and only one airing, producers had to come up with a concept that could be summed up in one line.

Movie of the Week focused on docudramas, based on recent events like *The Missiles of October* (the Cuban missile crisis) and *The Ballad of Andy Crocker* (Vietnam). The first docudrama, *Brian's Song*, aired on ABC in 1971.

Brian's Song chronicled the interracial friendship between Chicago Bears football players Gale Sayers and Brian Piccolo. Based on Sayers's memoirs, it ends with the heartbreaking death of Piccolo from cancer at age twenty-six. It was a sensation, capturing over 44 million viewers.

Brian's Song won the Emmy for Outstanding Single Program, and was the first made-for-TV movie to win a Peabody Award. Its success led to a deluge of docudramas from all three networks.

The ABC *Movie of the Week* premiered in 1969 on Tuesday nights at 8:30. By the 1971–72 season, it was the fifth-most-watched program. *Movie of the Week* was also used as a proving ground for pilots, for ABC series like *Marcus Welby, M.D.*; *The Six Million Dollar Man*; and *Starsky and Hutch*.

ABC's *Movie of the Week* produced an astounding one movie per week, for thirty-nine straight weeks—for six straight seasons.

Diller's made-for-TV movies began swallowing schedules. There were 50 made-for-TV movies in 1970; by 1975, there were over 120.

By 1973, ABC's entire prime-time programming strategy was designed around Diller's movie programming. He was promoted to vice president of prime-time programming that same year. Doubling down on his success, he added a second TV movie series (on Saturdays) and a third (on Wednesdays).

Diller became TV's first long-form mogul, decades before HBO.

In 1974, Diller moved from ABC to become chairman and CEO of Paramount Pictures, the place Goldenson had started so long ago. There, he became a mogul himself, overseeing hit films *Saturday Night Fever, Grease, Raiders of the Lost Ark, Indiana Jones and the Temple of Doom, Terms of Endearment,* and *Beverly Hills Cop.* Paramount also produced TV hits *Laverne and Shirley, Taxi, and Cheers.*

It was a logical decision because by 1973, CBS seemed unstoppable. *All in the Family, Mary Tyler Moore,* and *M*A*S*H* were firing on all cylinders. The Norman Lear spinoffs were on the way. Other than movies and sports, ABC seemed rudderless.

Diller returned to television in 1984, as chairman and CEO of a tiny would-be network called Fox Broadcasting Company.

Michael Eisner

While working in the programming department at CBS, Michael Eisner sent out hundreds of résumés. He received only one response—from Barry Diller. Diller hired Eisner, as assistant to the national programming director, in 1966. Eisner worked under Diller on film acquisitions, and eventually transitioned into development himself. Eisner became a powerhouse in the '70s, first as ABC's VP of daytime programming, then as SVP of prime time.

Eisner's biggest idea came to him while he was stuck in Newark Airport. He was reminiscing about a 1950s comedy series called *Mama* when it occurred to him that *Mama* was ripe for a remake. He brought the idea to showrunner Garry Marshall, whose CBS hit *The Odd Couple* was starting to wind down.

Marshall reimagined *Mama* as a different family in the '50s.

The result was 1971 pilot *New Family in Town.* It featured a Milwaukee high school student named Richie Cunningham and his family.

Despite Eisner's enthusiasm, ABC turned it down.

In the meantime, George Lucas told Marshall he was producing a movie called *American Graffiti*. He watched Marshall's pilot, and decided to borrow his lead actor, Ron Howard. When *American Graffiti* was a box office smash in 1973, Eisner again pushed ABC to revive his baby.

Eventually Eisner got his way, and the show reappeared as *Happy Days*.

The biggest boost to the show came from Garry Marshall's new character: Arthur Herbert "Fonzi" Fonzarelli, aka "the Fonz," a hoodlum Marshall described as "a combination of the Lone Ranger and Joe DiMaggio."

Happy Days premiered in January 1974. It was an immediate hit, beating out *Maude*. When asked about the success of the show, CBS's Fred Silverman said, "We sell to adults in prime time, not to children."[2] He would soon eat his words.

In addition to *Happy Days*, Eisner developed hits *Welcome Back, Kotter* and *Barney Miller*. Eisner began to view himself as the logical successor to Martin Starger, the then-president of ABC Entertainment.

But ABC leadership didn't go with Eisner, hiring Fred Silverman instead.

In 1976, Diller, now chairman of Paramount, recruited Eisner from ABC and made him president and CEO of the studio.

Eisner soon became CEO of the Walt Disney Company, and bought ABC in 1996.

CHAPTER 44

ROONE ARLEDGE

Roone was surely the only television executive of his time who would have dared to put sports in prime time. All of the money the athletes are making, all the big money in sports, none of that would be happening if not for Roone.

—DICK EBERSOL

R oone Arledge was the final piece of Goldenson's trifecta, and pioneered television sports, which began when NBC's *The Gillette Cavalcade of Sports* debuted in 1944.

Boxing was a hallmark of television in the '40s, with as many as five or six shows a week. As it had on radio, sports began on television with boxing, with Willie Pep's defeat of Chalky Wright for the world featherweight title. Boxing was perfect for early television: the ring was square, the space was confined, the stories were clear, and the sport barely needed to be explained.

Baseball soon followed, with the first televised World Series in 1947, between the New York Yankees and the Brooklyn Dodgers. NBC hoped for half a million viewers, but they got 3.8 million.

Football didn't rise to prominence until 1962, when James Aubrey made a $4.65 million deal with the NFL to broadcast all regular-season games. Aubrey warned affiliates that sports leagues would price themselves out of the market. But in 1964, he laid out another $28 million for NFL broadcasting rights.

Aubrey saw the power of sports, though he didn't know how to harness it. The man who did came to ABC in 1960. He brought sports from radio to television, and turned static games into high drama. He introduced pre- and postgame shows, color commentary, multicamera quick cuts, and slow-motion replay. Nearly every innovation of sports on TV was connected to Roone Arledge.

Early Career

Roone Arledge left the Army in 1955, and got a job as a stage manager for NBC New York. He soon developed a pilot called *For Men Only*, loosely based on *Playboy* magazine.

Though NBC didn't want the show, ABC VP Ed Scherick liked Arledge. He was further impressed when Arledge named every athlete on the walls of Ed's office.

In 1960, Scherick hired Arledge as assistant producer for ABC college football.

The next year, Arledge wrote a now-legendary memo saying, "We are going to add show business to sports."[3] He and Scherick did just that in 1961.

Wide World of Sports

> *Spanning the globe to bring you the constant variety of sport—the thrill of victory—and the agony of defeat . . . the human drama of athletic competition. . . . This is ABC's Wide World of Sports!*

Originally a minor weekend show, *Wide World of Sports* turned sports into great programming, introducing both slow motion and instant replay. It used then-new satellites to televise live events from around the world. As its innovations grew, so did its audience.

Scherick and Arledge hired commentator Jim McKay from CBS, and eventually Muhammad Ali and Howard Cosell. The success of *Wide World of Sports* earned Arledge the VP of ABC Sports in 1964.

The Olympics

Arledge acquired the American TV rights to the 1964 Winter Olympic Games for Innsbruck, in what became one of the most lucrative relationships in broadcasting TV. It cost $200,000, and was a visionary deal. In 2011, for the same set of rights, NBC paid over $4 billion.

Arledge was made president of ABC Sports in 1968.

Arledge and McKay faced their most trying moments during the 1972 Summer Games in Munich. They also became part of the biggest story in the world, with coverage so thorough that it would propel Arledge to legendary status.

A terrorist group called the Black September Organization took eleven Israeli athletes hostage. Arledge directed seventeen straight hours of coverage perfectly, as McKay reported on a global story that soon became a massacre. As the entire world watched, McKay delivered grim news: "They are all gone."

All eleven hostages had been executed. The story was led by ABC Sports.

Monday Night Football

> *I want everybody in the news business to think of ABC before they go anyplace else. If it costs us an extra few thousand dollars to do that, what does it mean?*
>
> —ROONE ARLEDGE

In 1970, the jury was out. No one knew if football would be successful on prime time. NBC and CBS were reluctant to disrupt their prime-time schedules, so NFL commissioner Pete Rozelle went to Goldenson and Arledge, who were willing to roll the dice.

Goldenson trusted Arledge throughout his career, but especially in the $8.5 million deal with the NFL. ABC got the rights to thirteen games, which would appear on *Monday Night Football.*

Arledge changed the nature of football on TV. He increased instant replays to keep the show moving. He doubled the number of cameras on the field. He brought on Howard Cosell and Don Meredith to inject drama into the broadcasts. Even play-by-play announcers Frank Gifford and Keith Jackson eventually become stars.

Monday Night Football began on September 21, 1970. It was an immediate smash, with a 35 share. In a win for network budgets, it also eliminated the need for two hours of scripted shows.

Cosell was always controversial, a brash figure viewers loved or hated. When Goldenson called Arledge to tone down Cosell, Arledge asked for four more weeks. Cosell lasted on ABC for fourteen years.

In 1974, John Lennon appeared on *Monday Night Football* with Governor Ronald Reagan, who explained the rules of the game to expatriate John during their interview with Cosell. In 1980, Cosell was the first to announce John Lennon's murder on national TV.

Arledge described his philosophy in a 1976 interview: "The image that ultimately appears on the tube is what TV is all about, so for me the most rewarding and exciting part of my job is making pictures and words that move people."[4]

Roone Arledge and ABC News

While sports were putting ABC back on the map, ABC News was still stuck in the mud. With fewer affiliates than NBC or CBS, it was simply hard to compete.

Arledge had proven his mettle at the '72 Munich Games, covering the hostage crisis masterfully. He was hungry to oversee news as well as sports, and made his ambitions known at ABC. The idea of giving one executive both divisions was an unprecedented gamble.

But, having already gambled on Arledge with *Monday Night Football*, Goldenson took another bet and gave him the keys to News. Goldenson later called it "throwing the deed to the family farm on the casino table. I couldn't be sure we'd win—but if we did, I thought we would win big."[5]

Of having the head of sports become the head of news, ABC news star Ted Koppel would say, "Our reaction when Roone came in was hostility, suspicion. We saw Roone as something of an interloper."[6]

Interestingly, Arledge's elevation at ABC News contributed to Silverman's defection in 1978. Silverman, too, had asked to run ABC

News in 1977. He was told that it was inappropriate to have the same head of news and entertainment.

The doubters would eat their words: while president of ABC News, Arledge created *World News Tonight, Nightline, 20/20, Primetime Live,* and the number one Sunday news program in the country, *This Week.*

Arledge built the ABC News bench by recruiting stars David Brinkley, Hugh Downs, Barbara Walters, and Diane Sawyer, taking ABC News from a loss into profit in 1990.

In 1986 Arledge gave up ABC Sports to focus on News, and his *World News Tonight* began a ten-year domination of network news.

Arledge won thirty-seven Emmy Awards, including the first-ever Lifetime Achievement Emmy Award. Sports journalist Ralph Wiley called Arledge "the Mark Twain of TV sports" and once wrote, "Look up 'visionary' in the dictionary, and there's a picture of Roone Arledge."[7]

Arledge's performance in both sport and news is unparalleled. He made sports more lyrical, and news more personal. He brought humanity to his shows, and professionalism to their production, with an unmatched eye for talent.

Goldenson's Legacy

When the Big Three became targets of corporate raiders in the 1980s, Goldenson led ABC's 1985 merger with Capital Cities Broadcasting. It was the smartest deal of the three. He retired the following year, and was inducted into the Television Academy Hall of Fame in 1987.

ABC and Cap Cities would get a new owner in the '90s, the partner Goldenson had selected so many years ago. The Walt Disney Company now dates ABC's birth from the arrival of Leonard Goldenson.

CHAPTER 45

TOO BIG TO FAIL

As the 1970s drew to a close, the Big Three networks basked in their success. They were a closed club with a revolving door, a cartel selling oxygen to a captive audience of millions. Executives might move among the three, but the general public had nowhere else to go.

Like the Big Three automakers, the networks were unassailable.

There were rumblings in the distance. Sony was hawking a new VCR technology as a product for the "TV viewer who had everything." *Broadcast* magazine referred to it as a "time shift machine," predicting it "would make the idea of prime-time viewing obsolete."[1]

But why would people go to all the work of recording a program, just to watch it after everyone else had?

It was just a blip on the radar. Home video would never touch the Big Three.

Meanwhile, in areas with bad TV reception, entrepreneurs had taken to wiring up neighborhoods with cable-based TV service. But no one who got a decent signal would ever pay for television.

Cable would never touch the Big Three.

In 1975, one minor company had made news, broadcasting the blockbuster title bout between Muhammad Ali and Joe Frazier to closed-circuit theaters. It was a nice stunt, but the company's core business was showing uncut movies. And that simply wasn't a real business.

HBO would never touch the Big Three.

The only real threat the Big Three could see was deregulation, if for some crazy reason a new administration somehow weakened their monopoly.

But Jimmy Carter had too many problems of his own to take on the TV business. And his likely challenger, Ronald Reagan, was an actor; he was one of them, for God's sake.

Washington would never touch the Big Three.

So the rulers of the Big Three ended the 1970s in a state of good cheer. The path ahead was clear, as unsullied and triumphal as a coronation.

On the long, strange journey since 1900, no one had ever been more wrong.

APPENDIX: ANCESTORS OF TELEVISION

number of inventors and cultural forces were key precursors of television.

Speed Kills

Before the advent of the telegraph, nothing came quickly but weather and illness. Then as now, early access to vital information, such as who had won a war, made fortunes possible, enabling trades against those who were not in the know.

Among the first to see this was the Rothschild banking family. With members in Germany, Austria, England, Italy, and France, the family created an early communications system to coordinate their actions for profit when news broke. The Rothschild network included carrier pigeons and specially trained couriers who traveled as swiftly as possible. In a time when mail took a week, the Rothschilds could transmit a letter in a day.

Eventually noblemen and kings used the Rothschild network too, sharing their information in an effective subsidy for the network.

As the Battle of Waterloo raged in 1815, the war between England and France became a climactic economic event. Because of the Rothschilds' communications network, they knew the result of the battle two full days before the British cabinet.

Knowing the British market would rebound, Nathan Rothschild began buying British government bonds. He held his position until British bonds had soared, netting profits equivalent to almost $1 billion today.

The Rothschilds had created an information network that foreshadowed the Internet, for their own private use—a forerunner of the private networks and dark pools in modern times.

Shortly thereafter, a middle-aged British writer deployed another technology to do the opposite: to democratize communication, and to get his work into as many hands as possible.

Dickens

A few decades after Waterloo, steam-powered printing presses brought on an explosion of affordable newspapers and magazines. It was an exponentially more powerful method of distributing content than had ever existed before.

In a time of rampant poverty and horrific labor conditions, this represented a potential revolution: an entire population desperate for meaningful stories during a period of massive disruption.

One visionary novelist saw an opportunity in publishing novels as installments in magazines. In 1836, his serialized *The Pickwick Papers* was published in England. In its wake, many classic novels were published as serializations, including *Anna Karenina, Crime and Punishment, Madame Bovary,* and *Huckleberry Finn.* Serialization remade the publishing business, and the era of Charles Dickens began.

Dickens's strategy was ingenious for a host of reasons. It reduced the cost of what readers had to pay, thereby increasing his potential audience. It allowed Dickens to end each installment with a *cliffhanger,* a dramatic ending that pulled his audience back for the next installment. Installments allowed Dickens more time to write and to gauge reader response as he worked. Ultimately, the approach gave him leverage: Dickens granted exclusive rights to certain publishers, and took ownership of publishers in exchange for rights to his content.

All this publishing innovation might have been worthless if not for one thing: Dickens was a great author, writing stories that reflected the world of his audience. Technology made his stories widely available at good prices, aligning creative, technology, and business as nothing had before.

Dickensian literature became the lingua franca of generations. Nearly forty years after his death, his characters still permeated the zeitgeist, as people described each other as "Dickensian" types.

One hundred years later, Dickens's innovations would inspire the cable era of television—a model built on cliffhangers, wide reach, and serialization.

But television needed telecommunications—and that began with Samuel Morse.

Morse

Samuel Morse was an inventor, a painter, and a geographer. His signal achievements were the dot-dash code that bears his name, the single-wire telegraph, and winning the brutal fight he waged to get Congress to fund it.

Like the many inventors who would succeed him, he would fight to control the inventions he developed. Unlike most of them, he would prevail.

In the 1830s, Morse began working on a device called the "electric telegraph." He did this in isolation, unaware that other inventors were in the game as well.

While traveling home from France on a ship called the *Sully*, Morse told fellow passengers about his idea. Five years later, he learned that a pair he'd spoken to on the ship now claimed to have invented his device and were in America demonstrating it.

Morse sent letters to the captain and passengers of the *Sully* declaring the priority of his invention over that of the pair. He also took to the press, emphatically relaying the story of his invention and all that it had cost him. Eventually he won and began a battle with Congress to get the first telegraph line laid.

Congress thought the telegraph was a waste of money, and Morse began an agonizing fight for funding that took years to procure. Even though he had previously lost his young wife, Morse said his fight with Congress was worse: "I can truly say that I have never passed so trying a period."[1]

Eventually, the bill passed Congress—89 to 83—and Morse's test telegraph line from Washington to Baltimore was laid. On May 24, 1844, Morse sent his first message. The text was biblical: "What hath God wrought?" It was a good question.

The consequences of Morse's first telegraph message in 1844 were seismic. It was the first time in history that two places could communicate instantly. The *New York Sun* called the telegraph "the greatest revolution of modern times and indeed of all time, for the amelioration of Society."[2]

Morse's telegraph would be nicknamed the Lightning Line by a fascinated public.

It was an ancestor of the Internet, capturing the American imagination as much as its successor would. The code that bears Morse's name would be memorized by generations.

Later, Morse would say, "The condition of the inventor is, indeed, not enviable." But electronic distribution had begun.

Bell

The first statement Alexander Graham Bell delivered on his disruptive invention was prosaic: "Mr. Watson—come here—I want to see you." More importantly, Mr. Watson could hear each word clearly from another room.

Scholars would later argue that Bell had not been first—that he may have bribed the patent office to beat another inventor to the punch. In any event, his patents were arguably the most valuable of all time and set the stage for the birth of a giant, when the Bell Company became AT&T in 1885.

Like those of any industrial giant, Bell's actions were closely followed. In 1880, he filed a confidential brief for a device called a "photophone," and rumors spread that Bell had developed a method of television, of "seeing by telegraph."

The photophone was actually a precursor to fiber optics and a distant ancestor of the Internet. Bell would call it his greatest invention, even more important than the telephone.

But it didn't matter. The market was frothy, and Bell rumors validated that "remote seeing" was possible.

Thus did the frenzy for television begin.

Marconi

The man who began modern media technology was born in 1874, the son of an Italian aristocrat. His father not only provided him with a library but grudgingly subscribed to all the leading scientific journals of the day. Marconi devoured them.

Inspired by Ben Franklin, Marconi and a friend built a homemade lightning conductor, and prayed for a storm. When one came, their contraption worked: the lightning flash triggered a bell to ring. As discussed earlier, Marconi soon became obsessed with sending telegraphs without wires. Knowing he was in a race against time, he started on his invention in 1894 and simply did not stop.[3]

In 1899, Marconi set up an office in New Jersey, creating the Marconi Wireless Company of America. The Marconi Company would dominate radio for two decades, until the American government decided radio needed to be controlled by domestic hands, and the Marconi Company was subsumed by RCA.

In 1900, Marconi patented a new form of telegraph, one he claimed would not be limited by the planet's curvature. In 1901, he proved it, using his system to transmit a wireless signal 2,100 miles. Even Thomas Edison, who had doubted the claim, had to admire Marconi's feat.

In 1909, Marconi won the Nobel Prize for physics. When he died in 1937, radio wireless stations throughout the world went silent for two minutes, returning to the silence that had reigned before his birth.

ACKNOWLEDGMENTS

Researching 100 years of media is not a minor undertaking. I was fortunate to have a lot of help.

My wife, Ann Marie, a TV and Film graduate herself, helped me a great deal with research and editing.

My teaching assistant Jeff Leathers was essential in helping work through the outline of the book.

Ryan Holiday and Nils Parker were critical in turning a seventy-five-page outline into an actual book proposal.

My teaching assistant Drew Eller was with me for countless hours, helping to tame thousands of pages of research into the stories of Sarnoff, Farnsworth, and RCA.

Lisa Crawford of the Annenberg School was with me for Paley, CBS, and the general bedlam of TV's entrepreneurs.

Brian Huh came on to research the '60s, including *The Twilight Zone* and *Star Trek*, and anything else that needed doing.

Michael Tunney was with me throughout Part 5 on the 1970s. He was critical in getting this book done on time, in a series of fourteen-hour days as the deadline loomed.

Bryce Paul was an incredible source of clarity, with a range of editorial suggestions that greatly improved the book.

Ellen Lohman's copyediting was likewise indispensable, remedying flaws and suggesting numerous improvements.

Many thanks to the execs who were kind enough to sit for interviews. Though most of their insights interviews appear in Volume 2, they were critical in mapping the arc of the story of this Volume 1. In particular, I owe a debt to Chris Albrecht, Preston Beckman, Kevin Beggs, Charlie Collier, Sandy Grushow, Warren Littlefield, John Penney, and Terry Winter.

There was only one interview essential to Volume 1: many thanks to Norman Lear for his thoughts on television and America.

I'm also grateful to my Television Academy colleague Thomas Sarnoff, for sharing his amazing recollections of his father, David, and of the earliest days of TV.

Many thanks to my colleagues on the Television Academy's Board of Governors, to its unbeatable staff—and to my extended family of the past fifteen years, the members of the Interactive Media Peer Group.

Thanks also to my colleagues at the University of Southern California, the greatest media university in the world. In particular, thanks to David Baron, Ali Sarafoglou, Bonnie Chi, and Larry Auerbach.

And for a range of assists, many thanks to Ryan Aguirre, Barbara Chase, Jennifer Cramer, Matt Dorff, Marc Johnson, Wendy Keller, Nick DeMartino, F. J. Lennon, Patty Mann, John Maatta, Gregory Markel, Bruce Rosenblum, Jay Samit, Bernadette Simpao, and Karalee Vint.

Many thanks to my friend Chris Tellez, the best creative director I know, for his work on the many iterations of this book cover.

A heartfelt thanks to Mr. Jeff Sotzing of Carson Entertainment Group, for his permission to base that cover on my childhood hero, his uncle.

And big thanks to my mom for taking me to NBC that day.

More from the Author

This book, *TELEVISION: Volume 1,* covers the invention and rise to power of television. It begins circa 1900 and ends circa 1978, with the three broadcast networks at the height of their power.

TELEVISION: Volume 2 will cover the cable age and the rise of the entrepreneur, including the stories of CNN, ESPN, MTV, FOX, NBC's Must See TV, HBO, AMC, FX and Netflix.

TELEVISION: Volume 3 will cover the broadband age and the rise of the audience, including Google, YouTube, multichannel networks such as Maker Studios and Fullscreen, Twitter, Facebook, and immersive media pioneers in virtual, augmented and mixed reality.

To get updates on the *TELEVISION* book series, please sign up for my monthly e-mail newsletter at www.SethShapiro.com/newsletter, or at www.SethShapiro.com.

In addition to updates on the *TELEVISION* series, you'll receive innovation case studies on companies like Uber, AirBnB, Amazon, and Netflix, virtual/augmented/mixed reality, and other major trends and perspectives on the business and cultural landscape.

My podcast is called *The New New Thing.* It focuses on the innovations that have changed the game in their respective fields. More about the show is available at *www.newnewthingshow.com.*

ABOUT THE AUTHOR

Two-time Emmy® Award winner Seth Shapiro is a leading advisor in business innovation, media, and technology. He has worked with clients including the Walt Disney Company, Comcast, DIRECTV, Intel, Interpublic Group, NBC, Showtime, RTL, Telstra, Verizon, Universal, Slamdance Studios, Goldman Sachs, government bodies, NGOs, and a range of startup and early-stage ventures.

Shapiro is an Adjunct Professor at the USC School of Cinematic Arts, a Governor of the Television Academy, a member of its Executive Committee, and Principal of New Amsterdam Media LLC. He has served as a frequent expert witness, including before the FCC, and has been quoted in outlets including *The Economist*, the *New York Times*, the *LA Times*, CNBC, the *Boston Globe*, Bloomberg, the Associated Press, PBS, and the U.K. *Daily Mail.*

As Head of Production at DIRECTV Advanced Services, he launched over twenty-five services, including TiVo by DIRECTV and the NFL Sunday Ticket Interactive Service.

Shapiro sits on a variety of advisory boards and on the Producer Guild's New Media Council. He is a magna cum laude graduate of New York University and was Adelbert Alumni Scholar at Case Western Reserve University.

NOTES

PART 1: NBC and the Battle for Television

2. David Sarnoff

1. Erik Barnouw, *Tube of Plenty: The Evolution of American Television* (Oxford: Oxford University Press, 1990).

2. Interview of Thomas Sarnoff with the author, April 29, 2016.

3. Eugene Lyons, *David Sarnoff: A Biography* (New York: Harper & Row, 1966).

4. Eugene Lyons, *David Sarnoff: A Biography* (New York: Harper & Row, 1966).

5. David E. Fisher and Marshall Jon Fisher, *Tube: The Invention of Television* (Berkeley: Counterpoint, 1996).

6. Daniel Stashower, *Boy Genius and the Mogul: The Untold Story of Television* (New York: Crown Archetype, 2002).

7. Alexander B. Magoun, *Television: The Life Story of a Technology* (Baltimore: Johns Hopkins University Press, 2009).

8. David Sarnoff, *Looking Ahead: The Papers of David Sarnoff* (New York: McGraw Hill, 1968).

3. Radio Corporation of America

1. Daniel Stashower, *Boy Genius and the Mogul: The Untold Story of Television* (New York: Crown Archetype, 2002).

4. Sarnoff vs. Armstrong

1. Erik Barnouw, *Tube of Plenty: The Evolution of American Television* (Oxford: Oxford University Press, 1990).

2. Lawrence Lessing, *Man of High Fidelity: Edwin Howard Armstrong* (Philadelphia: J. B. Lippincott, 1956).

3. Edwin Armstrong: The Creator of FM Radio (The First Electronic Church of America, n.d.), http://fecha.org/armstrong.htm.

4. Daniel Stashower, *The Boy Genius and the Mogul: The Untold Story of Television* (New York: Crown Archetype, 2002).

5. Daniel Stashower, *The Boy Genius and the Mogul: The Untold Story of Television* (New York: Crown Archetype, 2002).

6. From Radio to Television

1. Daniel Stashower, *Boy Genius and the Mogul: The Untold Story of Television* (New York: Crown Archetype, 2002).

2. Edwin Armstrong: The Creator of FM Radio (The First Electronic Church of America, n.d.), http://fecha.org/armstrong.htm.

3. Tim Wu, *The Master Switch: The Rise and Fall of Information Empires* (New York: Knopf, 2010).

4. Harry Henderson, *Communications and Broadcasting* (New York: Chelsea House, 1997).

7. The Alpha and Beta of Television

1. "Paul Nipkow," Bairdtelevision.com (n.d.), http://www.bairdtelevision.com/nipkow.html.

2. Alexander B. Magoun, *Television: The Life Story of a Technology* (Baltimore: Johns Hopkins University Press, 2009).

3. R. W. Burns, *British Television: The Formative Years* (Stevenage, UK: IET, 1986).

4. David E. Fisher and Marshall Jon Fisher, *Tube: The Invention of Television* (Berkeley, CA: Counterpoint, 1996).

5. Harry Henderson, *Communications and Broadcasting* (New York: Chelsea House, 1997).

8. Philo Farnsworth

1. Daniel Stashower, *Boy Genius and the Mogul: The Untold Story of Television* (New York: Crown Archetype, 2002).

2. Daniel Stashower, *Boy Genius and the Mogul: The Untold Story of Television* (New York: Crown Archetype, 2002).

3. Malcolm Gladwell, "The Televisionary," *New Yorker*, May 27, 2002, http://www.newyorker.com/magazine/2002/05/27/the-televisionary.

4. Paul Schatzkin, *The Boy Who Invented Television: A Story of Inspiration, Persistence, and Quiet Passion* (Terre Haute, IN: Tanglewood Books, 2004).

5. Gary R. Edgerton, *The Columbia History of American Television* (New York: Columbia University Press, 2007).

6. Paul Schatzkin, *The Boy Who Invented Television: A Story of Inspiration, Persistence, and Quiet Passion* (Terre Haute, IN: Tanglewood Books, 2004).

7. Alexander B. Magoun, *Television: The Life Story of a Technology* (Baltimore: Johns Hopkins University Press, 2009).

9. Farnsworth vs. Sarnoff

1. Tim Wu, *The Master Switch: The Rise and Fall of Information Empires* (New York: Knopf, 2010).

2. Daniel Stashower, *Boy Genius and the Mogul: The Untold Story of Television* (New York: Crown Archetype, 2002).

PART 2: Columbia Broadcasting System

10. William Paley

1. Sally Bedell Smith, *In All His Glory: The Life and Times of William S. Paley and the Birth of Modern Broadcasting* (New York: Random House, 2002).

2. Sally Bedell Smith, *In All His Glory: The Life and Times of William S. Paley and the Birth of Modern Broadcasting* (New York: Random House, 2002).

3. Nancy J. Woodhull and Robert W. Snyder, Eds., *Media Mergers* (New Brunswick, NJ: Transaction Press, 1997).

4. Ben H. Bagdikian, *The Media Monopoly* (Boston: Beacon Press, 2000).

5. William S. Paley, *As It Happened: A Memoir* (New York: Doubleday Books, 1979).

6. Sally Bedell Smith, *In All His Glory: The Life and Times of William S. Paley and the Birth of Modern Broadcasting* (New York: Random House, 2002).

11. Sarnoff vs. Paley

1. Sally Bedell Smith, In All His Glory: The Life and Times of William S. Paley and the Birth of Modern Broadcasting (New York: Random House, 2002).

2. Jim Cox, American Radio Networks: A History (Jefferson, NC: McFarland, 2009).

12. Inventing CBS

1. David Halberstam, *The Powers That Be* (Champaign: University of Illinois Press, 2000).

2. R. L. Hilliard and M. C. Keith, *The Broadcast Century and Beyond: A Biography of American Broadcasting* (Waltham, MA: Focal Press, 2010).

3. Sally Bedell Smith, *In All His Glory: The Life and Times of William S. Paley and the Birth of Modern Broadcasting* (New York: Random House, 2002).

4. Sally Bedell Smith, *In All His Glory: The Life and Times of William S. Paley and the Birth of Modern Broadcasting* (New York: Random House, 2002).

13. Broadcast News

1. John Douglas and Mark Olshaker *The Cases That Haunt Us: From Jack the Ripper to JonBenet Ramsey, the FBI's Legendary Mindhunter Sheds Light on the Mysteries That Won't Go Away* (New York: Scribner, 2000).

14. Edward R. Murrow

1. David Halberstam, *The Powers That Be* (Champaign: University of Illinois Press, 2000).

2. David Halberstam, *The Powers That Be* (Champaign: University of Illinois Press, 2000).

15. Television Takes Off

1. Gary R. Edgerton, *The Columbia History of American Television* (New York: Columbia University Press, 2007).

2. Gary R. Edgerton, *The Columbia History of American Television* (New York: Columbia University Press, 2007).

3. Sally Bedell Smith, *In All His Glory: The Life and Times of William S. Paley and the Birth of Modern Broadcasting* (New York: Random House, 2002).

4. David E. Fisher and Marshall Jon Fisher, *Tube: The Invention of Television* (Berkeley: Counterpoint, 1996).

5. Gary R. Edgerton, *The Columbia History of American Television* (New York: Columbia University Press, 2007).

6. David Halberstam, *The Powers That Be* (Champaign: University of Illinois Press, 2000).

7. William Strauss and Neil Howe, *Generations: The History of America's Future, 1584 to 2069* (Quill, 1991).

PART 3: Television and the 1950s

18. Jackie Gleason

1. William A. Henry, III, *The Great One: The Life and Legend of Jackie Gleason* (New York: Doubleday, 1992).

2. William A. Henry, III, *The Great One: The Life and Legend of Jackie Gleason* (New York: Doubleday, 1992).

3. Sally Bedell Smith, *In All His Glory: The Life and Times of William S. Paley and the Birth of Modern Broadcasting* (New York: Random House, 2002).

4. Andrew Bergman, "Television; Jackie Gleason: A Yardstick of the Common Man," *New York Times*, July 5, 1987, http://www.nytimes.com/1987/07/05/arts/televison-jackie-gleason-a-yardstick-of-the-common-man.html.

5. William A. Henry, III, *The Great One: The Life and Legend of Jackie Gleason* (New York: Doubleday, 1992).

6. Jack O'Brian, "Positive Ideas on Returning Comic Gleason," *St. Petersburg Times*, January 4, 1958, https://news.google.com/newspapers?nid=888&dat=19580104&id=5fpSAAAAIBAJ&sjid=koADAAAAIBAJ&pg=7314,1335064&hl=en.

7. William A. Henry, III, *The Great One: The Life and Legend of Jackie Gleason* (New York: Doubleday, 1992).

8. Brad Darrach, "A Fond Goodbye to the Great One," *People*, July 13, 1987, http://www.people.com/people/archive/article/0,,20096724,00.html.

9. Andrew Bergman, "Television; Jackie Gleason: A Yardstick of the Common Man," *New York Times*, July 5, 1987, http://www.nytimes.com/1987/07/05/arts/televison-jackie-gleason-a-yardstick-of-the-common-man.html.

19. *Your Show of Shows* and Ernie Kovacs

1. "Star-Studded Assembly Attends Kovacs' Funeral," *St. Petersburg Times*, January 15, 1962.

20. Lucy and Desi

2. Stefan Kanfer, *Ball of Fire: The Tumultuous Life and Comic Art of Lucille Ball* (New York: Knopf, 2003).

3. Stefan Kanfer, *Ball of Fire: The Tumultuous Life and Comic Art of Lucille Ball* (New York: Knopf, 2003).

4. Michael Kantor and Laurence Maslon, *Make 'Em Laugh: The Funny Business of America* (New York: Hachette, 2008).

5. Jess Oppenheimer, *Laughs, Luck—and Lucy: How I Came to Create the Most Popular Sitcom of All Time* (Syracuse, NY: Syracuse University Press, 1999).

6. Stefan Kanfer, *Ball of Fire: The Tumultuous Life and Comic Art of Lucille Ball* (New York: Knopf, 2003).

7. Stefan Kanfer, *Ball of Fire: The Tumultuous Life and Comic Art of Lucille Ball* (New York: Knopf, 2003).

8. Stefan Kanfer, *Ball of Fire: The Tumultuous Life and Comic Art of Lucille Ball* (New York: Knopf, 2003).

9. Stefan Kanfer, *Ball of Fire: The Tumultuous Life and Comic Art of Lucille Ball* (New York: Knopf, 2003).

21. Quiz Show Scandal

1. Charles Van Doren, "All the Answers," *New Yorker*, July 28, 2008, http://www.newyorker.com/magazine/2008/07/28/all-the-answers.

2. David Halberstam, *The Powers That Be* (Champaign: University of Illinois Press, 2000).

22. American Broadcasting Company

1. Leonard H. Goldenson, "Archive of American Television" (interview by Marvin Wolf, May 14, 1996), http://www.emmytvlegends.org/interviews/people/leonard-h-goldenson.

2. Gary Edgerton, *The Columbia History of American Television,* Columbia Histories of Modern American Life (New York: Columbia University Press, 2007).

3. Gary Edgerton, *The Columbia History of American Television,* Columbia Histories of Modern American Life (New York: Columbia University Press, 2007).

23. Westerns

1. Cecil Smith, *Los Angeles Times,* September 1975.

24. Murrow vs. McCarthy

1. Gary R. Edgerton, *The Columbia History of American Television* (New York: Columbia University Press, 2007).

2. A. M. Sperber, *Murrow: His Life and Times* (New York: Bantam, 1987).

3. All quotes in this section are from Murrow's RTNDA speech, at http://www.rtdna.org/content/edward_r_murrow_s_1958_wires_lights_in_a_box_speech.

4. David Halberstam, *The Powers That Be* (Champaign: University of Illinois Press, 2000).

PART 4: Television in the 1960s

25. Kennedy and Television

1. Thomas Mallon, "Ambassador in Spite of Himself," *New York Times,* December 21, 2000, https://www.nytimes.com/books/00/12/31/reviews/001231.31mallont.html.

2. Gore Vidal, "Coached by Camelot: Why Do We Still Want to Defend J.F.K.?," *New Yorker,* December 1, 1997, 84.

3. Tip O'Neill and William J. Novak, *Man of the House: The Life and Political Memoirs of Speaker Tip O'Neill* (New York: Random House, 1987).

4. Leonard H. Goldenson, *Beating the Odds: The Untold Story Behind the Rise of ABC* (New York: Scribner, 1991).

5. David Halberstam, *The Powers That Be* (Champaign: University of Illinois Press, 2000).

6. Louis Menand, "Masters of the Matrix," *New Yorker* January 5, 2004, http://www.newyorker.com/magazine/2004/01/05/masters-of-the-matrix.

7. Gary R. Edgerton, *The Columbia History of American Television* (New York: Columbia University Press, 2007).

8. Hugh Sidey, "The Lesson John Kennedy Learned from the Bay of Pigs," *Time*, April 16, 2001, http://content.time.com/time/nation/article/0,8599,106537,00.html.

28. LBJ and Vietnam

1. Doris Kearns Goodwin, Lyndon Johnson and the American Dream: The Most Revealing Portrait of a President and Presidential Power Ever Written (New York: St. Martin's Griffin, 1991).

2. Philip T. Neisser, Tales of the State: Narrative in Contemporary U.S. Politics and Public Policy (New York: Rowman and Littlefield, 1997).

3. Thurston Clarke, Ask Not: The Inauguration of John F. Kennedy and the Speech That Changed America (New York: Holt Paperbacks, 2005).

4. Daniel C. Hallin, The Uncensored War: The Media and Vietnam (Berkeley: University of California Press, 1989).

29. Nixon and Ailes

1. Evan Thomas, *Being Nixon: A Man Divided* (New York: Random House, 2015).

2. Evan Thomas, *Being Nixon: A Man Divided* (New York: Random House, 2015).

3. Evan Thomas, *Being Nixon: A Man Divided* (New York: Random House, 2015).

4. Richard M. Nixon, *RN: The Memoirs of Richard Nixon* (New York: Warner Books, 1979).

5. Brian Alexander Pavlac, *A Concise Survey of Western Civilization: Supremacies and Diversities throughout History* (Lanham, MD: Rowman & Littlefield, 2010).

6. "The Kitchen Debate Transcript," CIA.org, http://www.foia.cia.gov/sites/default/files/document_conversions/16/1959-07-24.pdf (accessed May 10, 2016).

7. Richard M. Nixon, *RN: The Memoirs of Richard Nixon* (New York: Warner Books, 1979).

8. David Brock and Ari Rabin-Havt, *The Fox Effect: How Roger Ailes Turned a Network into a Propaganda Machine* (New York: Anchor Books, 2012).

9. John Cook, "Roger Ailes' Secret Nixon-Era Blueprint for Fox News," *Gawker*, June 30, 2011, http://gawker.com/5814150/roger-ailes-secret-nixon-era-blueprint-for-fox-news (accessed May 10, 2016).

31. *The Twilight Zone*

1. Janet Wasko, *A Companion to Television* (London: Wiley-Blackwell, 2010).

32. *Star Trek*

1. Don Page, "'Star Trek' Lives Despite Taboos," *Toledo Blade*, August 15, 1968, https://news.google.com/newspapers?nid=1350&dat=19 680815&id=QPFOAAAAIBAJ&sjid=nQEEAAAAIBAJ&pg=7135,2042 483&hl=en.

2. Nichelle Nichols, *Beyond Uhura: Star Trek and Other Memories* (New York: G. P. Putnam's, 1994).

3. Jan Johnson-Smith, *American Science Fiction TV: Star Trek, Stargate, and Beyond* (Middletown, CT: Wesleyan University Press, 2005).

4. Abby Ohlheiser, "How Martin Luther King Jr. Convinced 'Star Trek's' Lt. Uhura to Stay on the Show," *Washington Post*, July 31, 2015, https://www.washingtonpost.com/news/arts-and-entertainment/wp/2015/07/31/how-martin-luther-king-jr-convinced-star-treks-uhura-to-stay-on-the-show/.

33. Aubrey's Wasteland

1. Kenneth Janda, "'Vast Wasteland Speech' Holds True after All These Years" (edited version of Newton Minow's speech to the National Association of Broadcasters on May 9, 1961, printed in the *Chicago Tribune*, April 24, 2001, p. 17), American Government and Politics, http://www.janda.org/b20/News%20articles/vastwastland.htm.

2. Paul Rosenfield, "Aubrey: A Lion in Winter," *Los Angeles Times*, April 27, 1986, http://articles.latimes.com/1986-04-27/entertainment/ca-23815_1_jim-aubrey.

3. Paul Rosenfield, "Aubrey: A Lion in Winter," *Los Angeles Times*, April 27, 1986, http://articles.latimes.com/1986-04-27/entertainment/ca-23815_1_jim-aubrey.

4. Richard Oulahan and William Lambert, "The Tyrant's Fall That Rocked the TV World: Until He Was Suddenly Brought Low, Jim Aubrey Ruled the Air," *Life Magazine*, September 10, 1965.

5. David Halberstam, *The Powers That Be* (Champaign: University of Illinois Press, 2000).

6. David Halberstam, *The Powers That Be* (Champaign: University of Illinois Press, 2000).

7. William Boddy, *Fifties Television: The Industry and Its Critics* (Champaign: University of Illinois Press, 1992).

8. Murray Kempton, "The Fall of a Television Czar," *New Republic*, April 3, 1965, 9–10.

9. Paul Rosenfield, "Aubrey: A Lion in Winter," *Los Angeles Times*, April 27, 1986, http://articles.latimes.com/1986-04-27/entertainment/ca-23815_1_jim-aubrey.

10. Martin Kasindorf, "How Now, Dick Daring?" *New York Times Magazine*, September 10, 1972.

11. "The Return of Smiling Jim," *Time*, October 31, 1969, http://content.time.com/time/magazine/article/0,9171,839128,00.html.

12. Murray Kempton. "The Fall of a Television Czar," *New Republic*, April 3, 1965, 9–10.

PART 5: Television in the 1970s

34. Norman Lear and American Life

1. Norman Lear, *Even This I Get To Experience* (London: Penguin Press, 2014).

2. Norman Lear, *Even This I Get To Experience* (London: Penguin Press, 2014).

3. Interview with the author, March 23, 2016.

4. Norman Lear, *Even This I Get To Experience* (London: Penguin Press, 2014).

5. Norman Lear, *Even This I Get To Experience* (London: Penguin Press, 2014).

6. Interview with the author, March 23, 2016.

7. Norman Lear, *Even This I Get To Experience* (London: Penguin Press, 2014).

8. Norman Lear, "Archive of American Television," interview by Morrie Gelman, *Norman Lear*, February 26, 1998.

9. Christine Acham, *Revolution Televised: Prime Time and the Struggle for Black Power* (Minneapolis: University of Minnesota Press, 2004).

10. Norman Lear, "Archive of American Television," interview by Morrie Gelman, *Norman Lear*, February 26, 1998.

35. Mary, Grant, and MTM

1. J. K. Armstrong, *Mary and Lou and Rhoda and Ted: And All the Brilliant Minds Who Made The Mary Tyler Moore Show a Classic* (New York: Simon & Schuster, 2013).

2. Grant Tinker, *Tinker on Television: From General Sarnoff to General Electric* (New York: Simon & Schuster, 1994).

3. J. K. Armstrong, *Mary and Lou and Rhoda and Ted: And All the Brilliant Minds Who Made The Mary Tyler Moore Show a Classic* (New York: Simon & Schuster, 2013).

4. J. K. Armstrong, *Mary and Lou and Rhoda and Ted: And All the Brilliant Minds Who Made The Mary Tyler Moore Show a Classic* (New York: Simon & Schuster, 2013).

5. J. K. Armstrong, *Mary and Lou and Rhoda and Ted: And All the Brilliant Minds Who Made The Mary Tyler Moore Show a Classic* (New York: Simon & Schuster, 2013).

6. Yael Kohen, *We Killed: The Rise of Women in American Comedy* (New York: Macmillan, 2012).

7. J. K. Armstrong, *Mary and Lou and Rhoda and Ted: And All the Brilliant Minds Who Made The Mary Tyler Moore Show a Classic* (New York: Simon & Schuster, 2013).

8. Robert J. Thompson, *Television's Second Golden Age: From* Hill Street Blues *to* ER: Hill Street Blues, Thirtysomething, St. Elsewhere, China Beach, Cagney & Lacey, Twin Peaks, Moonlighting, Northern Exposure, L.A. Law, Picket Fences, *with Brief Reflections on* Homicide, NYPD Blue *&* Chicago Hope, *and Other Quality Dramas* (Syracuse, NY: Syracuse University Press, 1997).

36. *M*A*S*H*

1. Larry Gelbart, *Laughing Matters : On Writing MASH, Tootsie, Oh, God!, and a Few Other Funny Things* (New York: Random House, 1999).

2. Larry Gelbart, *Laughing Matters : On Writing MASH, Tootsie, Oh, God!, and a Few Other Funny Things* (New York: Random House, 1999).

3. Deborah Starr Seibel, "'Funny Business: TV Laugh Tracks Can Still Cause Frowns, but the Studios Feel a Need to Be Humored," *Chicago Tribune*, April 16, 1992, http://articles.chicagotribune.com/1992-04-16/features/9202030928_1_laugh-tracks-audience (accessed May 10, 2016).

4. Jitendar Canth, "Review of M.A.S.H. Season 3," MyReviewer.com, March 20, 2004, http://www.myreviewer.com/DVD/57819/MASH-Season-3-UK/57838/Review-by-Jitendar-Canth (accessed May 10, 2016).

5. Larry Gelbart, *Laughing Matters : On Writing MASH, Tootsie, Oh, God!, and a Few Other Funny Things* (New York: Random House, 1999).

37. PBS

1. Malcolm Gladwell, *The Tipping Point: How Little Things Can Make a Big Difference* (Boston: Little, Brown, 2000).

2. Laurie Oullette, *Viewers Like You? How Public TV Failed the People* (New York: Columbia University Press, 2002).

38. Watergate

1. Charles J. Abbott, "Nixon: 'Cool Contempt,' not Press Pandering," *UPI*, May 29, 1987, http://www.upi.com/Archives/1987/05/29/Nixon-cool-contempt-not-press-pandering/9037549259200/ (accessed May 10, 2016).

2. Anthony Summers and Robbyn Swan, *The Arrogance of Power: The Secret World of Richard Nixon* (New York: Penguin Books, 2001).

3. "Covering Watergate 40 Years Later with MacNeil and Lehrer," PBS.org, http://www.pbs.org/newshour/bb/politics-jan-june13-watergate_05-17/ (accessed May 10, 2016).

4. "Covering Watergate 40 Years Later with MacNeil and Lehrer," PBS.org, http://www.pbs.org/newshour/bb/politics-jan-june13-watergate_05-17/ (accessed May 10, 2016).

5. Evan Thomas, *Being Nixon: A Man Divided* (New York: Random House, 2015).

39. Stanton's Last Stand

1. David Halberstam, *The Powers That Be* (Champaign: University of Illinois Press, 2000).

2. David Halberstam, *The Powers That Be* (Champaign: University of Illinois Press, 2000).

3. David Halberstam, *The Powers That Be* (Champaign: University of Illinois Press, 2000).

40. ABC and Silverman

1. S. B. Smith, *Up the Tube: Prime-Time TV and the Silverman Years* (New York: Viking Adult, 1981).

2. S. B. Smith, *Up the Tube: Prime-Time TV and the Silverman Years* (New York: Viking Adult, 1981).

3. Gary Edgerton, *The Columbia History of American Television,* Columbia Histories of Modern American Life (New York: Columbia University Press, 2007).

4. S. B. Smith, *Up the Tube: Prime-Time TV and the Silverman Years* (New York: Viking Adult, 1981).

5. S. B. Smith, *Up the Tube: Prime-Time TV and the Silverman Years* (New York: Viking Adult, 1981).

41. Johnny Carson and *The Tonight Show*

1. Laurence Leamer, *King of the Night: The Life of Johnny Carson* (New York: Avon Books, 2005).

2. Laurence Leamer, *King of the Night: The Life of Johnny Carson* (New York: Avon Books, 2005).

3. Laurence Leamer, *King of the Night: The Life of Johnny Carson* (New York: Avon Books, 2005).

4. Johnny Carson, *American Masters* (transcript, April 5, 2014), PBS, http:// tv.ark.com/transcript/johnny_carson__american_masters/918/ KQED/Saturday_April_05_2014/699033/

5. Johnny Carson, *American Masters* (transcript, April 5, 2014), PBS, http:// tv.ark.com/transcript/johnny_carson__american_masters/918/ KQED/Saturday_April_05_2014/699033/

6. *Pioneers of Television: People Johnny Carson* (2014), http://www.pbs.org/ wnet/pioneers-of-television/pioneering-people/johnny-carson/

7. Ed McMahon. *Here's Johnny!: My Memories of Johnny Carson, The Tonight Show, and 46 Years of Friendship* (Nashville, TN: Rutledge Hill, 2005).

8. Laurence Leamer, *King of the Night: The Life of Johnny Carson* (New York: Avon Books, 2005).

9. Henry Bushkin, *Johnny Carson* (Boston: Houghton Mifflin Harcourt, 2013).

10. Gore Vidal, *Point to Point Navigation* (New York: Vintage Books, 2007).

11. Gore Vidal, *Point to Point Navigation* (New York: Vintage Books, 2007).

42. *Monty Python, SNL,* and *SCTV*

1. George Perry, *The Life of Python: The History of Something Completely Different* (Philadelphia: Running Press, 1995).

2. Luke Dempsey, *Monty Python's Flying Circus: Complete and Annotated . . . All the Bits* (New York: Black Dog & Leventhal, 2012).

3. Richard Ouzounian, "Python Still Has Legs," *Toronto Star,* July 16, 2006.

4. "Eric Idle," Public Broadcasting Service (PBS), podcast, http://www-tc.pbs.org/montypython/media/montypython_ericidle_podcast.m4v

5. John Cleese and Eric Idle, *Monty Python: Almost the Truth–The Lawyer's Cut*, DVD, directed by Alan Parker (London: Eagle Rock Entertainment, 2009).

6. Laurence Leamer, *King of the Night: The Life of Johnny Carson* (New York: Avon Books, 2005).

7. Doug Hill and Jeff Weingrad, *Saturday Night: A Backstage History of Saturday Night Life* (Untreed Reads Publishing, 2014).

8. Doug Hill and Jeff Weingrad, *Saturday Night: A Backstage History of Saturday Night Life* (Untreed Reads Publishing, 2014).

9. Tom Shales and James Andrew Miller, *Live from New York: The Complete, Uncensored History of Saturday Night Live as Told by Its Stars, Writers, and Guests* (Boston: Little, Brown, 2015).

10. Dave Thomas, *SCTV: Behind the Scenes* (Toronto: McClelland & Stewart, 1997).

43. Goldenson, Diller, and Eisner

1. Gary Edgerton, *The Columbia History of American Television*, Columbia Histories of Modern American Life (New York: Columbia University Press, 2007).

2. S. B. Smith, *Up the Tube: Prime-Time TV and the Silverman Years* (New York: Viking Adult, 1981).

44. Roone Arledge

1. Elliot J. Gorn and Warren Goldstein: A Brief History of American Sports (Urbana: University of Illinois Press, 2013).

2. Bill Carter, "Roone Arledge, a Force in TV Sports and News, Dies at 71," *New York Times*, December 6, 2002, http://www.nytimes.com/2002/12/06/obituaries/06ARLE.html?pagewanted=all.

3. Elizabeth Jensen, "TV Executive Revolutionized the Coverage of News, Sports," *Los Angeles Times*, December 6, 2002, http://articles.latimes.com/2002/dec/06/local/me-arledge6/2.

4. Bill Carter, "Roone Arledge, a Force in TV Sports and News, Dies at 71," *New York Times*, December 6, 2002, http://www.nytimes.com/2002/12/06/obituaries/06ARLE.html?pagewanted=all.

5. Ralph Wiley, "Arledge's World Flowed with Ideas," *ESPN.com*, http://espn.go.com/page2/s/wiley/021209.html.

45. Too Big to Fail

1. "Something for the TV Viewer Who Has Everything," *Broadcasting*, November 3, 1975.

Appendix: Ancestors of Television

1. Kenneth Silverman, Lightning Man: The Accursed Life of Samuel F. B. Morse
    (New York: Knopf, 2010).

2. Kenneth Silverman, Lightning Man: The Accursed Life of Samuel F. B. Morse
    (New York: Knopf, 2010).

3. Gavin Weightman, Signor Marconi's Magic Box: The Most Remarkable Invention of the 19th Century & the Amateur Inventor Whose Genius Sparked a Revolution (Cambridge, MA: Da Capo, 1981).

SELECTED BIBLIOGRAPHY

Armstrong, Jennifer Keishin. *Mary and Lou and Rhoda and Ted: And All the Brilliant Minds Who Made the* Mary Tyler Moore Show *a Classic*. New York: Simon and Schuster, 2013.

Barnouw, Erik. *Tube of Plenty: The Evolution of American Television*. Oxford: Oxford University Press, 1990.

Bushkin, Henry. *Johnny Carson*. Boston: Houghton Mifflin Harcourt, 2013.

Castleman, Harry, and Walter J. Podrazik. *Watching TV: Six Decades of American Television*. Syracuse, NY: Syracuse University Press, 2003.

Edgerton, Gary R. *The Columbia History of American Television*. New York: Columbia University Press, 2007.

Fisher, David E., and Marshall Jon Fisher. *Tube: The Invention of Television*. Berkeley, CA: Counterpoint, 1996.

Gelbart, Larry. *Laughing Matters: On Writing* M*A*S*H, Tootsie, Oh, God!, *and a Few Other Funny Things*. New York: Random House, 1999.

Godfrey, Donald G. *Philo T. Farnsworth: The Father of Television*. Salt Lake City: University of Utah Press, 2001.

Halberstam, David. *The Powers That Be.* Champaign: University of Illinois Press, 2000.

Henry, William A., III. *The Great One: The Life and Legend of Jackie Gleason.* New York: Doubleday, 1992.

"Johnny Carson: King of Late Night." *American Masters.* PBS. Aired May 14, 2012. Television.

Kanfer, Stefan. *Ball of Fire: The Tumultuous Life and Comic Art of Lucille Ball.* New York: Knopf, 2003.

Leamer, Laurence. *King of the Night: The Life of Johnny Carson.* New York: Avon Books, 2005.

Lear, Norman. *Even This I Get to Experience.* London: Penguin, 2014.

Lyons, Eugene. *David Sarnoff: A Biography.* New York: Harper & Row, 1966.

Oppenheimer, Jess. *Laughs, Luck—and Lucy: How I Came to Create the Most Popular Sitcom of All Time.* Syracuse, NY: Syracuse University Press, 1999.

Paper, Lewis J. *Empire: William S. Paley and the Making of CBS.* New York: St. Martin's, 1987.

Schatzkin, Paul. *The Boy Who Invented Television: A Story of Inspiration, Persistence, and Quiet Passion.* Terre Haute, IN: Tanglewood Books, 2004.

Schwartz, Evan I. *The Last Lone Inventor: A Tale of Genius, Deceit, and the Birth of Television.* New York: HarperCollins, 2003.

"The Seventies." *CNN Original Series.* Premiered June 11, 2015. Television.

Shales, Tom, and James Andrew Miller. *Live from New York: The Complete, Uncensored History of* Saturday Night Live *as Told by Its Stars, Writers, and Guests*. Boston: Little, Brown, 2015.

Shatner, William. *Star Trek Memories*. New York: HarperCollins, 1993.

Silverman, Kenneth. *Lightning Man: The Accursed Life of Samuel F. B. Morse*. New York: Knopf, 2010.

"The Sixties." *CNN Original Series*. Premiered May 29, 2014. Television.

Smith, Sally Bedell. *In All His Glory: The Life and Times of William S. Paley and the Birth of Modern Broadcasting*. New York: Random House, 2002.

Smith, Sally Bedell. *Up the Tube: Prime-Time TV and the Silverman Years*. New York: Viking Adult, 1981.

Solow, Herbert F., and Robert H. Justman. *Inside Star Trek: The Real Story*. New York: Pocket Books, 1996.

Stanyard, Stewart T. *Dimensions behind the Twilight Zone: A Backstage Tribute to Television's Groundbreaking Series*. Toronto: ECW, 2007.

Stashower, Daniel. *Boy Genius and the Mogul: The Untold Story of Television*. New York: Crown Archetype, 2002.

Thomas, Dave. SCTV: *Behind the Scenes*. Toronto: McClelland and Stewart, 1997.

Thompson, Richard. *The Second Golden Age of Television*. Syracuse, NY: Syracuse University Press, 1997.

Weightman, Gavin. *Signor Marconi's Magic Box: The Most Remarkable Invention of the 19th Century and the Amateur Inventor Whose Genius Sparked a Revolution*. Cambridge, MA: Da Capo, 2004.

Weiner, Tim. *One Man against the World: The Tragedy of Richard Nixon.* New York: Henry Holt, 2015.

Wu, Tim. *The Master Switch: The Rise and Fall of Information Empires.* New York: Knopf, 2010.

Zicree, Marc Scott. *The Zone Companion.* Los Angeles: Silman-James, 1992

Printed in the USA
CPSIA information can be obtained
at www.ICGtesting.com
LVHW020535230823
755981LV00001B/62